RASPUTIN

The Memoirs of his Secretary

by Aron Simanovitch
(aka Aaron Simanovich)

Translated and annotated by Delin Colón
Edited by Bryna Kranzler and Delin Colón

Cover design by Siri Nadler
@cargocollective.com/siricreative

Delin Colón is also the author of:
Rasputin and The Jews: A Reversal of History

Publication and Translation Notes:

Aron Simanovitch's memoir was originally published in Russian (in Riga) in 1928, under the title *Rasputin and the Jews*. When he moved to Paris, in the 1920s, he had his book translated into French by S. de Leo and Madame de Naglovska. It was published in Paris, in 1930, as *Raspoutine par son secrétaire Aron Simanovitch* (*Rasputin by his Secretary Aron Simanovitch*). The book has subsequently been translated into Spanish and Hebrew, as well. In the early 1940s, the Nazis published a heavily revised version of Simanovitch's memoir in German, twisting his words to depict Rasputin as a pawn of the Jews in their so-called conspiracy for world domination.

This is the first English translation. The editing of Simanovitch's manuscript involved reorganizing and consolidating information that was scattered over several chapters. The original French manuscript seems to describe events as he thought of them, rather than by chronology or even topic. In this translation, there is an attempt at chronology within each chapter heading, by topic, rather than cover-to-cover. Many of his two and three-page chapters were consolidated into one, reducing his fifty-six chapters to eleven, while providing more continuity, clarity and flow. There were, in addition, many redundancies in the original work which were omitted. His thoughts, assessments and accounts of events remain intact. Simanovitch wrote his memoirs more than a decade after Rasputin's death, relying on his memory of people, dates (which are rarely provided), and places.

The annotations (except for one by Simanovitch) are this translator's attempt to either place information in context, correct misinformation, or provide background.

~ Delin Colón

Contents

Acknowledgements

Since the cover is the public face of a book, as well as the reader's first encounter with it, it is only natural that I first thank the designer responsible for this book cover, Siri Nadler of Siri Creative at cargocollective.com/siricreative, a graphic design company based in Nashville, Tennessee. I am ever grateful for her patience, skill, artistry, time and effort in producing a book cover I had not imagined but immediately loved.

Bryna Kranzler, author of *The Accidental Anarchist*, deserves kudos for her valuable editorial assistance, comments and suggestions. Her guidance, insights and assessments were spot on. I would be remiss if I didn't also thank her for giving my book priority at a time when she was immersed in other projects. Ms. Kranzler did not only edit, but also lent me her strength, courage, motivation and humor when my own were waning. Her assistance and encouragement were priceless.

My husband, David, always has my eternal gratitude. His gentle and affectionate efforts to prod me to work kept me from my usual modes of procrastination, and his ability to make me laugh often lent me much needed perspective. He knew just when to give me the solitude to work and when to push me outdoors for a revitalizing whiff of nature. His selfless love and devotion provided me with a nurturing, stress-free environment in which to write.

My belated father, Alex Linowitz, deserves the credit for telling me about his great uncle, Aron Simanovitch, whom I must also thank for hovering in the ether in my early days of translating his work. Whatever his failings as an objective chronicler of history, he is redeemed by his up-close and personal view of Rasputin as a three-dimensional human being with many endearing qualities. Simanovitch was one of the few writers to depict Rasputin as a victim of the aristocracy rather than the other way around.

~ Delin Colón

Foreword

Prophet, healer, mystic.

Libertine, Svengali, scoundrel.

Mention the name "Rasputin" and even someone without any knowledge of Russian history will have an immediate and visceral reaction.

The image of Gregori Yefimovitch Rasputin that has come down through history is of a man so manipulative and evil that he used his privileged access to Tsar Nicholas II and his Empress, Alexandra, to bring down the Romanov dynasty.

But as any student of human nature knows, the laws of physics don't apply to history: Not every action has an equal and opposite reaction. While Rasputin did, indeed, influence and attempted to influence Tsar Nicholas II's decisions (as did others, as Nicholas II was so weak-willed that he was often swayed to the last advice he received), had the Tsar heeded Rasputin's counsel on more occasions, Russia might not have entered into the Great War, and the Tsar might have lowered the temperature of the brewing revolution.

Just as each generation creates the heroes and villains it needs, Rasputin was a reflection of his unique time and place; had he not existed, someone would have had to invent him. The fact that he cultivated his reputation as filthy and debauched, and flaunted his power only made it easier for those who hated or feared him to demonize him.

Rasputin was introduced to Tsar Nicholas II and Tsarina Alexandra when the Romanovs faced both internal and external threats to their rule, and feared for the life of their son, Tsarevitch Alexei Nikolayevich, whose hemophilia had to be kept from the Russian population. This was a time when Russian society was predisposed toward the mystical, so the arrival of a peasant with mysterious healing powers fit the narrative of the age. Add to these factors that Nicholas II, who ascended to the throne upon his father, Alexander III's, assassination, was not psychically strong enough to lead Russia during challenging economic and political times, and you have a perfect storm of circumstances that led to the downfall of the dynasty and the 1917 Russian Revolution.

Rasputin: The Memoirs of his Secretary, the translated and annotated diaries of Aron Simanovitch, Rasputin's personal secretary and, arguably, the man who knew him best during his years in Petersburg, makes an important contribution to our understanding of historical events. It reminds us that even cataclysmic, history-changing decisions are made by human beings, with all their strengths, flaws and biases, who view the world through a prism constructed of their past experiences and whose light is refracted by their personal desires. This gives readers the opportunity to judge Rasputin and his actions for themselves, while at the same time presenting an insider's view of "Peyton Place in Petersburg."

If *Rasputin: The Memoirs of his Secretary* were a work of fiction, Aron Simanovitch might be considered an "unreliable narrator." He contradicts himself, and acknowledges that he aligned himself with Rasputin for personal motives – to enhance his business as a jeweler, and to improve the lot of his fellow Jews. However, his proximity to Rasputin gave Simanovitch unique access and insight into events and discussions that rarely become part of the historical record. By translating and annotating her great-great uncle's diaries to expose the humanity of historical personages who, for most people, exist only in textbooks, Delin Colón has provided readers with the color commentary on a unique period of history.

Bryna Kranzler
author, *The Accidental Anarchist*
www.TheAccidentalAnarchist.com
Bryna@CrosswalkPress.com

Translator's Introduction

Aron Simanovitch was my paternal great grandmother's brother. He was born on February 15, 1872 in Vilna, Poland. Little is known about his youth. According to a 1903 Belarus census, Aron's brother, Khaimysl, was a gold and silver merchant. Aron was listed in the 1911 census as dealing in watches, although he also dealt in gold, silver and, later, diamonds. Both brothers resided in the Mozyr district of Minsk at that time. Ellis Island ship records show that, on his 1923 visit to the U.S., Aron listed the residence of another brother, G. Semenovitch[1] of New Jersey, as his destination. He made a second trip to New York in 1934 and then returned to his home in Paris.

Simanovitch began working as Rasputin's unofficial 'secretary' or business manager in 1907, after having met him several years earlier. His published account of Rasputin's activities has been sometimes discredited by historians due to his inclusion of outlandish court gossip and no little exaggeration of his own importance in the court and in political events. However, the examples of Rasputin's aid to disenfranchised Jews are substantiated by many reliable sources and are indisputable.[2] Simanovitch's story has also been dismissed because his own reputation was suspect. Although he was a jeweler, he also ran gambling parlors which were frequented largely by the military, the nobility and government officials — many of

---

[1] As the original surname is translated from Cyrillic Russian characters, there are different spellings that appear: Simanovitch, Simanovich, Semenovich, Shimanovitch, Simanovitsch, etc.

[2] See *Rasputin and The Jews: A Reversal of History"* by Delin Colón

the people about whom he wrote. It is, however, these activities which place him in the center of the action. More importantly, Simanovitch's account has been disregarded because he was a Jew who, through his decade-long association with Rasputin, had to resort to bribing officials to save the careers, families, homes, educations, and lives of countless Russian Jews who, at that time (and for centuries before) were denied basic human rights.

The anti-Semitic veil through which the aristocracy viewed Aron is evident in their memoirs and testimonies to the Provisional Government's Extraordinary Commission, through their references to him as "the Jew Simanovitch" or, more commonly, "the Yid[3] Simanovitch." He claims to have been unaware of any prejudice on the part of many aristocrats of the "Young Court," however that was because it only manifested behind his back. Some regarded Simanovitch as a criminal (although no particular 'crimes' are ever cited) merely because the Tsar's secret service described him as such. It seems that the only 'crime' he committed was that of circumventing unjust laws, usually with bribes, in order to aid the oppressed Jews, and the poor in general. Due to his profession as a jeweler, Simanovitch was one of the few privileged Jews permitted to live outside The Pale of Settlement,[4] the ghetto to which most Jews were confined.

The irony in Simanovitch's preface to his memoir is that he explicitly states he does not want to compromise anyone or speak about events for which he has few details. However,

---

[3] "Yid" is a derogatory term for "Jew."

[4] The Pale of Settlement, home by law to 95% of Russia's Jewish population, was established by Catherine the Great in 1791 and encompassed parts of Poland, Latvia, Lithuania, Ukraine, Belarus – most territories between the Black Sea and the Baltic. It was abolished after the 1917 Revolution.

he does exactly that in some chapters containing intimate information about the royals, which he claims to have learned from Rasputin himself. Many of these statements about the royal family are nothing more than the popular gossip of the time. In this vein, one must remember that gossip was the predominant social pastime of that era, akin to the chatter on Twitter today. Many memoirs of that era were rife with unsubstantiated rumors. Princess Catherine Radziwell's gossip-laden books about European royalty, as well as her hand in promoting the anti-Semitic hoax *Protocols of the Elders of Zion*, are examples of that formerly popular genre of historical fabrication.

The rumors, however, are instructive. As they spread quickly in the Russian Empire and were often accepted as truth, they provide a window to the generally held perceptions and beliefs of the general population, true or not, and sometimes offer the motive for their actions. However, the value of Simanovitch's story, gossip aside, is in his affectionate description of Rasputin as a friend and human being — and, in particular, his efforts to help the severely oppressed Jews of Tsarist Russia, despite the prevailing anti-Semitism characterized by the unjust laws of the time. This part of Simanovitch's story is historical fact and well documented by numerous historians and biographers, including many who knew Rasputin personally. It is notable that most accounts of Rasputin's life contain at least one reference to his efforts on behalf of Jews, whether the authors viewed those activities as positive or negative, important or unimportant.

Ultimately, even the dubious events and sections of Simanovitch's memoirs are a lively read and can be enjoyed as works of fiction, just like numerous books and films that have depicted Rasputin as an oversexed, demonic Svengali. It's telling that few are ever indignant over the fabrications surrounding Rasputin's life, but vehemently take umbrage at groundless rumors about the Romanovs.

On that note, I leave you to Aron Simanovitch's account of his time with Rasputin.

Delin Colón
June, 2012

Important Persons

Bonch-Bruevich, Vladimir – (b.1873-d.1955) expert on Russian sectarianism, politician, Bolshevik
Gapon, Father George – (b.1870-d.1906) Priest who led a peaceful demonstration of workers presenting a petition for better conditions and pay, starting the 1905 revolution.
Gunzburg, Horace and Moishe – Jewish barons who were philanthropists and equal rights advocates.
Guseva, Chionya – (also Khionya) religious fanatic who tried to assassinate Rasputin in 1914
Iliodor – born Sergei Trufanov, an anti-Semitic monk and priest who befriended Rasputin, then turned against him.
Khvostov, Alexei – (b.1872-d.1918) anti-Semitic Minister of Internal Affairs from 1915-1916
Orbeliani, Princess Sofia – (b. 1875-d.1915) lady-in-waiting to the Tsarina.
Rasputin, Dmitri (Mitya) – (b.1897-d.1933) Grigori's son.
Rasputin, Grigori Efimovitch – (b.1869-d.1916) wandering spiritual pilgrim who served as spiritual advisor to the Tsar.
Rasputin, Matryona (Marya) – (b.1898-d.1977) Grigori's elder daughter.
Rasputin, Praskovya – (b.1870-d.1936) Grigori's wife.
Rasputin, Varvara (Varya) – (b.1900-d.1924) Grigori's younger daughter.
Romanov, Maria Feodorovna – (b.1847-d.1928) Dowager Empress, mother of Tsar Nicholas II and widow of Tsar Alexander III.
Romanov, Tsar Nicholas II – (b.1868-d.1918) last Tsar of Russia, son of Tsar Alexander III.
Romanov, Tsarina Alexandra – (b.1872-d.1918) German wife of Tsar Nicholas II, known before her marriage as Princess Alix of Hesse, granddaughter of Queen Victoria of England.

Romanov, Tsarevitch Alexei – (b.1904-d.1918) son of Tsar Nicholas II, heir to the throne.
Romanov, Grand Duke Nikolai Nikolayevich – (b.1856-d.1929) uncle to Nicholas II, Commander-in-Chief of Russian Armies, avid anti-Semite, married to ***Grand Duchess Anastasia*** of Montenegro who, with her sister, found Rasputin and brought him to Petersburg to introduce to the Tsar.
Romanov, Grand Duke Dmitri Pavlovich – (b.1891-d.1941) cousin to Nicholas II, grandson of Tsar Alexander II, one of Rasputin's murderers.
Ruzsky, Nikolai – (b.1854-d.1918) General of the Third Army, Commander-in-Chief of the Northern Front.
Sazanov, Sergei – (b.1860-d.1927) Minister of Foreign Affairs from 1910 to 1916.
Shcheglovitov, Ivan – (b.1861-d.1918) Minister of Justice from 1906 to 1915.
Simanovitch, Aron – (b. 1872-d.1944) Jewish secretary to Rasputin from 1907 to 1916, jeweler by trade.
Simanovitch, Ioann (John) – (b.190?-d.197?) Aron's youngest son
Simanovitch, Semyon (Salomon) – (b.1901-d.1943) Aron's eldest son
Sliosberg, Genrikh (also Henry Sliozberg) – (b.1863-d.1937) Jewish attorney, administrative law advisor to Minister of the Interior; offered free legal services to victims of anti-Semitic discrimination.
Stolypin, Pyotr – (b.1862-d.1911) Prime Minister 1906-1911.
Sturmer, Boris – (b.1848-d.1917) Prime Minister, Minister of the Interior and Foreign Affairs.
Vyrubova, Anna – (b.1884-d.1964) lady-in-waiting, confidante and best friend of Tsarina Alexandra.
Witte, Count Sergei – (b.1849-d.1915) Prime Minister from 1905-1906, also Finance Minister and served under Tsar Alexander III. As Finance Minister, he introduced the

gold standard and, in 1905, represented Russia at the signing of the Portsmouth Treaty in 1905, ending the Russo-Japanese War.
Yussupov, Prince Felix – (b.1886 –d.1967) nobleman from a wealthy family, married Irina, daughter of the Tsar's cousin, was one of Rasputin's murderers.

Preface by the Author

In writing these memoirs, I intend to focus solely on my observations of the stormy period of Russian history, which include the start of the Great War[5], the extraordinary ascent of Rasputin to power, the fall of the Romanov dynasty, and the first rumblings of the revolution.[6] It is not my intention to expose or compromise anyone. I have carefully avoided biased interpretations of the events I observed.

Moreover, I have limited myself to writing about my own personal experiences with the Imperial Court, or those confided to me by Rasputin. The Imperial Couple kept no secrets from him. The Tsar and the Tsarina confessed everything, as though he were their conscience. As confidant and advisor to Rasputin, I learned many of these things. This is how I know my narrative to be true. And it is only for this reason that I attempt to relate the facts of the Imperial Family's intimate life, untold until now.

It is possible that I've committed, here and there, minute errors in names and some details. I never took notes and therefore had to rely on my memory.[7] But the main points of my narrative remain solidly intact. Innumerable legends

---

[5] World War I, also known as "The Great War."
[6] There was one failed revolution in 1905, whose "rumblings" persisted until the successful 1917 overthrow of the Tsar.
[7] Simanovitch is better described as a personal assistant or business manager than 'secretary.' He purposely didn't keep notes and burned what records he did have, so as not to be targeted in anti-Semitic raids, as well as to protect others who had aided Jews.

have sprung up regarding Rasputin's personality. My goal is not to compete with the promoters of scandalous stories, but to make my own observations based on the real man, as I knew him.

As for my personal activities, I do not pretend that my behavior was always good or just. I did, however, aim for goals that seemed to me to be good and just at the time. I employed the means available to me which seemed the most effective. I sought, above all, not to forego any opportunities that promised to further the privileged position I occupied at Rasputin's side. I was his advisor, and the Emperor himself appointed me secretary to his 'favorite'.[8]

~ Aron Simanovitch

[8] There is no evidence, reference or documentation to suggest any official appointment of Simanovitch. It is more likely that it was a relationship the Tsar simply tolerated. Rasputin is often referred to as the Tsar's 'favorite.'

A. Simanovitsch

Aron Simanovitch

Chapter 1

My Introduction to the Imperial Court

Allow me first to say a few words about myself: For more than 10 years, I occupied a position, in Petersburg, that one could certainly call 'unique'. For the first time in Russian history, a simple Jew from the provinces was received by the Royal Court and had some influence over affairs of state. The upper classes of that time posed no serious obstacle despite their profound anti-Semitism. They sought my advice and assistance even though I was a Jew; however, most of my activities consisted of trying to aid my oppressed people, and lighten their load.

My success in Petersburg has generally been attributed to my bond of friendship with Rasputin. It has been said that it was Rasputin who cleared the way for my introduction to the Imperial Court. This is not exactly true. My friendship with Rasputin was certainly very precious to me, but the truth is that I had established connections with Petersburg society before Rasputin arrived in that city. And this is how I did so:

I was an established jeweler in Kiev and knew many influential people. Living in the provinces, I acquired a lot of experience in dealing with the police and other bureaucrats. I became adept at the art of manipulating these state officials. However, life for all Jews in Kiev, meant tolerating all sorts of vexations and humiliations. So, in 1902, I moved to Petersburg, temporarily leaving my family in Kiev to manage my thriving business. In Petersburg, I often met people for whom I previously had performed important services. Most had not forgotten my assistance and remained ready to oblige by helping me to get established in the city. Due to several among them, I was later able to escape certain death, as well as save the lives of my children.

In 1905, at the first worrisome reports of a pogrom in Kiev,[9] I hurried back to join my family. My stores had been ransacked. My business managers and many of my relatives had been massacred. My own life and that of my immediate family were in grave danger. But General Mavrin[10], who led the pogrom, and Zichotzki, the police prefect, took us under their protection and, thanks to them, my family and I escaped to Berlin.[11]

As we were leaving Kiev, in front of the synagogue, we saw the corpses of Jews massacred during their holy service. This horrible spectacle left such an indelible impression that, after arriving in Berlin, it took me some time to recover. It was then that I firmly resolved to engage in the struggle, using any and all means, to defend the lives and rights of myself, my family and my fellow Jews. I decided to actively support the causes and interests of my people. Only now, and for the first time, am I making a public report of what I attempted and accomplished, taking full responsibility for my actions, and ready to accept any attacks or accusations.

---

[9] In October, 1905, a hostile mob at Kiev City Hall blamed Jews for Russia's ills and incited a pogrom, massacring 100 Jews, injuring 300 others, and destroying 20 to 30 million rubles worth of property, over three days, while authorities stood by and watched. Author Sholem Aleichem witnessed this event and recreated it in his novel *In the Storm*.

[10] General in the Imperial Russian Army who often carried out or instigated pogroms.

[11] Simanovitch, as part of his "art of manipulating and corrupting" officials, regularly paid those officials for protection.

My wife was from a family of Jewish entrepreneurs who were builders. They were serious workers and businessmen. Many of her relatives were artisans in Petersburg, with the support[12] of Count Witte.[13] They congratulated me when I established my first business relations there. Some of them occasionally received work orders from the Imperial Court. But just the same, they led a modest life and didn't mix with high society. I, on the other hand, was a completely different kind of man. I eagerly and assiduously frequented the circles of little theaters, cabarets, and the races where I met people from the most diverse social strata. As everyone knows, the passion for gambling is a force that puts people at ease with each other, causing them to overlook social and national differences. The search for pleasure renders us, its prey, amiable in social relations. I quickly learned my way around this world and developed my client list from the contacts that I made each day.

Thanks to my facility for creating amicable relationships despite social differences, I soon made contact with many members of the Imperial Court and interested them in doing business with me. In this fashion, my relations with them grew more intimate and I quickly learned, up close, the sort of lives the aristocracy lived. I arrived in Petersburg with business experience and a knowledge of life at just the right moment to help well-situated people who didn't know how to obtain credit or buy and sell valuable objects. (Petersburg society was extraordinarily ignorant with regard to any sort of business affairs.)

[12] This 'support' would have been in the form of letters of introduction, business contacts, etc.
[13] Count Sergei Witte was Prime Minister from 1905-1906, also Finance Minister and served under Tsar Alexander III.

My friendship with two brothers, the Princes Wittgenstein, was of capital importance to me. Gritzko and Nicholas Wittgenstein were bodyguards to Tsar Nicholas. Through them, I met: Princess Orbeliani, influential handmaiden to Tsarina Alexandra; the Caucasian Princes Utscha Dadiani and Alek Amilachvani; then, little by little, the entire corps of officers of the Imperial Bodyguard. Later, I made the acquaintance of all of the Imperial handmaidens — the celebrated Anya Vyrubova, Mlle Nikitina, Mme von Dehn and the Princess Astaman-Galitzina.

Having access to the Imperial Palace allowed me to become familiar with nearly the entire Court. Monsieur Poincet, Imperial Maitre d', was very instrumental for me to know, as he enjoyed considerable contact with everyone associated with the Royal Court. Monsieur Poincet and I began a chess club that was, in reality, a political circle. The two Wittgenstein princes, who were always short on money, were also members. In this way, I managed to involve influential personalities of the Royal Court in my various enterprises.

The fate of the Wittgenstein brothers, descendants of the Hohenzollerns[14], was tragic. One was killed in a duel over a woman of questionable morals; the other, married to the bohemian Lisa Mallaska who was celebrated for her great beauty, choked on a chicken bone. Both were very close to the Tsar, permitted to eat at his table and to pass leisure time with him. After their deaths, Prince Utscha Dadiani,[15] well liked by the Court, became a member of our chess club. He was a regular in the salon of Princess Sofia Tarkhanova. One of the daughters of the Princess had

---

[14] The Hohenzollern dynasty, from 1415 to 1918, ruled Brandenburg, Prussia and Germany, at varying times.
[15] The House of Dadiani was a Georgian family of nobles dating back to the 11th century.

married Prince Gelovani[16] whom I elected president of my club, just as he had desired.

The first time I was presented to the Tsarina's maids of honor was at the home of Princess Orbeliani, formerly Nicholas II's favorite mistress. By then, the princess was already paralyzed.[17] Despite her former liaison with the Tsar, she enjoyed the good graces of the Tsarina who often took her for rides in her car. The Tsarina rarely displayed jealousy despite having serious reason to do so. At the home of Princess Orbeliani, I was presented to the Tsarina's maids of honor, first and foremost as a jeweler, a salesman and connoisseur of diamonds. They soon couldn't do without me. My pockets were always stuffed with jewels to sell. I was in the good graces and confidence of people in high places, and was initiated into many secrets of the Imperial Court. I acquired assurance and self-confidence especially when I saw that my ties to the people of the Court impressed others, and this led to my desires and requests being taken into consideration by the government. Many people sought my company and put themselves at my service. I, in turn, sought to be useful to them.

It was also at Princess Orbeliani's home that the Tsarina first accorded me an audience. She often gave me orders for jewelry which I filled with the utmost diligence and conscientiousness. She was happy with me and accorded me her confidence. Knowing her taste for economizing, I put very low prices on the jewels she bought from me. After making her choice, she sought the counsel of the Court jeweler, Monsieur Fabergé,[18] asking him if my price

---

[16] Varlam Gelovani, of the noble House of Gelovani (traceable to the 11th century) was a Georgian lawyer and politician

[17] Princess Orbeliani was afflicted with a hereditary, progressive spinal disease that eventually resulted in her paralysis.

was reasonable. And when the jeweler was stunned at the low price, she rejoiced. Naturally, what was most important to me was to be in the Empress' good graces. She often bought jewels on credit, which she paid off in installments, as befitted her frugal ways. I willingly accepted these conditions which pleased her greatly. Those in her entourage also wanted favorable prices, which I gave them graciously. The result was that these people always endeavored to show me their gratitude.

[18] Peter Carl Fabergé was court jeweler to the Romanov dynasty, best known for his bejeweled Fabergé eggs.

Grigori Efimovitch Rasputin
His early years in Petersburg

Rasputin before World War I

Chapter II

Rasputin's Arrival at the Court

Nicholas II showed an avid interest in the spirit world and, in general, for all that was supernatural. The Imperial Family's religious mysticism was not unusual in Russia. Almost all of the aristocracy were imbued with similar tendencies. The Imperial Family was merely a product of its environment. Pure religion, abstract faith, prayer with no response, and questions with no solutions could not satisfy these people. They wanted to touch the heavens, feel God and embody him in a direct and permanent union.

In this way, pure religion with prayer to an unknown and silent God gave way to a pagan adoration, a cult of icons, with superstition replacing faith, and prayer becoming a rite. The aristocracy's faith was misplaced in objects, rituals and living men. It was very attractive to have permanent contact with a saintly man, an emissary of God — to have celestial counsel, a prophet to secure the path to heaven. And these ignorant people, elevated by destiny to a superior social class, sought every means of realizing this goal. So, the fact that a simple, illiterate Siberian peasant became a friend and counselor to the Tsar's family, penetrating the core of the Imperial Palace and breaking through class barriers, is not particularly surprising, considering that the Court was so favorable to things of that nature.[19]

---

[19] Many tsars before Nicholas II, as well as other European royalty, consulted mystics, wise men, or had 'holy fools.'

Hundreds of monks and holy men had passed through the Court before Rasputin's arrival. Many spiritualists, hypnotists, astrologers and oracles had approached Nicholas II. Courtesans, exploiting the Tsar's weakness, brought them from far and wide. There was a constant search for miracle makers, hermits and preachers who embodied a celestial force, transmitted the word of God, absolved people of sins, healed illnesses, and gave some direction for the future.

Many were zealous about finding these questionable people with supposed powers, to introduce to the Tsar. Consequently, Rasputin's appearance at the palace was not an unusual event. Just like other miracle men before him, he was found and brought to the Tsar by ladies of the Court who sought to curry the Emperor's favor. Their Majesties eagerly met with these 'miracle men' and sought their advice. They scrupulously followed any counsel given, but without success. After many meetings, communal prayers and religious teachings, the Imperial Couple's interest in each prophet waned, making room for the next.

This penchant for mystics presented a great danger to Nicholas II's security because, upon hearing the slightest mention of some soothsayer, fortuneteller or hypnotist, he wanted to meet them. This explains how so many charlatans and suspicious people who otherwise would not have dared approach a tsar, easily gained access to him. One had only to mention Papus[20] or Philippe[21], occultists who had had a great influence on him, to gain an audience.

---

[20] Gérard "Papus" Encausse, was an occultist and French physician who counseled Nicholas II a few times in the early 1900's.

[21] Anthelme Nizier Philippe, also known as "Maitre Phillippe de Lyon", was a French occultist healer, though not a medical doctor, who spent some time in Petersburg.

Rasputin owed his unprecedented success to the Emperor's penchant for the supernatural. Nicholas II always looked into the world beyond for the solution to his doubts.
The Tsarina, a German, was an adamant believer who, after embracing the Russian Orthodox Church, became morbidly attracted to the superficial trappings of the rites and rituals of her new religion. The two spiritual dispositions of this couple required reconciliation in the form of one incarnation which arrived in the form of Rasputin, man of God, maker of miracles, and mediator between the sinful earth and the clemency of heaven. Nicholas II was a distrustful man, as well as headstrong and clever. However, he showed great respect for those who appeared to possess supernatural powers. He felt better in their company, listening to their teachings and counsel. Many attributed this bizarre fact to the head wound inflicted on him by the sword of a Japanese prince, when he voyaged to Japan.[22]

Among those who interested the Tsar in their supernatural powers, I must include Countess Nina Zarnekau, daughter of the Prince of Oldenburg, who was very close to Nicholas II. He had her evoke innumerable spirits and questioned them about the future that awaited him. I tried once, without success, to utilize his penchant for my own ends. One of my good friends, the Rumanian violinist Goulesko, the golden-haired boy of all Petersburg, gave a party for some occasion. He invited a number of people to come taste the dishes of his country, particularly the "Rumanian soup." Among those invited were the Caucasian Princes —Nicholas Nizheradze, chamberlain to

---

[22] In May, 1891, when Nicholas II was still heir to the throne, he was making an official visit to Japan when one of the Japanese policemen on security duty attacked him with a sword. Nicholas' head wounds were slight but left scars.

the Tsar; Ivan Nakaschidse, member of the counsel of the Red Cross; Prince Utscha Dadiani; Alexander Eristov, aide to the Emperor; Prince Orbeliani, governor general of Koutais (and father of the aforementioned lady-in-waiting), and others.

After a rich feast, generously accompanied by wine, we wanted to continue the party elsewhere. We telephoned Countess Zarnekau and she invited us to her place. That is when the party really started. We were all quite drunk, our hostess included, when Prince Alex Amilakvari, darling of the Tsar, suddenly arrived from Tsarskoye-Selo, in a royal car, with an order from His Majesty to bring the Countess immediately to the Palace. She did not dare refuse the invitation of the Emperor, but regretted interrupting the party. We made all sorts of jokes about the Countess' spiritual talents when the idea came to me to beg her to intercede, through the spirits, on behalf of Russian Jews. The spirits were to advise the Emperor to revoke all laws hostile to Jews. However, to my regret, the Countess did not dare evoke the spirits for a political end. It may also be that she didn't wish to act on my request because, as everyone knew, the Court was extremely anti-Semitic.

Long before Grigori Rasputin's 1905 appearance at the Tsar's Court, fantastic rumors spread about this mysterious man, following letters from Grand Duchess Anastasia, wife of Grand Duke Nikolai Nikolayevich, [23] and from her sister Militza who was married to Grand Duke Pyotr Nikolayevich. The two Grand Duchesses had made a pilgrimage to a celebrated convent in Kiev. In giving their news, they spoke of the marvelous "staretz,"[24] a very

[23] Grand Duke Nikolai Nikolayevich, uncle to Tsar Nicholas II, was Supreme Commander-in-Chief of the Russian armies.

[24] A 'staretz' is an elder of the Russian Orthodox monastery who is a spiritual advisor and teacher. Rasputin never claimed to be a

respectable man whom they wanted to bring to Petersburg. This man, they said, was neither monk nor priest, but possessed an extraordinary spiritual force.

The people of the Russian Court were very ignorant and superstitious. In this way, the nobles were on the same level as the peasants. Most of the people around the Tsar were very narrow-minded, with no practical experience, and totally incapable of finding solutions to the simplest questions of daily life. Vyrubova, Orbeliani and other ladies of the Court told the Tsar and Tsarina what they had learned of Rasputin. The Imperial Couple had been going through a difficult period. They were oppressed by valid fears regarding their family, the Court, and the future of their dynasty due to the rising threat of revolution. When word of Rasputin's miracles reached their ears, it awakened the hope that he might come to their aid. Above all, they hoped for a cure for Tsarevitch Alexei, heir to the throne, who was gravely ill. It had been said, among the Imperial Couple's entourage, that the Tsarina had transmitted to her children impure blood that engendered illness and brought unhappiness.[25]

The Tsar and Tsarina often quarreled because both were extremely nervous. Sometimes the Tsarina would go for weeks without speaking to her husband. She suffered bouts of hysteria. The Tsar drank a lot, looked worn, half-asleep and lost mastery of himself. It was in this troubled atmosphere that the news of the miraculous cures of Rasputin arrived at the Court. It was said that he could cure grave illnesses with the aid of mysterious herbs. This gave the Tsar and Tsarina new hope. The order was given to bring Rasputin, immediately, to the Imperial Palace.

---

monk or a staretz, but was more a 'strannik' or a spiritual pilgrim.

[25] The Tsarevitch was afflicted with hemophilia.

The groundwork was laid for Rasputin's arrival at the Court. A superior willpower and a singular energy distinguished him from questionable seers, psychics and spiritualists who had passed through the Court. In addition, he had no desire for financial gain. His ambition derived from a real need for power, and his strong nature required that he deploy it. He loved to command and direct people. Before his arrival in Petersburg, this tendency had already been observed, despite his modest lifestyle, but once in Petersburg, this trait was more pronounced following his fabulous success.

Rasputin arrived in Petersburg nine years before the Great War.[26] These are the events as he told them to me: Grand Duchess Anastasia, wife of Grand Duke Nikolai Nikolayevich, and her sister Militza, married to Grand Duke Pyotr Nikolayevich,[27] had both made pilgrimage to Kiev and stayed at the hotel of St. Michael's Convent. One morning, in the convent's courtyard, they noticed a simple fellow cutting wood to earn his bread. It was Rasputin. He had already made several pilgrimages to different holy places, and had just come from his second journey to Jerusalem.

Rasputin gazed penetratingly at the two women and greeted them politely. They asked him different questions and thus engaged him in conversation. The ladies found this unknown person altogether interesting. He spoke to them of his pilgrimages and his life. He had seen much. He had twice made the long trip from Tobolsk to Jerusalem on foot; he knew all the big convents, all the important Russian churches, and he knew many interesting things about certain famous monks. His conversation captivated

---

[26] World War I (1914-1918).

[27] Grand Duke Pyotr Nikolayevich Romanov (b.1864-d.1931) was brother to Grand Duke Nikolai Nikolayevich Romanov.

the attention of the two *grandes dames,* and his comments on religious questions impressed them. This first encounter ended with an invitation to join the ladies for tea. He quickly took them up on their invitation. The Grand Duchesses, who were traveling incognito, were bored in Kiev. Rasputin's stories brought them the distraction they sought. It pleased them to receive him at their lodgings, this strange man of unusual appearance.

Rasputin explained to his new friends that he was simply a poor man from the village of Pokrovskoie, in the province of Tobolsk. His father was still alive and was responsible for dispatching boats on the Tura River.[28] His family consisted of his wife, Praskovya, his son Mitya, and two daughters, Marya and Varya.[29] Rasputin was convinced that, despite his illiteracy and lack of education, he was going to preach to people in public places. He was proud of his talent for making predictions, which easily surpassed that of missionaries, men of the church and wise theologians. He bragged, particularly, of his knowledge of canon law, and it was undeniable that his knowledge of religious matters stunned even bishops and reputable theologians.

Rasputin's visits to the *grandes dames* from Petersburg became increasingly frequent. They were pleased to see him, invited him to their table, and were quite amiable toward him. There was something in his personality that worked in his favor. Women, especially, submitted to his influence, almost without realizing it. When Rasputin learned just who his new friends were, he worked harder to gain their favor, the importance of which he fully

[28] His father was also a farmer and a carter, delivering people and packages with his horse-drawn cart.
[29] Their proper names were Dmitri, Matryona and Varvara. His first child, a son, died in infancy.

understood. Of course, he couldn't have had the slightest suspicion of the great role he would be called upon to play in the Imperial Court, but he soon saw that marvelous opportunities were opening up for him.

Rasputin told his new friends that he knew how to cure all illnesses, feared neither devil nor sorcerer, and could predict the future to avoid pending danger. He spoke with fire and conviction, flashing his big, grey eyes in a persuasive fashion that filled his two listeners with enthusiasm and respect. They were convinced, due to their superstitious natures, that they had found the miraculous man they had sought and waited for in their hearts. One night, one of the ladies asked him directly, "Can you cure a young boy afflicted with hemophilia?" Rasputin responded with the greatest assurance. He said he was quite familiar with this mysterious illness and described the symptoms with stunning precision. His description coincided, on every count, with the illness of the Tsarevitch. He even named the plants that he would use for the cure. The Grand Duchesses were profoundly impressed. They rejoiced at the thought of rendering an unforgettable service to the Sovereigns, by helping to cure their son. They confided to Rasputin that the heir to the throne had inherited this disease. At that time, it was still a secret outside of the Court's society. Rasputin offered to cure him. It was in this way that the knot was tied, not to be undone until many years later, upon the death of this miraculous man, and the torment of the second revolution.[30] The reign of Rasputin began.

---

[30] The first revolution was in 1905, by citizens seeking better working conditions; the second revolution was the famed Bolshevik (or Russian) Revolution of 1917, which saw the Tsar overthrown.

~~~~~~~~~

When Rasputin arrived in Petersburg, on foot, he stayed in a convent, hosted by his old friend, Father Theophan. This sparked the unfounded rumor that he was recommended to Grand Duke Nikolai Nikolayevich by Father Theophan.[31] Rasputin later left this lodging to live in the apartment of General Lokhtin[32], on Nikolayevskaya Street. The General's wife, Mme. Lokhtina, was an eccentric woman who was only marginally sane. She drew attention to herself with the little white silk top hat she constantly wore. She was very devoted to Rasputin and taught him to read. From there, he went to live on Jamakaya Street with Sazanov,[33] a relative to the Minister of Foreign Affairs [Sergei Sazanov]. Later, Rasputin had an apartment at 64 Gorochovaya Street, where he lived until his death.

Rasputin's arrival at Tsarskoye-Selo[34] was awaited with great impatience, yet he was received with a certain reserve. Grand Duchess Anastasia[35] was already waiting for Rasputin in Petersburg and, upon his arrival, took him to the Empress. He made a good impression, spoke of his life with a calm and dignified air, and avoided bragging about his supernatural gifts. He knew that the Grand Duchesses had already paved the way for him. From his first encounter with the Tsarevitch, he proved himself confident and sincere in his care of the ill child. He had the

---

[31] Also written Feofan, Archbishop in the Russian Orthodox Church.

[32] Vladimir Lokhtin was an engineer in charge of paved roads in Tsarskoye-Selo, and held the civil position of Actual State Councilor, corresponding to the military rank of general.

[33] Georgy Petrovich Sazanov was a journalist, economist and magazine publisher.

[34] Tsarskoye-Selo, or the Tsar's Village, was one of the imperial residences of the Romanovs.

[35] Wife of Grand Duke Nikolai Nikolayevich.
~~~~~~~~~

gift of calming people with his firm but tranquil demeanor. He demonstrated his art of healing with the Tsarevitch, Prince Alexei who lay on his bed of suffering.

The poor child often had violent nosebleeds for which the doctors could find no remedy. The great loss of blood weakened him and this greatly anguished his parents. Days and nights of this terrible agitation would pass. Little Alexei was very fond of Rasputin whose curing power over the prince was successful. Then, one day, the nosebleeds began again. Rasputin took from his pocket a fistful of bark which he boiled in water and spread over the young boy's face, so that only the eyes and mouth were visible. A miracle happened; the blood stopped flowing.

Rasputin gave me a detailed account of this incident that marked his debut as a healer to the Imperial Palace. He made no mystery of the fact that the herb was nothing more than common oak bark, which has the ability to stop hemorrhages. The Sovereigns learned from this that there existed Siberian, Chinese and Tibetan herbs that had marvelous healing power over certain illnesses. Rasputin could also heal without the aid of plants. Then, he would rely solely on his conjuring[36]. If someone complained of tenacious migraines, fevers, or any discomforts, Rasputin would place himself behind the patient, take the patient's head between his hands, murmur something that no one could understand, give him a good thump, and say, "Go, now!" And the sick person felt well. I, myself, experienced his conjuring and I can only certify that the effect was gripping.

When I first met him in Kiev, Grigori was not yet known in Petersburg but, later, I met him in the capital at the home of

---

[36] Rasputin, when not using herbs, primarily used prayer to heal.

Princess Orbeliani with whom I was on very good terms. Afterward, I saw him often at the home of Vyrubova[37]. From the time of our first meeting, I was always greatly impressed by his eyes. His steel grey eyes were deep set under his arched eyebrows. Rasputin's eyes not only charmed, but also awakened a sense of malaise and worry. His gaze was firm and penetrating. Few could look at him without lowering or averting their eyes. A power of suggestion was hidden there, which people who were easily influenced could not resist. His appearance was that of a real Russian peasant. He was of average height, with big shoulders, and was quite vigorous. His long, brown hair was thick and heavy. It fell over his shoulders, giving him the appearance of a monk or priest.

Rasputin had a bump on his forehead. He tried to hide it with his hair. He always carried a comb and often ran it through his hair, which was so shiny it seemed impregnated with oil. His beard, on the other hand, was very unkempt. He rarely brushed it. In general, he was clean and bathed often, but at the table, his lack of manners showed. He rarely used fork and knife, but instead plunged his dry bony fingers into his plate. He devoured huge mouthfuls, like an animal, which was somewhat unpleasant to witness. His mouth was very large and, instead of teeth, he had blackened stubs. During meals, he often had food in his beard. He never ate meat, sweets or cake, but preferred the potatoes and fruits his admirers sent. Where his wardrobe was concerned, he remained faithful to the peasant style. He wore a Russian shirt, with a silk belt, baggy pants, high boots and a peasant's undershirt beneath his shirt. In Petersburg, he gladly wore the silk shirts embroidered for him by the Tsarina and his numerous admirers. In addition, he generally wore his high shiny

[37] The Tsarina's confidante and chief lady-in-waiting.

boots. Though far from a moderate man, he did not care for cognac, liqueurs or hard alcohol. He preferred Madeira and port to all other wines, having grown accustomed to the wines of the south when he lived in the convents. He could consume unbelievable quantities.

The future held little interest for him and he did not concern himself with it. He was an extremely carefree man who lived from day to day. The Court underwrote all of his needs, but he was lonely and out of his element in the capital city. Despite his close personal relationship with the Tsar's family, he felt alone. Having a passionate temperament, he reveled in strong and profound emotions. He loved wine, women, music, and dancing, as well as long discussions. He found none of those at the Imperial Palace. The Court led a closed life, separated from everyone and everything, disguising their vices and passions under a mask of hypocrisy and feigned decency. The severe and rigid etiquette of the Court was only a thick veil for human weaknesses, which were just as prominent there as elsewhere. That was not Rasputin's style. In front of the Tsar and Tsarina, he did not freely show his true nature.

Rasputin was friendly to me and I found him quite agreeable as well. I noticed that he and I had a common appreciation for useful relationships and reciprocated courtesy. We immediately formed a bond of friendship. As Rasputin had no sense concerning the material side of life, during the course of which he often had to beg for food and housing from others, he never occupied himself with financial matters. This was, for me, a favorable opportunity. His private life was completely unruly and he was incapable of directing an orderly household. In the beginning, his means of livelihood were by the Tsar's generosity, which was irregular and uncertain. For this reason, he needed my help. I took upon myself the concern for his material well-being. Rasputin was happy and grateful not to have to bother with this. I soon became indispensable to him. I provided for all of his daily expenses. I saw to it that the most important supplies were delivered to his home. I always made sure he had everything that he and his family needed. We had a tacit agreement regarding this. Nicholas II knew that his 'favorite' would not be disturbed by any material worries for as long as I was charged with his care. Rasputin accepted my services without ever looking for ulterior motives to my actions. He never once asked where the money came from. If he had need of something, he simply asked me and troubled himself no further about it.

His lifestyle consumed large sums of money. However, I always arranged the procurement of what was needed. By the Tsar's order, the Minister of the Interior was made to hand over five thousand rubles per month for Rasputin,[38] which was a drop in the bucket considering the very costly parties he held at restaurants. Neither were my own means sufficient to cover all of these expenses. That is why, in order to procure the necessary money for Rasputin, I squeezed different sources which I will never reveal for fear of doing wrong to my fellow Jews.

My life experience and knowledge of the capital were essential to him. I helped initiate him to life in Petersburg. Everything was new and strange to him, so much so that he followed my advice on every occasion. I became, in this way, his secretary, aide and protector. In the end, Rasputin undertook nothing of importance without consulting me. I knew all of his business and secrets. When Rasputin was insubordinate to others, I chided him and he took on the air

---

[38] 5,000 rubles, in 1911, was about $2500 U.S. dollars which, at this printing, would now be equivalent to approx. $62,500 U.S.

of a guilty schoolboy. The public knew nothing of this side. One thing I knew: through Rasputin, I could obtain almost anything from the Tsar, the Tsarina, the ministers and most of the powerful people of the country.

Rasputin was only mildly sympathetic to the men of the church. He sincerely believed in God, but he was not a hypocrite. He prayed very little.[39] Yet he enjoyed discussing God and religious questions at length and, despite his lack of culture, had a penchant for philosophy. He also loved to teach. However, he spoke very little and most of the time, in short, choppy sentences which were often incomprehensible. Everyone had to listen attentively because he wanted his listeners to be aware of the importance of his words. The moral and emotional lives of men interested him profoundly. He was a connoisseur of the human soul, an ability that was of great use to him. Regular work was not his style. He was rather lazy yet, when needed, could accomplish hard physical labor.

As for Rasputin's female admirers - it would be more correct to say "worshippers" - they can be categorized into two groups. Some believed in his supernatural gifts, his holiness, his divine mission; others were just being fashionable or hoped to obtain, through his intervention, favors for themselves or their families. Rasputin had worshippers who visited him on holidays to give him their best wishes and prostrate themselves before him, their arms embracing his tar-polished boots. He said, laughing, “On those days I purposely polish my boots with much tar so the elegant ladies who roll at my feet will soil their silk dresses."

---

[39] Rasputin may not have prayed in Simanovitch's presence and Simanovitch, being Jewish would not have accompanied him to church. Accounts by others say he prayed often.

Rasputin's friends often joked that he had his own council of ministers that was more reliable and capable than the Tsar's. This "Council of Ministers" was special. It was composed entirely of women. Old Mme Golovina was, in a way, president. She lent Rasputin the mantle of her authority and relations with Petersburg's high society. Her daughter, Munya, served as intermediary between the high clergy and Rasputin. Vyrubova helped, with her usual decisiveness, to nominate new ministers. Mme Nikitina, another lady-in-waiting to the Tsarina, was in constant contact with the Council President.

One of the Voskoboinokov sisters had the Imperial Palace as her stomping grounds, while the other had important contacts in military circles. Akilina Laptinskaya was our news reporter. She procured all the latest news and was up to date on all the gossip. A woman of unpredictable temperament, she secretly watched Rasputin's adversaries. All the other ladies scrupulously carried out, with total devotion, the missions and important services Rasputin charged them with.

Mme Von Dehn, the Tsarina's beautiful lady-in-waiting, was German by birth and had married a German-Russian naval officer. She was one of the influential members of Rasputin's group. She respected him especially for his stance in favor of a separate peace with Germany, but was also generally quite attached to him. Whenever they met at the Imperial Palace, they did not speak to each other. However, they often saw each other at the home of Rasputin's friend, Kushina, who was referred to as 'the Beautiful One.' I was sometimes invited to these delightful, intimate soirées.

The prodigious success of Rasputin with the Imperial Couple made him an idol. Civil servants were ecstatic.

One word from Rasputin was sufficient to give a state official a decoration, promotion, or some other important advantage. Of course, he was constantly assailed with requests from officials of all types. All of them tried to gain his support. Rasputin was more powerful than any high dignitary. They did not have to have any knowledge or special talent to obtain a brilliant career, thanks to him. Rasputin's whim was sufficient. Promotions that would not have been possible without long years of service, were given in a day or even an hour. For some, he obtained positions which they would never have dreamed possible. He was an all-powerful magician with an easy-going manner. One could count on him more than on any general or dignitary. No other 'favorite' of an emperor had ever held such power in Russia.

Between 10 a.m. and 1 p.m., Rasputin received those in need, at his apartment. Every day the crowd was huge enough to make any cabinet minister envy the peasant from Pokrovskoie. Sometimes, up to two hundred people came through the little apartment in a single day. One could find people of all circumstances and professions. There was a general who Grand Duke Nikolai Nikolayevich had struck with his own hand, a functionary disciplined for having abused his administrative powers, etc., etc. Others came begging for some favor or well-paid position. Still others brought complaints or denouncements. Jews came seeking protection from the police or military authorities. But the men disappeared in the crowd of women who came to Rasputin under diverse pretexts.

Even when he had not slept all night, due to his nocturnal amusements, he still received the crowd that filled the dining room, antechamber, and receiving room that was almost devoid of furniture. He would enter, greeting people sincerely. He would cast an eye about him and say,

"You come to me for help. I will help all of you -- yes, all." He almost never refused his support regardless of any principle. He did not ask if the person was deserving of his protection, nor if he had the ability to fulfill a certain position. To those who had been upbraided for some word or deed, he said, "The condemnation and subsequent fear you have suffered are punishment enough." For Rasputin, the deciding factor was that the person making the request had need of him. He always helped, when possible, in one way or another, and he loved to humiliate the rich and powerful to show that his sympathies lay with the poor and the peasantry. If military generals were among the crowd closing in on him, he sarcastically told them, "Generals, you are accustomed to being served first. Nevertheless, I see here, Jews who have been deprived of all rights. I will first attend to their needs. Come, Jews, I will do everything for you." After finishing with the Jews, Rasputin took care of the others, leaving the generals for last. To each person, at every meeting, he stated, "All beings are dear to me. Everyone should help each other and offer his hand."

If Rasputin had had the least interest in it, he could have amassed a great fortune. It would have been easy to ask for monetary compensation from those for whom he procured favors. However, he never asked for money. He received, in return, gifts, clothing, or soirées in his honor. He only accepted money when it was going to be passed along to some destitute individual who needed it. Often, if a rich man were present when a poor one was asking for help, he would instruct the wealthy one to give money to the poor man. He willingly helped any of the peasants who came to him. Often, he sent the poor to the homes of millionaire Jews (such as Gunzburg, Solovichik, Manus, Kaminka, and others), with a note instructing the latter to help the needy individuals who stood before them. These demands were often extreme ones.

When Gunzburg[40] visited Rasputin, he would voluntarily take all the money he had on him and distribute it to the poor who were there. At these times, Rasputin would announce, "A rich man has come to share his wealth with the poor." Once, I tried to interest Grigori in different business investments, but he declined my offers. Because he accepted no money, one had to find a subtle way to thank him for his services. By nature, he had a good heart and rarely turned away anyone in need. In very serious cases, he showed great delicacy and good will to help as much as possible. He questioned the needy, made them describe their situation in detail, and if he could not be of assistance, this caused him great pain. He took upon himself the causes of the offended and oppressed, and supported those who came with complaints against a powerful person.

In Petersburg, Rasputin did not try to acquire the habits and ways of high society. In aristocratic salons, he behaved with incredible insolence and a perfect lack of inhibition. He exaggerated, by design, his crudeness and lack of education. Truly, it was a strange sight to see these princesses, countesses, famous actresses, powerful ministers and high dignitaries pressing around this peasant filled with drink. He treated them like lackeys and servants. The slightest pretext was good enough reason to insult aristocratic ladies, with a vocabulary that would barely have been fit for a stable. His arrogance was grotesque. He spoke loudly, teased everyone and gave free rein to his moods.

With women and girls, he behaved with the greatest

---

[40] The Gunzburgs (also Ginzburg/Guenzburg) were Jewish barons who were scholars and philanthropists. They were at the forefront of those working for equal rights for Jews. There is no indication which Gunzburg is referred to here.

impudence, and the presence of mothers or husbands did not bother him in the least. His ways would have offended even a whore. Despite that, it was rare that anyone appeared offended by his attitude. It was disgusting to see these scenes but Rasputin's hosts were used to it and tolerated all of it with unequalled patience. He was feared, which is why he was flattered and catered to. As for me, I am convinced that Rasputin deliberately showed himself to be insolent and ill-bred to express his hatred of the nobility. He insulted and made clowns of aristocrats, saying they were dogs and that he didn't believe they had a single drop of Russian blood in their veins. Nevertheless, when he spoke to peasants or to his daughters, one never heard a bad word uttered.

A mixed social circle usually gathered at Rasputin's dining table. Each visitor brought a plate of delicacies such as caviar, prize fish, fruit and fresh rolls, but never meat. Potatoes, sauerkraut, and black bread were served, with a steaming samovar in the center of the table. There was always a full bowl of salty crackers as well. Rasputin loved these crackers and offered them to the other diners, among whom were a number of candidates for ministerial or administrative positions. These crackers became renowned in Petersburg. There were provisions of all sorts. Every person who came to his lodging was invited to drink and eat as much as he wanted.

One was often witness to strange scenarios at these gatherings. He was accustomed to sitting at the table, ignoring his silverware and using his fingers to feed large handfuls of food to his worshippers, who wished to show him that this gave them pleasure. Rasputin would throw morsels of black bread in a bowl of fish soup, take them out with his fingers, and distribute them to his guests who accepted these soggy morsels and ate them enthusiastically. Women kissed his hands that were covered with the remains of a meal, and paid no attention to his black, repulsive fingernails.

His two nieces, Nyura and Katya did the cleaning. He never wanted to have domestics in his house. Grigori's daughters lived in his apartment, in the farthest room, and never entered the rooms where he received visitors. The girls' rooms were well furnished and were connected to the kitchen, where Nyura and Katya lived. As for the rooms Rasputin reserved for his personal use, they were practically empty, containing only a few ordinary pieces of furniture. The table on which he ate had no cloth. It was only in his office that he had a few leather chairs. In fact, that was the only one of his rooms arranged in a relatively comfortable way. It was there that Rasputin spent his leisure time with aristocratic ladies or bureaucrats. These interviews were conducted with the greatest simplicity, and Rasputin would finally see the lady out, saying, "So, little one, all is in order now!"

After these visits, he would go to the public baths across the street. Whatever promise was made to the lady, he fulfilled scrupulously. It was obvious that Rasputin could not tolerate women who were too eager. On the other hand, he assiduously chased those who wanted nothing to do with him. Women asking a favor often offered themselves to him, believing that without this sacrifice they would gain nothing from him. In these cases, Rasputin played at being indignant, lectured the woman at fault, but did not hesitate then to accept her solicitation. When he was teased about his weakness for women, he generally responded that it was not his fault that many influential people threw their mistresses and even their wives into his arms, in order to gain his favor. These women entered into intimate relations with him with the consent of their husbands or lovers.

Once a year, Rasputin's wife, Praskovya, came to Petersburg to see her children, but never for more than a short visit. At such times, Rasputin changed nothing in his behavior, but treated this self-effacing country woman, whom he loved in his own way, in a friendly fashion. She rarely preoccupied herself with her husband's amorous adventures, and had the custom of saying, with an indifferent gesture, "He should do what he wants. He has enough to go around." Praskovya seemed flattered when, in her presence, Rasputin kissed his aristocratic admirers. He, who was usually extremely stubborn and would go on a rampage over nothing… he who was impatient over the least contradiction, and who was quick to go after his adversaries with his bare hands, showed himself to be very accommodating toward his wife. They had a good and cordial understanding and never did differences arise between them.

Rasputin's father also came to Petersburg once, to see for himself his son's success. He spent little time in the capital, quickly returned home, and died shortly thereafter.[41]

Rasputin's son, Dmitri, a good and peaceful boy who was not gifted, had difficulty learning. After two years at the seminary, he returned to Pokrovskoie to farm the land like a simple peasant. He still lives today[42] with his mother and wife. During the war, he reached the age of military service. However, his father did not want him to go to the front, and instead procured a job for him as nurse's aide in the imperial infirmary.

---

41 Efim Rasputin, Grigori's father, died in 1916.

42 Circa 1928. In 1920, the communists took Praskovya's home and, in 1930, she and Dmitri were exiled further into Siberia.

~~~~~~~~~

Rasputin often said he possessed a 'force' of a particular nature, whereby he could obtain the goals he proposed, and save his life at a critical moment. Skeptics did not believe this, but Rasputin really did have that special faculty. Many times, I had the opportunity to observe how this force manifested in him, and how he put it to use. It is not my intention to explain it or to say whether it was hypnosis or magnetism. There has been much debate and speculation on this topic. I simply wish to communicate my own observations, and the facts, as I know them.

Several cases of healing will give a clear idea of Rasputin's marvelous power. The first involved my youngest son, Ioann,[43] who had long suffered from a serious illness that seemed incurable.[44] His right hand had a nervous tremor and the entire right side of his body was paralyzed. He was confined to bed for several months out of each year. After I heard Vyrubova and the other ladies speak of Rasputin's healing gift, I repeatedly asked him to help my son. Either he paid no attention to my pleas, or he hesitated. Then, one day, he came to my home on business and saw my son in his sad state. He was seized with pity for the boy. His eyes never left the lad, as he ordered me to bring my son to his home the following day. He recommended coming early, before he had gotten out of bed. My son was to wait for him alone in the adjacent room while I was to wake Rasputin without showing myself. I did as he advised. I drove my son to Rasputin's, sat him in a dining room chair, knocked on Rasputin's bedroom door, and immediately left the apartment. One hour later, my son returned home. He was happy and cured. The illness never returned.

---

[43] John

[44] Ioann suffered from St. Vitus' Dance, a neurological disorder typified by jerky movements.
~~~~~~~~~

This is Ioann's account of what happened: Rasputin emerged from his room, approached my son and sat down, facing him. He placed his hands on Ioann's shoulders, stared straight into his eyes in a penetrating way, and suddenly began to shake violently. Rasputin's trembling and jerking diminished little by little, until it stopped.[45] Then, he leapt up from his chair and shouted, "Go, you little rascal! Go home! And, if you don't, you'd better watch out!" The boy jumped to his feet, laughed joyously, and came running home, happy.

I also had personal experience with Rasputin's power. For many years, I had been an incorrigible gambler, and spent most of my nights in gambling parlors. Once, I was so caught up in the fever of betting, that I stayed at the gambling table for three days in a row. It just so happened that, at that time, Rasputin needed me for an important business matter. He telephoned and even went to my home, but could not find me. When we saw each other again, he asked what had happened to me. I admitted to him that I had lost a lot of money and was stubborn about staying at the table until I won it back. Rasputin listened closely. When I'd finished my story, he smiled in a strange way.

He said, "I will give you money. Go play!"

This proposition surprised me and I refused to risk his money.

"Instead of gambling your money away," he said, "you'd do better to buy a new brain!"

---

[45] This description is reminiscent of 'empathic healing' whereby the healer absorbs and then releases the symptoms of the ailing person.

Rasputin invited me to sit at his table and stated, in an imperious tone, "Sit down! We will drink together!"

I accepted his invitation. He brought out a bottle of wine and filled two glasses. I was about to bring my glass to my lips when Rasputin stopped me and gave me his to drink instead. Then he mixed the wine in both glasses and told me to drink at the same time as he did. After this enigmatic ritual, there was a brief silence.

Finally, he said, "Do you want me to tell you something? You will never gamble again. It is over. Go where you want. I'd like to see if you disappear again for three days."

As he spoke, his gaze transfixed me. I felt uncomfortable, but very impressed. Rasputin got up and left the room, leaving me alone and greatly embarrassed. From that day until Rasputin's death, I never bet on the cards although I continued to own a gambling parlor. I abstained from the racetrack as well, which saved me tremendous amounts of time and money. When Rasputin died, this strange power ceased to exert its influence on me and I resumed gambling.

He said he had done the same for the Tsar, with regard to his drinking. The Tsar, as everyone knew, was a big drinker. He was only in a sober state until about ten o'clock in the morning. The rest of the time, he was generally drunk. Sometimes, at the regiment parties, he drank until he passed out and the officers had to carry him to his car.

Rasputin was everything to Nicholas II. He was completely involved in the intimate lives of the Imperial Family. He was unnerved, however, by the Tsar's sexual instincts which, apparently, exceeded the norm. Rasputin treated him as if he were a child. He yelled and railed against the Tsar, shouting orders. The Tsar tried to follow his advice, not at all upset at how he was spoken to. Many times, I asked Rasputin why he did not completely cure the Tsar of his alcoholism, since he only prohibited the Tsar's consumption of alcohol for a few weeks at a time — but never for longer. He never quite responded to the question, his explanation being so vague that I got the impression that it was not convenient to completely cure the Tsar, as the latter's weaknesses were useful to Rasputin. They allowed him to conserve his power over the Imperial Family.

The Tsar often spoke with Rasputin about the difficult programs of abstinence imposed upon him. He usually asked if his 'sentence' could be abbreviated. For example, when Rasputin prohibited him from drinking for a month, the Tsar wanted it reduced to two weeks. When the Tsar went to General Headquarters, this injunction would be sent in writing, and stayed in effect for the prescribed duration. Rasputin required the Tsar's absolute sobriety when at Headquarters. As for curing the Tsar of his love of drink or other weaknesses, this was not in the interest of Nicholas II's darling. In any case, that was my conviction.

There is no question that Rasputin would have lost some influence had the Tsarevitch fully recovered from his illness. While the state of the boy's health improved considerably after each of Rasputin's treatments, it was not a definitive cure. However, Rasputin persuaded the Tsar that the boy's illness would not torment him beyond his 18th year.[46] Then, he would be released of all suffering. The Tsarevitch could not do without Rasputin. At the least sign of aggravation, for the least discomfort, the miracle

---

[46] Tsarevitch Alexei was 13 years old when he was murdered with his family in 1918.

man would be summoned for his inexplicable power over the young boy. Even a brief conversation on the telephone could assuage the child's insomnia, fever, or chills. This explains the immense consideration Rasputin enjoyed from the Tsarina. Her maternal love made her a slave to this man.

Rasputin knew how to take full advantage of the benefits that accompanied these exceptional circumstances. Despite his lack of culture, he was very clever and adroit. It is not surprising that he would want to conserve this fantastic power as long as possible. Most of the Tsar's entourage — the high dignitaries of the Court, the ministers and generals, were motivated similarly to keep their status and favor. They worried little about the interests of the people or the country. In fact, the difference between them and the Siberian peasant consisted solely in that they lacked his extraordinary talents, and had no influence on the Tsar.

Gathering of followers at Rasputin's apartment. Rasputin is center. The unkempt man seated to the right of him is his father, Efim. The third and tallest woman in white, from the upper left is Anna Vyrubova. Lili Dehn, another of the Tsarina's confidantes, stands behind Rasputin, by the left door jamb, with a large plume in her hat. Seated on the floor is Akilina Laptinskaya.

Rasputin at home in Pokrovskoie with family and neighbors

Rasputin's family home in Pokrovskoie.

Rasputin at home in Pokrovskoie with his children. (from left to right) Matryona (Marya), Rasputin holding Varvara (Varya), and son Dmitri (Mitya).

Chapter III

The Rumors and the Two Courts

The hostility between the Court of Nicholas II and that of his mother, the Dowager Empress,[47] grew to lethal proportions. Nearly all the Tsar's relatives unreservedly attached themselves to the Old Court of his mother. The animosity between the two Courts did not begin with Rasputin's arrival, but dated from long before. Some claimed that it stemmed from the Dowager Empress' discontentment at seeing her eldest son on the throne. In the Crimea, rumor had it that there was a plot to give the throne to George, second son of Alexander III, and the apple of his mother's eye.[48] Some troops of the Palace Guard were said to have been party to this. However, the plot was never executed for whatever reason.

It was no secret that the Tsar's family opposed some of the concessions he made to the liberal movement. Once Nicholas II signed the decree for the Constitution in 1905, his relatives rose up against him in a tempest of indignation. This attitude was further propagated by the Tsar's indecisive politics in the following years. Count Witte, father of the 1905 Constitution, told me on many occasions that he, too, feared the vengeance of the Old Court. Everyone at Tsarskoye-Selo[49] knew that, in keeping

---

[47] The Dowager Empress, Maria Feodorovna, was Nicholas II's mother and widow of Tsar Alexander III.

[48] When George died, in 1899, Mikhail became her choice for tsar.

[49] Tsarskoye-Selo was a town on the outskirts of Petersburg that housed a number of palaces inhabited by the Imperial Family and

with the promise the Tsar had made to his father, the mother Empress and her people demanded that he maintain absolute power. Otherwise, they insisted, there could be a bad turn of events. Some of his friends even dared to counsel the Tsar to put his relatives in their place.

Those loyal to the Emperor, notably those who remained by his side during this struggle with the Old Court, accused him of housing and feeding his most ardent enemies. Even Rasputin hardly agreed with the Tsar on this point. He was well aware that their own bond was like a loaded weapon pointed at the Tsar's head and he knew that the Tsar's family hated him no less than they did the Emperor. This conviction made Rasputin a sworn enemy of the Old Court and the entire sovereignty. He did not miss an opportunity to pit the Tsar against the Grand Dukes. However, Nicholas II did not dare take severe measures against his family members. He feared them and tried to be amiable in any conflicts or differences with them. Rasputin did not hide his discontent in this regard and often bitterly reproached the Tsar:

"Why don't you act like a Tsar is supposed to act? You are one, you know! If I were Tsar, I would show you how to behave. No one thinks of you. No one needs you. Your family will kill you. You don't know how to win their hearts. They are all hostile toward you. And you... you're content to say nothing."

He wanted to push the Tsar to defend himself, to resist, but the Tsar did not have the resolve to battle his enemies. It was only when a member of the Imperial House committed some grave error that some sanction was pronounced against him; and even then, the punishment inflicted was so

---

other nobility.

benign that everyone was shocked at the timidity of the Emperor. Nothing showed his weakness more than the assassination of Rasputin. He could not find the courage to force the murderers to pay for their crime.

The hatred that the Tsar's family, the Old Court, felt for Rasputin is explained less by the friendship between the Tsar and the Siberian peasant than by the stalemate of certain projects fostered by the Grand Dukes. It was, of course, thanks to the benevolence of the Grand Dukes' Montenegrin wives[50] that Rasputin was introduced to the Court. The Tsar's family took an active part in the hunt for miracle workers and took great care to search in every corner of the empire. When Grand Duchesses Anastasia and Militza introduced Rasputin to the Imperial Couple, they made a grave error. He showed himself to be stronger and more intelligent than his predecessors. Although Rasputin enjoyed the warm support of the Grand Duchesses for many years, once he saw that their benevolence was no longer necessary to maintain his foothold, he turned his back on them.

Two reasons drove him to do this. The animosity between the Old Court and the Young Court had intensified, and the majority of the Grand Dukes' families were on the side of the Dowager Empress. Consequently, Rasputin felt obliged to distance himself from them. In addition, his confidence had grown strong and his thirst for power would not tolerate any intermediary between himself and the Imperial Couple. He no longer required protectors, and it was no longer necessary to exhibit humiliating displays of devotion to them. From then on, he was his own master.

---

[50] Grand Duchesses Anastasia and Militza of Montenegro were married to the Tsar's uncles.

Grand Duke Nikolai Nikolayevich became Rasputin's sworn enemy and conducted merciless campaigns against him. One of his most dangerous devices involved false rumors which compromised the Imperial Family. Nevertheless, this ploy did not have its desired effect. Actions against Rasputin met the same fate. Even the full powers of the Commanding General of the Russian Armies did not give Nikolai Nikolayevich the most remote chance of interfering with Rasputin's power.

When the Old Court realized that the Tsar was beyond their influence, they turned against the Imperial Couple. The Dowager Empress dreamed of placing her son, Mikhail, on the throne, after the death of George.[51] The birth of Nicholas' son, Tsarevitch Alexei, dashed those hopes. The Dowager Empress openly showed her hatred for the young Tsarina. The rift between the two grew greater due to Tsarina Alexandra's bold character and inability to be intimidated. In addition, the Grand Dukes, seeing that they could no longer influence the weak Nicholas as easily as before, became very irritated by the young Tsarina's stubbornness, and often lost their tempers. This both pained and aggravated Alexandra who came back with the rage of a lioness protecting, with all her strength, that which she loved most.

Eventually, this war between the Grand Dukes and Rasputin dragged official circles, the army, and the public into the heated dispute. But not all of the Grand Dukes took sides. The Tsar's cousins, Cyril, Boris and Andre, the sons of Grand Duke Vladimir, stayed away from the conflict.

---

[51] George died in 1899.

Nicholas II did not have confidence even in his own bodyguards. He always feared some treason from the Old Court. That is why he always appointed Tartars and Georgians as his guards. It was always the Georgian princes he felt most comfortable with as his guards. He felt affection for them and was less worried when they were on duty at the Palace. The Empress Mother herself had proposed that the Georgians be made palace guards, as they were known for their loyalty. In reality, she had hoped they would help her to put her second son, George, on the throne but Nicholas II gained their loyalty instead.

The Tsar knew well the weaknesses of these faithful guards. He knew they were uneducated and that they had an irresistible penchant for all sorts of excesses, especially for drinking and gambling. He willingly paid their gambling debts. For example, the Tsar's favorite among them, Prince Dadiani, once admitted to him, upon returning home from a wild party where there was no lack of drink, that he had put up his epaulettes on a bet, which signified that he gave his word to honor his debt. Nicholas II would indulgently close his eyes when their passion for gambling, their excesses and amorous adventures got these good and brave boys mixed up in some scandalous story. Their pranks amused him greatly. Nevertheless, he could also be certain that each one of them would sacrifice his life for him, without hesitation, and that they would shoot anyone to defend him. He was proud of their loyalty and, in return, treated them well. They lived a magnificent life, thanks to the Emperor, but abused his kindness and gentleness.

These palace officers often provoked scandals in pleasure establishments, but they were devoted to the Emperor, body and soul, and this compensated for all else. General Ruzsky and the Deputies Shulgin and Guchkov were very lucky to find not a single Caucasian guarding the Tsar when they demanded he sign his abdication. Otherwise, there is no doubt that not one of these men would be left alive. It is said that General Ruzsky went so far as to threaten the Tsar with a gun. For this to have happened, it must have been the coward Voyekov on duty, the commandant of the Palace who was constantly in a state of semi-drunkenness.

I was on the best terms with all of the officers in the Tsar's Bodyguard, and I never had any but the most cordial relations with them. One day, they invited me to meet them at the Guard's Room in the palace where we were to play cards. While we were playing, the Emperor suddenly wandered in, wearing his nightclothes. He lectured us adamantly about gambling, gave us each rolls of 20 kopeks and ten rubles, then sat down with us to play cards.

It is possible that the tension in the Imperial Court had causes much older and more profound, but there is no doubt that the terrible event I'm about to tell played a large role, as it led to a whole series of difficulties and complications. As far as I know, it never was made public knowledge, but the preciseness of my information has been confirmed by different sides, as well as by Rasputin himself. Many readers are familiar with the photograph of the Tsarevitch in the arms of one of his guards — a strapping sailor. At that time, a notice reported that the tsarevitch took a nasty fall on the Imperial Family's yacht, the *Standart*, and wounded his foot. Shortly afterward, the newspapers announced that the commander of the *Standart*, Commodore Tschagine[52] killed himself with a

---

[52] Also spelled Tchaguin and Chaguin. This story is a convoluted version of an incident where the "Standart" ran onto some rocks off the coast of Finland and the royal family had to be evacuated. Tchaguin, as captain, was reprimanded. Admiral Nilov, however,

revolver. It was said that the admiral killed himself because the heir to the throne had suffered an accident on a vessel that he commanded. But this could not have been a sufficient reason for suicide. What I learned was that there was no "accident" on the yacht. The young boy was rather at Tsarskoye-Selo where he was the victim of an attack. Members of the Old Court had begged Admiral Tschagine to recommend two sailors to be employed as common workers at the Imperial Palace of Tsarskoye-Selo. It was customary to choose, for such positions, only people who had served the Imperial Family or in homes known to the Court, even for the most ordinary work. It was the best way to obtain proven workers.

The two sailors recommended by Tschagine had previously served at the Anichkov Palace as gardeners. At Tsarskoye-Selo, they would remain in that trade. It would never have occurred to anyone that these two sailors had been commissioned to kill the Tsarevitch. One day, the young boy, accompanied by the Emperor's valet, was playing in the palace garden near where the two sailors were pruning a hedge. Suddenly, one of them threw himself on little Alexei and thrust a long knife into his leg. At the child's cry, the valet ran toward him and overpowered the fleeing sailor whom he strangled on the spot. As for the second sailor/gardener, he was seized and, by order of the Tsar, was immediately hanged with no prior formal proceedings.[53] It was then established that these sailors had been introduced to the Imperial Palace by Admiral Tschagine

---

was responsible for the family's security and was about to shoot himself when the Tsar stopped him. The Admiral was simply reprimanded. No one committed suicide over the incident.

53 All other accounts state that Alexei had bumped his leg disembarking from a boat prior to the photograph of the sailor carrying the boy. There is no documentation about such an attempt on Alexei's life and, as a hemophiliac, it is highly unlikely he would have survived such an attack.

who, fearing he would be charged as an accomplice in the attack, killed himself. He put a gun in his mouth and pulled the trigger. His head exploded into pieces. Tschagine left a letter for the Tsar, exposing the entire chain of events.

After this attempt, the Imperial Couple went through a terrible period. The little prince was in a grave state and improved very slowly. From this moment on, the Tsar and Tsarina never ceased fearing for their son's life. They believed their relatives were mounting new attacks against the child, but dared not confide this. The boy's mother didn't leave him for a moment. The Tsar also was profoundly shaken; he no longer knew which saint to devote himself to. This explains the bizarre characteristics that others saw in him at the time.

Letter from Rasputin to the tsarina, written in 1912, during the Tsarevitch's illness: "My Dear Mama - I received your telegram. Do not be sad. Pray. God gives his grace based on prayers, not sins. Have confidence and the prince will heal. I pray endlessly, but what can I do? Only God is all-powerful; he did not make man so. I cannot come now, perhaps during the Assumption. May God keep you. – Grigori."

~~~~~~~~

The story told to me about the birth of Tsarevitch Alexei is so fantastic that it doesn't seem believable. However, my sources are persons worthy of absolute trust. As everyone knows, the Tsarina, in her first years of marriage, bore only girls. This repeated ill luck provoked many comments and much mockery. Finally, the Royal Couple was at the point of abandoning all hope of having an heir. The Emperor was convinced that if his wife could only bear girls, the
~~~~~~~~

fault lay with him alone. I do not know what led him to this belief. Perhaps some clairvoyant suggested it to him. In any case, it was said that he renounced, for a while, his conjugal prerogatives and yielded his wife to another. Certainly, a deciding factor in this decision was that the birth of a son would eliminate his family's previously discussed plans to have him deposed.

The Emperor's choice was the Commander in Chief of the Tsarina's horse cavalry, General Orlov, a handsome man who was also a widower. The Empress, it is said, entered into intimate relations with him, at her husband's request. The goal of this union was successful.[54] The Tsarina gave the light of day to a son named Alexei. But the story doesn't end there. It seems that the Empress Alexandra had become passionately taken with this lover who, at first, had been imposed on her but then won her heart. However, Nicholas II was not prepared to tolerate this result of his attempt to produce an heir.

The delivery was painful and an operation was necessary, as the child was not in the normal birth position. As the Tsarina was very unhappy with Professor Ott, her birthing coach, she summoned her regular doctor, Dr. Timoyev, although he did not practice gynecology. He informed Nicholas II of the gravity of the situation and asked him to choose between mother and son, in case one had to be sacrificed. The Tsar responded, "If it's a boy, save him and sacrifice the mother." Thanks to the operation, the doctor succeeded in saving both mother and son. However, the crudely done surgery, combined with the Tsarina's

---

[54] This rumor about Count Alexander Orlov and the Tsarina was popular and circulated widely. However, the Tsarina never received male visitors alone in the palace, and was under guard by the secret police 24/7 when outside the palace. There is no evidence that Alexei was not the Tsar's son.

hysterical nature, caused her to stop fulfilling her wifely duties. She learned that she was the one chosen to be sacrificed in case only one of them could be saved. This made an indelible impression on her. Her relationship with Orlov continued.

When this became a public scandal, the Tsar resolved to send Orlov to Egypt but invited him to one more dinner before his departure. What happened between the two men, I never knew. All I was told was that Orlov was taken, unconscious, from the palace. Soon after, he was dispatched to North Africa, but he never arrived there, having died en route. His body was brought back to Petrograd and solemnly buried at Tsarskoye-Selo.

After the tragic death of Orlov, the Tsarina prayed at his grave for a whole year, often unable to hold back her tears. She never forgot to bring beautiful flowers. The Tsar did not try to stop her. During this period, she was subject to violent outbursts of hysteria. The Tsarina was convinced that the Tsar bore all responsibility for Orlov's death, and never forgot this. Her sorrow was profound and, for a long time, her husband was nothing more than a stranger to her. Eventually, they reestablished a good rapport, but even then, there were many times she wouldn't speak to him. On those days, they sent each other letters, via trusted friends or aides. Sablin, aide-de-camp and commander of the imperial yacht "Standart", was often the mediator between them.[55] Once he established peace, the Tsar and Tsarina appeared, once again, as a close couple. She always had a considerable influence over him but, in reality, who didn't?

---

[55] Sablin was second in command to Tschagine.

A letter about the Orlov incident from Rasputin in Pokrovskoie to the Imperial Court in Petersburg, reads: "My loved ones: Dunya told me everything. God will save us. I will come at Easter and fix everything. I cannot come before that. You must hide Mama's mistake; even for a peasant it would be shameful, and for a Tsar it is much worse. Let us wish that all will go well. It is already getting much better. God protect you. Do not worry about the children. — Grigori" (This letter constitutes proof of the tsarina's adultery.)[56]

The entire reign of Nicholas II was filled with events worthy of any sensationalist novel. In this, he surpassed his predecessors. There is no doubt that the Emperor himself brought much of this about. His conscience was tainted by more than one bad deed. He was involved in a confusing array of bloody acts and terrible crimes that went unexplained.[57] However, I will leave this subject to future historians and stick with relating my impressions of this decade, 1907 to 1917, which preceded the revolution.

~~~~~~~~

There was no delay to the diverse and fantastic rumors about Rasputin's personality and his visits to the Imperial Palace. One wondered, above all, what prompted the two grand duchesses and their ladies-in-waiting to introduce the Imperial Couple to this peasant who, the day before, was completely unknown to Petersburg. Many suspected that the arrival of Rasputin in Petersburg was not simply by chance, but that this man of strange genius had been brought to politically influence the Tsar.

---

56 Simanovitch's parenthetical note does not, of course, establish any evidence of adultery.

57 This is likely a reference to a variety of events such as the 1905 revolution, the pogroms, Russo-Japanese War, etc.
~~~~~~~~

Others thought Rasputin was Germany's instrument. It was widely thought that the Hohenzollerns[58] had a deep hatred of the Romanov dynasty, and that the German emperor wanted revenge for what he perceived as the Romanovs' ingratitude and lack of respect. The Hohenzollerns had been, for the prior two centuries, well-prepared to do battle with Russia. Germany had an extraordinary influence on Russia's economy, though it had none on Russian politics. The Russian Court did not like the Hohenzollerns, being of the opinion that Emperor Wilhelm II felt the Romanovs to be the one insurmountable obstacle to any conquest of Russia.

Did Grand Duchesses Anastasia and Militza, the two daughters of the King of Montenegro, bring Rasputin from Kiev in order to destroy Nicholas II? Some believed he was brought to the Emperor's side in the hopes that this ignorant monk would ruin the already precarious health of the prince. What would prompt the Tsarina's friend, Lady Vyrubova, to be used to Rasputin's advantage? There could be no question in their minds that it was a German influence. Yet it was Vyrubova who used all her influence to bring Rasputin to the Court. There was no desire of his that she did not take as an absolute order. She practically deified him and it was largely due to her, acting as faithful intermediary between him and the Imperial Couple, that he owed his unique situation. He often said that Vyrubova would follow him to the end of the world and, certainly, she was devoted to him, body and soul. Her mission was to act in the interest of the sovereigns and the dynasty, with the principal objective of curing the heir to the throne.

~~~~~~~~

58 The Hohenzollern Dynasty ruled Brandenburg-Prussia from 1415 to 1918, and Germany from 1871 to 1918.
~~~~~~~~

Rumors spread in Petersburg that Rasputin was having an affair with the Tsarina, and that he was behaving inappropriately with the daughters of the Tsar. These stories had no basis whatsoever. Rasputin never went to the Imperial Palace when the Tsar was not there. I do not know if this was his own practice or by wish of the Tsar. From time to time, he encountered the Tsarina at the military hospital built by Vyrubova, but always in the presence of her entourage. Neither was there a word of truth to the rumors involving the Tsar's daughters. Rasputin was always attentive to and protective of the Tsar's children. He was against the marriage of one of the daughters to Dmitri Pavlovich and warned them to guard against him. He even advised against extending their hands to him because he suffered from an illness easily spread by the slightest contact.[59] In the case where a handshake was unavoidable, Rasputin recommended that they wash immediately with an infusion of Siberian herbs. He also counseled the Tsarina about her stinginess. He hated seeing the Tsar's daughters poorly dressed simply because of their mother's excessive thrift. The Tsarina's stinginess was legendary in the Court. She sought to economize on even the smallest items. It was so painful for her to spend money that she even bought clothing on an installment plan.

The advice and counsel of Rasputin was generally wise and useful; he enjoyed the complete confidence of the Tsar's family. The imperial children had in him a true friend and good counselor. Sometimes he was discontented with them and did not hesitate to scold them. His relationship with them was exclusively that of a father with his

---

[59] Pavlovich suffered from chronic tuberculosis which became acute in the 1930s and eventually led to his death in 1941. It is not known if this is what Rasputin was referring to.

children. The Tsar's family wholly believed that Rasputin was God's emissary.

The infamous rumors spreading throughout the city often gave me occasion to speak with Rasputin about his relationship with the Tsarina and her daughters. This caused me much worry because I knew these rumors were based on nothing but malice. However, the young girls, good and pure as they were, did not deserve the shameful accusations of scandalmongers. Despite their high position, they were devastated by these attacks.

The most shameful thing, above all, was that even the Tsar's relatives and the Court took part in spreading these dirty little stories. Their attitude was especially undignified, as they knew well that these rumors were unfounded. Rasputin was indignant with regard to these stories, but having a clear conscience on this issue, he did not react. As for me, I judged the situation differently and thought he should counter these revolting rumors. I reproached him for not doing anything.

"What do you want of me?" Rasputin would cry. "What can I do? Is it my fault if they spread these rumors about me?"

"But the Grand Duchesses should not be maligned because of you. It could hurt them. Think hard about that! And the Tsarina is also suspected..."

"Go to the devil," Rasputin said. "I've done nothing wrong. People should know that no one soils the place where he eats! I serve the Tsar and I would never allow any such thing to happen. It would be the vilest ingratitude. And what do you think the Emperor would do to me if that were the case?"

"These stories start because you're such a skirt-chaser," I told him. "Leave the women alone. You don't spare a single one of them."

"Is it my fault?" he replied. "I don't take them by force. They come of their own accord, so that I may plead their case to the Tsar. What should I do? I am a healthy and vigorous man and I cannot resist the attraction of a pretty woman who seeks me out. Why wouldn't I take them? I don't go find them. They come on their own."

"But you have a bad reputation with the Tsar's relatives. All of Russia is rising up against you... the nobility and foreign countries as well. Believe me, in your own interest, it is time to put an end to all of that. If not, you risk losing everything."

Rasputin tossed aside all of my warnings, but when I became tormented by bad premonitions, I became more insistent. He said, "Be a little more patient. I am going to make peace with Wilhelm. Then I'm going on a pilgrimage to Jerusalem."

One day, we had a similar conversation in the presence of Vyrubova, the Voskoboinokov sisters, Mme von Dehn, Mlle Nikitina, and other ladies of the Court. I saw clearly that they held the same opinion, but simply did not have the strength or courage to speak frankly to him. The more Rasputin's star rose, the more his bond with the Imperial Family led to gossip, plots and intrigue. The nobility, bourgeoisie and Grand Dukes, on the one hand, and the press and liberal sectors of society, on the other, tried to discredit him in the eyes of the Russian people and the entire world. They tried to end his influence over the Tsar's family, at any cost. Rasputin offered them all an ideal target, vulnerable enough to kill with impunity, while appearing to perform a patriotic duty.

The rumor suggesting intimate relations between Rasputin and the Tsarina was, for unimaginable reasons, believed by all. This dealt a hard blow to the Imperial Family, and it could not be quelled due to the delicate nature of the issue and the speed with which rumors spread throughout Russia and the Court. I have always maintained that this romance novel theory of such a liaison is inane and absurd. Today,[60] this rumor has lost much of its credibility.

The widespread notion that Rasputin used the Tsarina to exert his influence the Tsar is somewhat erroneous. In reality, it was often the opposite. The Tsarina often used Rasputin to influence the Tsar for her own purposes, by invoking Grigori's name with her requests. Not only did the Tsar love and trust Rasputin, but he also considered him a saint and a seer whose advice was like law to him. Rasputin was, perhaps, the only man the Tsar trusted, and Nicholas II was typically very distrustful.

The Tsarina had been abandoned by most of society, during the Great War,[61] and she felt threatened by the increasing solitude. The one person she could always turn to and trust was Rasputin, especially when she wanted the Tsar to destroy their enemies or decide on a political action. The Tsar often consulted Rasputin on important affairs of state. And the little peasant from Tobolsk was insistent about his opinion, even to the point of raising his voice to the Tsar.

---

[60] Circa 1928

[61] World War I, then called the Great War, began in 1914.

Another rumor that found its way to the throne, during the war, targeted Rasputin as a German spy or, at least, an instrument of occult forces with German sympathies. This story had no basis whatsoever. Rasputin knew how to surround himself with people who were devoted to him, body and soul, serving him blindly and showering him with flattery. On the other hand, he also saw hate rise against him from all quarters, each day more intense and menacing. A venomous campaign was mounted against him. His enemies became greater in number and strength. But all efforts to turn the Imperial Couple against him were in vain. His enemies never attained this goal. On the contrary, the couple's affection for this man grew all the greater as they saw him hated and attacked. Neither the prayers nor threats of his adversaries could change that. The Tsar and Tsarina clearly saw the increasing dangers of their rapport with Rasputin but they did not want to be influenced by threats.

A merciless struggle ensued, in which the Tsar was up against his people, his family, and even his closest allies. The life of the Imperial Couple was poisoned by protests against Rasputin, by reproaches, by bitter accusations (often false), and by the growing hatred that surrounded them. However, the Tsar, though weak in other ways, was unshakeable with regard to this issue. Another would certainly not have hesitated to sacrifice not only a Rasputin but all that he held dear, to save his throne which was seriously in danger. Nicholas II chose the opposite: he accepted his own loss and that of his family, beginning the downfall of his own great empire.

Chapter IV

Rasputin's Politics

Rasputin's politics were completely original and very personal to him. They were uniquely 'Rasputinian.' He consistently stood against all war and told Nicholas II to beware of it. When they met alone, he spoke to the Tsar as to a small child, and the Tsar listened attentively, with deference, to Rasputin's counsel.

"Fear war!" Rasputin said. "You were born in a bloody century. Your reign began in blood.[62] Fear, fear war!"

Rasputin pressed this warning on the Tsar with increasing insistence and force, whenever foreign conflicts broke out during the years preceding the Great War. Each time, the odor of gunpowder and blood filled the European atmosphere.

Rasputin told Nicholas II, "You are the Tsar — your father's heir. Your father created a friendship with the French and you do not have the right to change your father's legacy. Are you stupid? If you had to be *elected* Tsar, no one would vote for you, as stupid as you are. I also have an heir — my son, Dmitri. He is stupid, too. I will leave to him a cottage and some cows and horses. *Your* father left you *all of Russia!*"

---

[62] This refers to Nicholas II's 1896 coronation celebration, 'the Khodynka Tragedy,' where overcrowding and souvenir seekers ended in a stampede and many deaths.

In his own inimitable language and fashion, filled with comparisons and examples, Rasputin tried to avert any rupture in the Franco-Russian alliance. However, he feared the Germans, seeing them as aggressive, and Wilhelm as ambitious. His philosophy was: "With France on one side, Russia on the other, and Germany between the two, as long as we get along with France, there will be no war."[63]

As much as he feared the Germans, Rasputin respected Wilhelm and often spoke of him in more esteemed terms than he did of other monarchs. Rasputin also knew that Wilhelm was curious about him, which flattered him. He loved his name to be spoken in the high spheres of foreign courts. Wilhelm knew Rasputin, and found him interesting. He considered Rasputin to be a natural-born diplomat, and once said to Nicholas II: "My father had Bismarck to advise him, and you have Father Rasputin."

Rasputin spoke as much against war with Germany as he did in favor of maintaining an alliance with France: "The Germans are our neighbors. Do not say 'fountain, I will no longer drink your water.' We cannot go to war against the Germans. Even if Russia took Berlin, we would not profit. Germany would cry on our shoulder and we would have to give it back as a gift."

Once when Rasputin was asked why he was more sympathetic toward the Germans than toward the French or English, he responded, in a joyous mood from drinking: "I cannot like the French because I know they don't like me. They are republicans and revolutionaries. I appear ridiculous to them. I can only work with monarchs. But kings should never make war. On the contrary, they should

[63] The Russo-Japanese War (1904-1905) had been over for five or six years, but WW I (1914-1918) would begin in two or three years.

develop a good rapport with each other. That is why Russia should make peace with Germany as soon as possible." His response clearly showed that while he knew the extent of his power, he also was aware of its limits.

Rasputin was really only indisposed toward the English. "The English are the most diplomatic people," he would say with a little smile. "They number twenty million but have four hundred million slaves. The English do not like us because we act with the fist while they use intelligence. They don't like us to fight, and we don't like them to be too clever."

But Rasputin feared the Balkan states the most. He considered them to be a hotbed of a future, sinister world. He warned the Tsar: "The Balkans, you see, are first a cloud, then thunder. Help them financially, but do not mix in their quarrels. When they fight, leave them to manage on their own. Just pay and be done with it."

Shortly before the Great War, Ferdinand, King of Bulgaria, came to Russia incognito, sent by Wilhelm, on a secret mission to persuade Nicholas II to remain neutral in the event of war. The Tsar did not want to receive Ferdinand, and it was only through Rasputin's intervention that he received an imperial audience.

"What do you want?" Rasputin asked Ferdinand. "You are king of many people. You are king of clouds and thunder. Be calm and do not make a move. If it's a matter of money, Papa will give you what you need."

Ferdinand was received by the Tsar, but the interview went poorly for him. After the meeting, a very content Grigori paced up and back in his room, rubbing his hands together and saying, "And King Ferdinand left with a red nose — with a very, very, very red nose…"

~~~~~~~~~

In the summer just before the Great War, Rasputin went home to his village in Tobolsk where there was an attempt on his life which I will recount later. He was in serious condition. Not fully recovered, Rasputin returned to the capital, but the war was already underway. He had obstinately struggled against war, and all the blood that flowed like a river was a great sadness to him. He felt impotent with regard to the unfolding chain of events. He always regretted that, when war was declared, he could not get to Petersburg due to the serious wound inflicted by Guseva.

This is Rasputin's letter to the Tsar, at the moment the Great War was declared: "Dear Friend, I repeat: a terrible tempest menaces Russia. It is a great sorrow, an unfathomable evil. Everything around us is obscured and no battle will pierce the fog. An ocean of tears. And so much blood! What can I say? I find no words. An indescribable horror. I know all those around you have been pushing you toward war, including your most loyal subjects. They do not see that they are teetering on catastrophe. Cruel is God's punishment. If he takes reason from one man, it is the beginning of the end. You are Tsar — father of your people. Do not let the enraged triumph, running toward their own loss, trailing the population behind them. Perhaps we will conquer Germany. But what will become of Russia? Upon reflection, one can see that there has never been a greater martyr than Russia. Russia will drown in her own blood. This misfortune is huge. The sadness is infinite. — Grigori"

A little later, when the war became a real worldwide catastrophe, Rasputin tried, once again, to save Russia and stop the torrents of blood. He renewed his efforts to
~~~~~~~~~

convince the Tsar. This time, however, it was not with advice of a separate peace, as many believed. He proposed to the Tsar a purely Rasputinian solution to the world conflict: “Take France’s side and dethrone Wilhelm, that crazy man who wants to own the whole world. We, the peasants, will take the weight of the war on our backs. We will tolerate what’s necessary, but do not spill any blood. Pay. Pay! End war and bring about peace. You are the Tsar, the anointed master, but you haven’t given life to anyone; why do you want to take it away?”

But the war only seemed to spread more and more, and Rasputin already smelled the scent of a national revolt. He was closer to the mentality of the peasants and soldiers, and understood them. He warned the Tsar that the soldiers would return from war as “wild beasts, howling.”

“The freedom of the peasants was not well-conceived,” he would say. “The peasants are free, it is true, but they do not own enough land. The peasant has a large family — about ten children — but the strip of land he is allowed is very small. The sons argue with their father that their little field, which they will have to share with their children someday, is already stretched too thin. Many go to the city to earn money, but find no work. When the war is ended, our sons will return to the paternal home and marry. But how will they live? You would have to expect conflicts and agitation. In earlier times, even the serf had an easier life. He was given food and the necessary clothing. Now, the Russian peasant receives nothing and must pay hefty taxes. His property can be seized and sold, right down to his last cow. As for his children, they go naked until their tenth year. They have neither shoes nor boots, and can only take pride in their rope sandals. If the peasant has no land, no life is possible for him in the village.”

"You must borrow foreign money," Rasputin told the Tsar. "Buy back all the land owned by the nobility. Divide it among the peasants and create communal schools in the teachers' homes. You will deprive no one. Everyone will be happy and living in peace — the nobles with their money and the peasants with their land. When the peasants have land, they will be rich. They will build schools and teach their children to read. But you must not permit the nobles to use the proceeds of the sale of their lands, on costly trips outside of Russia. That sort of thing should not be tolerated," he warned.

The primary goal, in Rasputin's mind, was to relieve the nobility of its political power, and to assure the peasantry of a decisive influence in the country's government. He dreamed of making Tsarevitch Alexei the emperor of the peasants. "Your son must become a tsar of the people," Rasputin told Nicholas II. "This is the only way you'll remain, throughout history, Nicholas the Great."

"Which is worth more to you?" he asked the Tsar. "One hundred fifty thousand rich landowners or one hundred fifty *million* rich peasants? Let the landowners take their money and build factories, or traffic in commerce. You are the Tsar of the people, and not the other way around. You are afraid of everyone and no one needs you. Let your heir be a Tsar of the people and you will be immortal and remembered as Nicholas the Great, and your dynasty will last another thousand years."

When Nicholas responded that he did not have the strength to do all that, and that the Grand Dukes would rise against him, Grigori slammed his fist on the table, yelling, "For once in your life, you too should hit the table with your fist, and write with your own hand! Otherwise, be careful that they do not cut you up in pieces and throw you out the window like the King of Serbia![64] Make them gifts of money, to members of your family, and send them on vacation abroad that they might amuse themselves. For the love of God, show the greatness of a Tsar. You are the most powerful of all orthodox tsars. All the people serve you — you, the anointed of God. And you are like a goat — one has to make such a fuss with you! Take all that is given and all that you own. You will do it all. Have no fear; no one will touch you. Your mujik[65] is always ahead of you with bread and salt, and you do nothing for him. And the city thinks of nothing but carnage. The blood of those dogs, the nobility, is always near you…"

Rasputin did not like the nobles who avoided and opposed him. In fevered moments, when enemies tried to discredit him and diminish his ties to the Tsar, he would run about the room, waving his fists, daggers in his eyes, bellowing: "They'll remember me, those dogs! It used to be the nobles, but now the Russian peasant has climbed to the top. We will take the land; we will take the money. And we will have a Tsar of the people! I will take everything from them. They want nothing to do with me? They want none of my advice? I will make them submit. I will show them what peasants are made of. The Tsar has but one peasant close to him, and everyone is dead set against that one. Some want to send me away; others want to kill me. I sense everything. I smell it all and I remember it all."

Rasputin also complained about the government not wanting to build a railroad to Siberia: "They are afraid of the train and the changes it will bring. They fear that the train will pervert the peasant. That is stupid! The train can

---

[64] King Alexander of Serbia married a woman of questionable background, as well as being considered unfit to rule, and both he and his wife were murdered and thrown out of a palace window.
[65] Also spelled 'muzhik' means Russian peasant.

help the peasant better himself. Without the train, he must stay in his corner of the world, since one cannot run around Siberia on foot. The Siberian peasant knows nothing of what is going on in the world. He does not hear the news of other places. Can you call that a life? Siberia is vast and the Siberian peasants enjoy its roominess, but in Russia, the peasants' children so rarely see white bread, that they consider it a luxury item. The men of the fields have nothing. They only have wheat flour at Easter. Even on the holidays, they only eat meat in small quantities. Clothing and shoes are all lacking and they can do nothing about it since there are no artisans out in the country. If a stranger comes to the village, they immediately chase him away. Why? Is it because he digs a hole, plows a trough, makes a horseshoe, sickle, boots, or other necessary objects? They fear the foreign artisan.

There seems to be a widespread fear of seeing the peasant grow accustomed to a comfortable life, chase money and demand his share of the land. They say it will lead to revolution! This is sheer nonsense! The nobility has more than their fair share. They do nothing but put sticks in the wheel spokes of those who want to do something for themselves. If they find an educated man who wants to undertake some enterprise, they treat him as a revolutionary. They cry from the rooftops that he is a rebel and they throw him in prison. They do not want schools. They want to keep the peasants in ignorance. The politics of these aristocrats will lead to no good."

To his contemporaries, Rasputin was nothing but a dirty, drunken peasant who became part of the Imperial Family and appointed ministers, bishops and generals, only to catapult them into disgrace. He was widely known through Petersburg's gossip columns which he dominated for a decade. People saw his life as one of disorder and excess, with his wild parties at the Villa Rode and his passionate dancing in the mixed company of aristocratic ladies and drunken gypsies. His outrageous hold on the Tsar and his family, his mesmerizing force and faith in his mission were astounding.

Once Rasputin had acquired an influence over the Tsar, he disdained little daily problems and petty worries. His ideas were sharply focused and he stubbornly worked to realize them. But Rasputin never forgot he was a peasant. He never pursued fame or glory, nor did he want an official appointment. He always remained the peasant, exaggerating his crudeness, especially in the company of those who scorned mujiks. He never lost sight of his millions of Russian brothers, dispersed in villages throughout the immense empire. His most ardent desire, and the goal toward which he worked with all of his soul's strength, was to come to their aid and break down the wall between them and the Tsar. In the course of the long hours Rasputin spent with the Imperial Family, he and the Tsar often discussed political and religious issues. He spoke of the Russian people and their suffering, painting vivid portraits of their lives. The Imperial Couple listened attentively and the Tsar thus learned many things that otherwise would have remained hidden from him.

Only a very few had the privilege of appreciating the profound qualities of spirit and character hiding under Rasputin's crude exterior. Unfortunately, some of those who could have benefitted from the mujik's influence on the Tsar allowed themselves to be put off by his appearance and his rowdy behavior. Rather than take the time to look more carefully at him, they remained distant and hostile. Most of those who did approach him saw him as a means to reach their own self-serving goals which were often unsavory. They had not the slightest desire to delve any deeper. The real Rasputin was of little interest to them.

It is undeniable that there existed, behind the mask of a crude peasant, a powerful and penetrating spirit, as well as an intelligence preoccupied with various political problems. When Rasputin arrived in Petersburg, he was already a self-made man. He had no education but he was one of those who follow their paths solely by their own sense of reason and logic, lending an attentive ear in order to divine the mysteries of life. He had been a carefree pilgrim who had traveled all of Russia and journeyed twice to Jerusalem, on foot. He had met all kinds of people from the most diverse social circles, and had had lengthy conversations with them. Thanks to his prodigious memory, he profited from these contacts by learning many things, such as the various lifestyles and priorities of people from different backgrounds. He often reflected on this subject. This was how, little by little, in the course of his long nomadic years, he developed his own unique philosophy.

~~~~~~~~

Rasputin was actively interested in the problems of the country's minorities. He did not approve of the government's politics regarding them, and he often railed against this tendency toward national chauvinism.

"What is this?" he would say. "Cutting the Tartars' throats, bayoneting the Armenians, stabbing the Georgians, and slicing open the stomachs of Jews? Who needs this carnage? The Tartar? The Armenian? The Georgian? The Jew? There should not be a difference in the eyes of the Tsar. They should all be equal before him. One can be a Tsar over many people, but one cannot force them to
~~~~~~~~

change religions. That is a great, great sin. Each believes in God, but in what way? That is his own affair. Every man who has faith is a good man, and one must love him."

The Imperial Family was indifferent to the problems of these four groups, although they seemed to bear no animosity. Traditionally, non-Slavic Russian palace guards and servants were considered safe, more attached to the monarchy, and less prone to subterfuge than other nationalities. The Georgians were in the Tsar's personal guard; the Tartars were court servants; the people of the Caucasus were nannies and caretakers; and the Jews were tradesmen of the court — tailors, plumbers, jewelers, and the like. Nevertheless, during the last years of the monarchy, under the influence of the Old Court at Anichkov Palace,[66] this system fell apart, little by little. The Grand Dukes chose prospects from the lesser nobility and bureaucrats, to perform these functions.

During his long pilgrimages across Russia, Rasputin came to know many regions populated by non-Russian minorities. He saw German colonies, Tartar villages, Polish Jews, Georgians and Armenians. He bore no ill feelings toward any of them and, partly due to my influence, he energetically took on the cause of oppressed people. "We are all equal in front of God," he used to say.

Rasputin was for the abolishment of all restrictions on minorities, and hoped to realize this goal, once the Great War ended. Those who became ministers, with Rasputin's help, originally promised to remove any laws restricting the rights of minorities, principally Jews. He not only wanted those laws removed, but wanted them more lenient

---

66 Anichkov Palace, home to many tsars, was where Nicholas II grew up and where his mother, the Dowager Empress, resided during his reign.

than for the general population. However, it often happened that, once in office, the ministers did not have the courage to keep their promises and, consequently, saw their new status rescinded. Then, Rasputin not only had the ministers against him, but also the Grand Dukes who felt that the Tsar should reach no solutions regarding minorities without first consulting the rest of the dynasty.

When the retreating Russian troops had to abandon Warsaw[67], an agitated Nicholas II telephoned Rasputin at 2:00 a.m. He said there was nothing to do but hang himself. "Wilhelm II," he said, "wants to make Poland an independent state. I cannot survive the shame of it."

Typical of his views, Rasputin replied, "You should have given Poland its autonomy, but don't lose heart. If you retake Poland, you will give her what she needs. They belong to the same Slavic race as Russians, and should, therefore, get along best with Russians."

Rasputin's opinions of foreign countries were based on what he saw of those minorities in Russia. He was often accused of being friendly toward the Germans. This accusation is not totally unfounded. His inclination, which seems strange for a peasant who had no knowledge of Germany, is simply explained by the fact that his opinions were based on his observations of German colonies in Russia. He was struck by their prosperity, as well as by their cleanliness, comfortable clothing and bountiful crops. The abundance of food on their tables also impressed him. He was additionally surprised to see that they drank not only tea, but coffee as well. Everything he noticed in the colonies made a profound impression on him, and he often spoke of them to Russian peasants. He advised young

---

[67] Russia retreated in late 1915.

Russian men to marry young German women because such marriages were happy ones. “The peasant is content when a German woman is in his house,” Rasputin said, “because there is order and nothing is lacking. The father-in-law is proud and brags to his neighbors, saying ‘look at what a wonderful worker my daughter-in-law is’.” His esteem for Germany further increased when he learned that most of Russia’s agricultural machinery and tools came from there.

Rasputin was a spokesman for immediate peace, even under the harshest conditions, and was of the opinion that any kind of peace had to be better than war. He reasoned that once Russia regained its strength, any disadvantageous conditions could be renegotiated. When it was suggested to him that peace was no longer a consideration, and that it was dangerous to even dream of it, Rasputin responded: “I fear nothing. What wrong have I done? No one has the right to annihilate human lives. Other men’s businesses involve money, houses or land; I only want to be an intermediary for peace. Papa[68] himself always told me that I am right and should remain neutral.”

Then he would be reminded of the Tsar’s declaration to continue the battle as long as there were German soldiers on Russian soil. Nevertheless, this objection did not trouble Rasputin: “It is quite possible that the Tsar said that. But he is the master of his word. If he gave it, he can also take it back. If he gave one order, he can replace it with another. He is the Tsar and he can do as he pleases. And how are you going to run all of the Germans out of Russia? Who will replace the German artisans and tradesmen?”

---

68 Rasputin called the Tsar “Papa” which is how many peasants thought of him.

It was useless to explain to him that the Tsar was only speaking of German soldiers, not of the German-Russians. Rasputin would only declare that there is no difference between German soldiers and the German citizens of Russia. “They are each like the other, pursuing a single goal,” he would say, “except one works with his fists, and the other with intelligence and money.”

Rasputin felt that Russian peasants sympathized with the Germans. He explained it this way: “Russians are accustomed to German merchandise. German manufacturers deliver good quality items and pleasantly cater to the buyer’s desires. The German knows how to work. If a German prisoner of war arrives in a village, the villagers all want him to stay at their houses because they know Germans are good workers.”

Rasputin sympathized not only with Germany, but with America as well. This inclination, like any other, was based more on emotion than logic. Many Russians had relatives in America and often received money from them. In letters, these relatives described life in the New World, in a way that was seductive to the Russian mujik. Many poor immigrants became rich farmers or found factory work there. Generally, they were satisfied with their lot. To the poor Russian, America sounded like a fairytale El Dorado. Rasputin, who always saw America in such a flattering light, often said we must live in peace and friendship with this country.

Chapter V

The Jewish Question

Rasputin was of great importance to me. He was my solution to the Jewish issues that occupied most of my time and became my principal worry. Never did he refuse me his support. To tell the truth, at first he was very reserved regarding any Jewish affairs. He paid more attention to my requests in other matters, and I thought he might not be well informed regarding Jewish issues. He often told me how the Tsar complained bitterly about the Jews. The ministers spoke to the Tsar endlessly of Jewish conspiracies, plots and revolutionary movements. Nicholas II was tormented by this subject, not knowing what to do with my people whom he suspected of all this subterfuge.

This tense period was filled with danger for all Russian Jews. I worried that Rasputin might align himself with our anti-Semitic enemies. I made desperate efforts, went to great lengths, to make him understand our problems. This meant wresting him from the influence of the Tsar who constantly berated the Jews. It was a matter of whether Rasputin would listen to the Tsar's accusations or my pleadings. Representatives of the Jewish world were aware of this tenuous and fearful situation, and appealed to me to do whatever it took to prevent Rasputin from siding with the anti-Semites which would have been disastrous.

By this point,[69] Rasputin had already reached the summit of his strange and extraordinary destiny, and his power was nearly as great as that of the Emperor. But Nicholas II had

---

69 Approx. 1911

developed a passion for reactionary groups, and even joined the League of Russian People,[70] which ordered the pogroms. If Rasputin had sided with these reactionary leaders who courted him avidly, the Jews would have had a much worse time of it. However, after a long time straddling the fence, Rasputin's sane comprehension of men prevailed. He became a friend and protector to the Jews, despising oppression in any form. Moreover, he supported me without reservation in my efforts to alleviate their burden.

The Tsar's passivity manifested itself unpleasantly with regard to the Jewish question. Certainly, he was a close friend to Rasputin who despised the reactionary leagues, but his friendship with Rasputin did not prevent him from giving his full support to those same organizations. That is why Rasputin did not openly attack these groups, but took every opportunity to show the Tsar their faults, to no avail.

~~~~~~~~~

Shcheglovitov, who was Minister of Justice for many years,[71] had a malevolent influence on the Tsar. He tried, with a singular stubbornness, to prove to the Tsar that all Jews, without exception, were poisoned by socialism. In his opinion, all of them belonged in an environment that would obliterate their faith in socialism. The murder of the Christian Yuschinsky boy furnished the Minister of Justice, as well as other anti-Semites, with a pretext to charge Mendel Beilis, a Jew, in the famous trial called "the ritual

[70] The League of Russian People was also known as the Union of Russian People and, in other circles, as the Black Hundred. Membership included many politicians, aristocrats, and military. Pogroms were instigated by this group.
[71] Ivan Grigorevich Shcheglovitov was Minister of Justice from 1906 to mid-1915.
~~~~~~~~~

murder case."[72] However, this trial did not have the expected result of casting more blame on the Jews, and the outcome was not a pleasant one for the accusers.

Rasputin hated Shcheglovitov and bluntly insulted him whenever they saw each other. Rasputin called him a "heart-eater" and decried his membership in the League of the Archangel Saint Michael[73] when, previously, he had been a socialist. The Minister, well knowing Rasputin's influence on the Tsar, was obliged to take the insults and provocations without responding. At the time of the Beilis trial, Rasputin told him: "You will surely lose this trial. Nothing good will come of this. Jews don't spill Christian blood; I know this better than you."

Before the trial even began, Rasputin had predicted an acquittal.[74] The proceedings launched a new wave of anti-Semitic propaganda which I begged Rasputin to persuade the Tsar to stop. He tried many times to speak to the Tsar about the Beilis trial, but was told to leave it alone. That greatly displeased Rasputin. He thought Nicholas II had some ulterior motive in lending an ear to Shcheglovitov's insinuations. Later, after the Tsar dismissed Shcheglovitov, the latter asked Rasputin to help him obtain a new ministerial position. Rasputin brusquely responded that only upon his death could Shcheglovitov even hope to

---

[72] Also known as a 'blood libel' case. Menachem Mendel Beilis was the Jewish superintendent of a brick factory and, in 1911, was accused of murdering the Christian schoolboy, Andrei Yuschinsky, in order to use his blood to make matzo.

[73] The Russian People's League of the Archangel Michael was a Black Hundreds organization which promoted anti-Semitism and pogroms (raids and killings in Jewish villages).

[74] Beilis spent two years in a brutal Russian prison before being released. The child's mother and boyfriend were found guilty of murdering the boy after he had witnessed a crime they'd committed.

become minister of anything. And, in fact, it was only after Rasputin's assassination that Shcheglovitov became Council President, though only for a very brief time.

Often, when the subject of the Jewish situation arose, the ministers would respond: "Unfortunately, Gurland[75] is against Jews." Gurland played a special role. A Jew himself, he was the son of an Odessa rabbi. In adulthood, he converted to Christianity. He became an avid enemy of the Jews, and came to be on good terms with all the ministers. He was, at the time, editor-in-chief of the government newpaper, *Russia*. He supported the Old Court and plotted openly against the Young Court. Despite that, he had some influence on the Tsar regarding the Jewish question. I often wondered if he, himself, prompted the Beilis trial. What is certain is that he was the official Chief of Anti-Semitic Propaganda. Meetings took place in his home, about how the 'ritual murder trial' could be used to exploit Jews.

Beilis, the only one accused in the ritual murder, was acquitted. However, Kiev's Chief of Police and some of his subordinates were charged with abuse of power in the affair and condemned to hard labor. A Jewish delegation, consisting of Rabbi Maso of Moscow, sugar manufacturer Leo Brodsky, and Petersburg financier Gerasim Schalit asked me to plead for mercy on behalf of the condemned Kiev police officials, which I did.

At this point, I would be remiss if I did not mention that Gerasim Schalit and his well-known family of Riga lumber merchants, Mark and Lipman Salomonovitz Schalit,

---

[75] Ilia Yakovlevich Gurland was a professor of constitutional law, before becoming council member to the Minister of the Interior from 1904 to 1907 when he became editor of the government's official newspaper.

always displayed a heartfelt interest in the suffering of their Jewish brethren. Even today,[76] with one in England and the other in France, no Russian would be refused their assistance. Here, I publicly pay homage to their spirit of brotherly generosity.

~~~~~~~~

The leading Jewish communities had great faith in me and in my efforts. They saw that, through my contacts and my aptitude for influencing governing bodies, I was able to open a dialog on the Jewish question. I held a series of conferences with eminent Jewish representatives regarding the acquisition of equal rights for Jews, and devoted all of my resources to this mission. I accepted this honorable task and, although the revolution prevented me from completing my mission, I am proud to have been able to help other Jews during such a trying period, and hope to have sweetened their lives to some extent.

One of the most energetic and warm defenders of Judaism was Moishe Gunzburg[77] who had made a fortune in Port Arthur and, once established in Petersburg, occupied himself with everything of concern to Jews. Mr. Gunzburg telephoned me one day during the war,[78] to invite me to his house as he had something important to tell me.

---

[76] Circa 1928

[77] Also spelled Ginzburg, Gintsburg. The Gunzburg family was known as prominent pre-revolutionary Jewish philanthropists, as well as advocates for equal rights. They funded legal defenses in other blood libel trials as well.

[78] When Simanovitch refers to 'the war' he means WW I. This incident dates somewhere between 1914, the start of WW I and late 1915 when the Tsar took over as Supreme Commander of all Russian Armies.
~~~~~~~~

"You have excellent contacts," Gunzburg told me, "and you have access to places never before penetrated by a Jew. Ask Rasputin, since you are so close to him, to support you. It would be a sin to let the opportunity escape us. I have come to the conclusion that Rasputin can obtain whatever he wants. He has the power to change the opinion of all the cabinet ministers. As for us, we must no longer tolerate that Nikolai Nikolayevich and his henchmen plunder and assassinate Jews who happen to be in his path at the battlefront or anywhere in Russia where Jews are so horribly oppressed. You will receive from us whatever you need to attain this goal. Go to work on this immediately and if you succumb, victim of your efforts in the good fight, the Jewish people will perish with you."

He felt that the situation justified the worst fears for Jews, and that we needed to take steps immediately to avert the pending danger. Above all, we had to stop this terrible persecution. In the course of this meeting, Gunzburg underscored the fact that the Great War had only aggravated the situation. One had the impression that Grand Duke Nikolai Nikolayevich wanted to take advantage of every opportunity to exterminate every last Jew. With the situation worsening each day, we understood the need to battle the enemy aggressively. The moment was favorable while we had excellent contacts in Petersburg. It was a question of making them act, not just to better the lot of *some* Jews, but for the *entire* Jewish population. Consequently, those in Jewish society applied pressure, used contacts and all means to obtain equal rights for all Russian Jews. There was no lack of money. Jewish philanthropists resolved to turn over large sums of money to those who could make this happen. If I had been able to get the Emperor to make considerable reforms, I would have been the richest man in Russia.

This meeting with Gunzburg had a profound impact on me. I promised to devote myself entirely to the cause when the rights and interests of our people were at stake, and we identified the steps to take. The first thing to do was win over the ministers in order to get the Tsar to enact the necessary measures. I felt that the Jewish representatives should meet with Rasputin. This way, they would know Rasputin's stance on the Jewish question. I offered to set up the meeting and Gunzburg accepted. I immediately approached Rasputin and told him that we hoped he would lend us his support in the struggle we had undertaken for the rights of Jews. He said he was in perfect agreement with me and was ready to meet the delegates. The meeting took place at Gunzburg's house to which I brought Rasputin at the appointed hour.

Numerous participants from the most eminent quarters of Jewish society were there, including Leo Brodsky, the attorney Sliosberg, Gerassim Schalit, Samuel Gourevitch, bank director Mandel, Warshavski, Poliakov, our host Baron Gunzburg,[79] well known for his charitable foundations, and others. Sliosberg was the only attorney present because Rasputin said he did not want to meet with any lawyers or socialists. He made an exception for Sliosberg because he found nothing to reproach him for. Rasputin saw that he was an honest Jew and so did not take umbrage at his profession as an attorney. Everyone gave Rasputin a warm and dignified welcome, worthy of his high position and the hope they placed in him. Some cried,

---

[79] Brodsky was a pioneer in the sugar industry; Slios(z)berg, an attorney who fought for equal rights; Schalit, activist and philanthropist; Gourevitch, journalist; Warshavski (Varshavsky) philanthropist who supplied the Russian army with food; Poliakov played a role in building Russia's railroads and was known for his Jewish philanthropy, however, he was dead by this time, so if this does not refer to his son, Simanovitch was mistaken.

and Rasputin was quite moved at this display of emotion. He listened attentively to our grievances and promised he would put everything in the works to resolve the Jewish question.

Then, he added: "You must all help Simanovitch to buy the people upon whom this all depends. Do as your fathers have done. They went so far as to negotiate financial affairs with the Tsar himself! What have you all become? You do not act like Jews used to. It is only by corruption and ruse that the Jewish question will be no more. As far as I am concerned, you can rest easy. I'll help you for as long as necessary."

This meeting with Rasputin, the all-powerful darling of the Tsar, made an enormous impression on these Jews. They were completely committed to the hope that our enterprise would be crowned with success.
The conference ended with dinner. Rasputin was about to take a seat next to the young and lovely Mme Gunzburg but our host, aware of Rasputin's reputation as a skirt-chaser, begged me to place myself between his wife and Rasputin. I did this willingly, which appeased the jealousy of our host. This little scene was not lost on any of the other diners. Those who noticed it were highly amused.

After this meeting with the representatives of Russian Jewry, Rasputin no longer made a mystery of his sympathy for my people, and willingly accepted their requests. For my part, I took advantage of his kind disposition. He often complained of coming up against the recalcitrant attitude of the ministers and other influential people the moment a Jewish matter was brought up. He asked me to introduce him to others who could keep him informed of the situations facing Jews. Rasputin and I came upon the idea of proposing candidates who would not be anti-Semitic or pro-war for Cabinet posts.

At that meeting, Rasputin told me that the Tsar was far from being as great an enemy of the Jews as was generally believed. However, it is true that the entire Imperial Family trembled in fear at the single word "Jew". The Tsar's children were raised to be afraid of Jews, as were generations before them. All of their entourage, beginning with their nannies, drove this into their minds, starting at a tender age. Rasputin told me that – and this is just one of many examples –Minister of Internal Affairs Maklakov, when playing with the Tsarevitch, was in the habit of intimidating him by saying, "Watch Out! The Jews will come to get you!" or something of that nature. Then, the little boy would scream in fear.

When we had succeeded in composing a list of sympathetic ministers, Rasputin brought up the Jewish question more frequently in his talks with the Tsar, but the latter had a deep repugnance to the topic. I finally had the occasion to state our case directly to the Tsar, on behalf of my fellow Jews, regarding the following matter: two hundred Jewish dentists were sentenced to prison. They were accused of having obtained their dental diplomas for the sole purpose of establishing residence outside the district assigned to Jews.[80] These were decent, peaceful, inoffensive men, many of whom were married and had children. I decided to take on their cause. I invited representatives of the condemned dentists to meet with me, and told them I wanted to arrange a meeting with Rasputin. They begged

---

[80] Known as the Smolensk Affair, in 1911, it actually involved 307 Jewish dentists who feared expulsion from their homes if it was found that their primary motivation in obtaining professional degrees was to live outside the Pale of Settlement. It was one of many such sweeps by the authorities.

Rasputin to support them against Minister of Justice Shcheglovitov.

Rasputin, sympathetic to them, but perplexed, said, "What can we do? I ask myself this. Shcheglovitov is so stubborn, so hard, that he goes so far as to modify the Tsar's orders when they're favorable to Jews. You must have Simanovitch handle this affair. He will devise some ruse to bring an end to Shcheglovitov. Ask him!"

We decided to present a plea for mercy the following Sunday when Rasputin would be at Tsarskoye-Selo. First, he would assist with the religious service where the entire Imperial Family would be present, and then he would lunch with Anna Vyrubova. That Sunday, I accompanied him. Everything went as foreseen. The Tsar, Tsarina and their children also dined with their lady-in-waiting. The Emperor was in a good mood. Vyrubova knew of our plans and promised to help us. After the meal, she said to the Tsar, "Simanovitch is here." The Tsar leaped up and jested, "Surely he's going to bend my ear."

Entering the room where I waited, he asked, "What do you want to say to me?"

Hiding my emotion, I explained that I wanted to sell, at a discount, a 110-carat diamond, and that I had offered it to the empress, but she thought the price too high.

"I cannot buy diamonds during war time," the Tsar said. "But certainly there's something else you wanted to ask. Speak."

At this moment, Rasputin entered and, hearing the Tsar's words, said, "You guessed."

"How many Jews are we talking about?" the Tsar asked.

"Two hundred," Rasputin answered.

"I knew it. Give me the petition."

I handed the Tsar our petition, which he perused. "Ah! They are tooth-pullers," he said. "But the Minister of Justice doesn't want to hear it. He doesn't want to pardon them."

"Your Majesty," I said, "how can the Minister be allowed to say 'I don't want to' when Your Majesty commands? He has no choice but to obey."

Rasputin pounded his fist on the table. "How dare they not follow your orders!" he bellowed.

The Tsar was visibly embarrassed.

"Your Majesty," I said, "permit me to propose that Your Majesty sign the petition and, when Your Highness has left, I'll hand it over to Taneev[81] who will do what is necessary."

The Tsar followed my advice and the dentists were absolved.[82] They took up a collection of 800 rubles, and bought Rasputin a mink coat. As for me, I received a Jewish honey cake, a bottle of red wine, and a silver Jewish goblet.

~~~~~~~~

[81] Taneev was Chief of the Emperor's Chancellery and Anna Vyrubova's father

[82] This incident, regarding the dentists, has been confirmed by historians such as Lucien Wolfe and in the memoirs of authorities such as General Alexandre Spiridovitch.
~~~~~~~~

After Sturmer, whom Rasputin and I had recommended, was nominated for Council President,[83] we reunited with Pitirim at the Alexander Nevski Convent regarding Sturmer's commitment to the Jewish question. Attending this meeting were Bishop Isidor, Sturmer, Rasputin and myself. All who took part swore they were ready to work to the limits of their capabilities to better the lot of Jews in Russia.

However, Sturmer turned to me and said: "You're a unique man, Simanovitch. The cause you support is certainly a just one, but you are taking the wrong path! Certainly, you must know that neither the other ministers nor I can even raise the question without the Tsar's consent. Any minister who would do that would rightfully fear for his life. It was different in the time of the former tsar.[84] Under his reign, the ministers had complete autonomy. They acted under their own authority. They also had more courage and did not go back on their word. But no one has confidence in the current Tsar. He, himself, is very wary of us, which makes it difficult to come to any agreement with him. If I could deliver the Jewish people from their atrocious situation, I would be sincerely happy. But I cannot undertake an initiative at the cost of my life. In Russia, a minister has to be officially anti-Semitic.[85] He cannot renounce anti-Semitism. It is only natural that you do not understand my desire to retain my position as minister, but you cannot ask me to do impossible things. I would gladly give the Jews my support, but the opportunity has to

---

[83] Sturmer became Council President in January, 1916

[84] Alexander III, Nicholas II's father.

[85] Anti-Semitism was government policy, with many laws restricting Jews from parts of Russia, from educations, occupations, etc. If an item was not mentioned in the law, it was considered illegal.

present itself. Since you have the Tsar's ear, you are the likely one to take the initiative. In effect, you are more powerful than the entire Council of Ministers, so do what you must to get the Tsar to order me to put the Jewish question on the agenda. If you have the Tsar present the issue, I will do what is necessary."

At that point, Pitirim made an unexpected proposition: "Listen, Simanovitch," he said. "Tomorrow, Rasputin and I are going to Tsarskoye-Selo where a holy service will be performed. A dinner will be served to the wounded. Bring cognac, wheat, sugar and jam for the soldiers in the hospital, and I will arrange for you to speak personally to the Tsar. That is certainly the best way to go. Listen to my advice. Tell him the truth. Tell him how the Jews are being persecuted, as you told us here. God will help you."

His proposition was welcomed by all present and I agreed to ask the Tsar for equal rights for Jews. I called the Voskoboinokov sisters[86] who confirmed that a holy service would be performed at the hospital the following day. The ladies asked me to meet with them immediately, as they wanted to place an order. Indeed, the heir to the throne, Tsarevitch Alexei, was to give gifts to the soldiers that day. I hastily went to the hospital where the Tsarevitch ordered twelve silver watches with chains, and an equal amount of silver saucers for teacups.

I procured these items and took them to the hospital the next day, arriving just at the end of the service. The Tsarevitch was enchanted with what I had brought, and the Tsarina told the Tsar that Alexei was pleased with me. Nicholas II turned to me and thanked me. Rasputin

[86] Rasputin found positions for the Voskoboinokov sisters at Vyrubova's military hospital. One of them was Protopopov's mistress.

understood that this was the moment to execute our plan. He rose and said to the Tsar, "You have, before you, a son of the Jewish people."

Nicholas looked at each of us with bewilderment and said, "I don't understand."

All those present looked at us curiously. Rasputin said to the Tsar, "I have begun it. It is for him to tell you the rest, himself."

I trembled with emotion and began with these words: "Your Majesty, I have lived in Petersburg for years, but neither my brothers nor my sisters — indeed, our people — know anything of your love for the city."

Pitirim interrupted: "You speak in terms that are too vague. If you're going to speak as a son of the Jewish people, you must be clear in your communication."

Seized with anguish, I pursued my objective: "Sire, my brothers, the Jewish people, anxiously await word from you regarding their fate. They are hoping for deliverance, for the right to education and place of residence. They expect nothing but your grace."

The Tsar listened to me attentively. I spoke in a choppy, disconnected fashion, but Nicholas II understood me. Those around us were quiet and awaited the Tsar's response. This was calming. I felt that the attendees sympathized with me.

But the Tsar said, "Tell your brothers I'll give them nothing."

At these words, I could no longer contain myself. Losing control, tears in my eyes, I begged him: "Sire, I plead with you — don't make me the bearer of that message. It's beyond my strength to bring that message to my brothers."

The Tsar looked at me kindly and calmly. With compassion in his voice, he said: "You misunderstand me. You must tell the Jews that, with regard to minorities in my kingdom, I do not differentiate between them nor do I favor one over another. However, we have eighty million peasants and one hundred million subjects of diverse national origin. My peasants are illiterate and not intellectually mature, unlike the Jews. Tell the Jews this: when my peasants have risen to the same degree as the Jews, then I will give the Jews whatever I accord to the peasants."

I answered, "As you wish, Your Majesty. I'll do whatever is necessary."

The next day, I begged Rasputin to receive the Jewish delegation as a witness to the fact that I did not shrink from the mission conferred upon me, that I presented our case to the Tsar himself, begging him to accord equal rights to Jews.

~~~~~~~~

Adversaries and reactionaries spied on and followed me relentlessly. They hoped to acquire information about my actions that would justify charges against me. They also investigated people I visited. In order to downplay the suspicions of espionage, I avoided holding any meetings at my house regarding Jewish affairs. We usually met in one of my social circles which I could easily escape to, in the middle of crowded rooms and in plain view of those following me. The actions of the police were very amusing. They were spying on me at the same time that government secret agents were watching them.[87]
~~~~~~~~

I had created a vast communication network to obtain information on the condition of Jews in all parts of Russia. In the last years preceding the revolution, this organization was completely in place. I spared not a cent. I had the names of all the rabbis, Jewish politicians and businessmen, even Jewish students. I was not only informing myself about the political leanings and social lives of my people, but also about their personal situations. This permitted me to make an impression on my clients once they presented themselves to me. Most often, I knew in advance who had sent them, but they were further impressed that I was well informed about their personal lives and needs. In order to help these Jews who came from all parts of Russia, I developed good relations with various political bodies, and I can honestly say that I never received the least money for any of my actions on behalf of my people. I did not want to compromise my reputation with the ministers or jeopardize my influence, which is why I earned my living by other means.[88]

The Jewish youth gave me the most to do. It is common knowledge that Jews were only accepted in very limited numbers in the universities and secondary schools.[89] It was very difficult to be admitted beyond the quota, and this cost an enormous amount of money. Not a day went by that I didn't receive a verbal or written request or even telegrams. I was begged to put myself to good use for Jewish youth who were stymied by these stringent rules in their aspirations to higher learning. Parents traveled

---

[87] It was not uncommon for bureaucrats to spy on each other in this atmosphere of sabotage, bribery, intrigue and plots wherein each tried to advance his position at the expense of others.
[88] Simanovitch was, first and foremost, a jeweler but also ran casinos and had investments.
[89] Jews were only permitted to comprise 3% to 5% of the student population in universities.

thousands of kilometers uniquely to consult me on this subject. Most were not rich, but they gave all they had for their children to be admitted to the schools.[90]

This is how I did it. Before the start of each scholastic year, groups of young Jews desiring to attend school in Petersburg would visit me. I would give them letters from Rasputin and introduce them to whichever cabinet minister had say in the matter, telling him that the Tsarina supported the requests of these young people. Rasputin's letters, which I dictated to him, were conceived in the following terms: "My Dear Minister — Mama[91] would like these Russian students to complete their studies in their own country so as not to have to go to a foreign land where they could become revolutionaries. They must stay in their country. — Grigori." My protégés would be admitted despite the imposed quota.

I gave precise instructions to all who addressed themselves to me, as well as the names of which officials to go to for support. But if this did not suffice to resolve the affair, I would have to intervene personally and get a letter of recommendation from an influential person such as a university professor, a lady of the court, an eminent man of the church, etc. Many requests allowing Jews admission to a school were made in the name of the Tsarina.

There were also quotas on housing for Jews. Each day, I received telegrams from the provinces from Jews asking me to obtain permission for them to live in Petersburg or

---

[90] For a Jewish student to be admitted beyond the allowable quota (3%-5%), the family had to pay the tuition of three Christian students in addition to their child. Some authorities could be bribed.

[91] Rasputin referred to the Tsar and Tsarina as Mama and Papa, which is how most peasants thought of them.

Moscow, or to take a business trip abroad, in addition to their time limit dictated by the quota.[92] I created a vast organization that occupied itself exclusively with these requests. For as long as I had influence in Petersburg, I obtained travel authorization for all Jews who came to me, without exception. Jewish businessmen, like the artisans, had the right to reside anywhere regardless of the quota, and to undertake trips necessary for business. It was easy for me to obtain safe passage for them. However, it sometimes happened that one would not have the required authorization to live in Petersburg. I would have that person send two telegrams requesting a permit to travel there: one telegram to me, and the other to the prefect of police. Then I would send back a quick response: "This is to inform you that, under new orders, you are attaché to the prefect's chancellery". This method was used by the police prefect in especially difficult cases, to avoid the question of right to residence. These Jews could live with their families in Petersburg without worry.

Jewish artisans could establish themselves wherever they wished to practice their trade.[93] All Jews who wished to avail themselves of this right had to take a test which was not especially difficult. I managed to gain a foothold in Petersburg's Artisan's Council established for this purpose, and gained influence over the choice of its members. Candidates I suggested were always admitted, and

---

92 The laws imposed stringent limits on the amount of time Jewish businessmen could spend abroad; in addition, Foreign Jewish businessmen traveling to Russia were subject to the same restrictions as Russian Jews. This blatant anti-Semitism prompted the U.S. Senate to terminate the Russo-American Treaty of Commerce in 1911.

93 Only certain artisans and professionals were permitted this privilege.

subsequently became my loyal allies. I managed to obtain permits to live in the capital, not only for those who had a real trade, but also for those who had not the least idea of the trade for which they took the government examination.[94] These people were on the registers as "workers."

As a jeweler, I could also employ workers and, although I had no workshop in Petersburg, I freely availed myself of this right. There was an empty room in my apartment in which I placed several workbenches even though no one worked there. These 'workers' practiced every available trade other than making jewelry. There were, among them, actors, singers, writers, and teachers. When Minister of the Interior Khvostov exiled me to Narym in Northern Siberia — I'll describe this event later — a veritable panic seized the people I'd been helping. They feared expulsion from Petersburg. However, I returned shortly and was warmly received by a crowd of hopeful Jews. They did not just rejoice for me or for them, but for the fact that a simple Jew had won a struggle against the all-powerful Minister of the Interior. The order that had me banished was revoked; this was evidence of the high favor the Tsar bestowed on me. On this occasion, I received innumerable telegrams of congratulation from all parts of Russia. Only a small number of people knew the real reason for my influence. All sorts of myths grew rapidly, regarding my position. Some thought I was some sort of Minister of Jewish Affairs, others saw me as representing American Jews.

If a pogrom menaced some town or province, I was quickly informed by local correspondents. In pre-arranged terms, the telegram, read: "Worried about your health. Send a

---

[94] To qualify for residence outside the Pale of Settlement, an artisan had to pass a government exam in his trade, and practice that trade only. If found to be practicing any other trades, the artisan would be banished to the Pale.

telegram." Upon receiving these words, I used my influence to have local authorities act against anti-Semitic propaganda. In this way, I succeeded in averting pogroms at Minsk and Vilna where Giers and Lubinov were the respective governors. As soon as I had taken these necessary steps, I sent this short reply to the rabbi or other influential Jew in the endangered village: "Hope all to be back in place tomorrow. Will give news as soon as I can leave." That signified that the village governor and local police authorities had been exhorted, by urgent telegrams, to intervene against agitators who favored a pogrom. In such cases, the chief of police would take the governor to personally visit the area and reassure the Jewish populace. The governor would call together the rabbi and most influential representatives of the Jewish community, and assure them that he opposed any pogrom.[95]

Jews generally showed very little inclination toward military service, which is understandable, considering that they were deprived of all of their rights and were severely oppressed. During the war, many young Jews came to me, asking to be exempted from military service. In order to help them dispense with their military duty, I made myself known to the Recruitment Commission, based in Luga, a town not far from Petersburg. All of the members of this commission had been named at Rasputin's suggestion. Whenever I sent to Luga someone whose papers bore the agreed-upon sign, he returned exempt from military service.

Jews holding a bachelor degree or a certificate from an approved school could matriculate to a university or superior school and were, therefore, exempt from serving in the military. However, there were also Jews who had

---

[95] There were, however, a number of areas where the governors themselves incited the pogroms.

not attended secondary school. It was for them that a school was founded, called the Institute of Agronomy and Hydrotechnics. Due to their enrollment, these students were excused from military service. In reality, however, there were only six hundred actual students attending the school, of which sixty percent were Jews. This would not have been possible if not for Rasputin.

Beletsky, private secretary to Under-Secretary of State Kryzhanovsky, was named Rector of the Institute. He was, moreover, a member of the administrative council of the reactionary Academic Union. Our Institute was founded as an intermediate step into the schools of higher learning. After a year, the students could easily gain entry to these schools. To repay Beletsky for his work in our Institute, I introduced him to Rasputin. Beletsky wanted to ask Rasputin to support his boss, Kryzhanovsky, for Council President, and arranged a meeting between Rasputin and Kryzhanovsky. This interview took place, but the Under-Secretary of State committed the grave error of declaring himself opposed to minorities,[96] and it was this statement that caused Rasputin, after the meeting, to declare that, in his opinion, Kryzhanovsky was absolutely not qualified to be president of the Council of Ministers.

~~~~~~~~

One day, the Jewish impresario Fischsohn came to me requesting a permit to stage Jewish operettas. It was not easy. Even within the limits of the districts assigned to Jews,[97] no Jewish theater had been tolerated. I decided, however, to take up the matter. I asked Fischsohn for a list of members in his troupe. He gave me forty names. When

---

96 Minorities were nationals of the Empire, but considered of non-Russian nationality.

97 The Pale of Settlement.
~~~~~~~~

I got to Tsarskoye-Selo, I presented my case to the Tsarina, telling her that I wanted to present Jewish plays in my home. To avoid all suspicion, I told her that Bishop Isidor, who understood Yiddish, would be present at the opening and could act as a sort of censor. The promise of Bishop Isidor's presence greatly pleased the Tsarina who, due to her English education, could not conceive that some Jewish plays could be a source of worry. I added that Rasputin, Prime Minister Sturmer, and other known personalities would be there. The Tsarina listened attentively and then asked, as was her habit, "What should I do?" I handed her the petition and she signed, "Granted. Alexandra." I immediately delivered it to the prefect of police. He was stunned but did not want to cause me any trouble as we were on good terms. The police permit was promptly issued.

When Fischsohn's troupe arrived in Petersburg, I threw a gala reception at my home. The Prime Minister, Bishop Isidor, Rasputin, Protopopov (Minister of the Interior), Globatschev (Chief of the Palace Police Dept.[98]), Beletsky (adjunct to the Minister of the Interior), and many others were my guests that evening. I had invited the entire Fischsohn troupe. One can imagine the surprise of the Jewish actors at the sight of all of these important people at my home. The company's prima donna, Klara Young, a talented artist, danced and sang beautifully. She was heartily applauded. The troupe's plays were then staged at the "Catherine" German Circle. The Petersburg debut of the troupe was, overall, a brilliant success, as much financially as artistically. Fischsohn received a permanent permit to play in all of Russia.

~~~~~~~~

[98] Chief of Petrograd security.
~~~~~~~~

A Jewish doctor, named Lippert,[99] was incarcerated in a German prison during the war. His wife, a relative of Count Witte, asked me if there was some way he could be exchanged for a German prisoner of war. I counseled her to see Rasputin in person. The excitement of this woman, at the thought of meeting Rasputin, had a comical impression on me. An audience with the Tsar did not excite people as much as an encounter with Rasputin. Mme Lippert addressed herself to Rasputin begging him to return her husband. For us, it was the first case of this type, and we wondered who could help us. When I suggested meeting with the Minister of Foreign Affairs, Rasputin, visibly embarrassed, said, "Sazanov? He'll throw us out!"

"Why?" I asked, somewhat surprised.

"He is for war, and I am against war," he said.

Rasputin knew that Sazanov was not favorably disposed toward him. The Minister had even tried, as had many others, to defame Rasputin in front of the Tsar, but had to withdraw his accusations after seeing how they displeased the Tsar. Rasputin did not like to ask his enemies for favors or support for his protégés. He only did so rarely, when there was no other choice. Rasputin finally consented. He told Mme Lippert, "Go find Sazanov."

Rasputin could barely write. However, he often sat down at his desk with an important air, and laboriously scratched out some confusing and incoherent lines. His handwriting was very bad and it took him a long time to formulate a letter. Mme Lippert waited, anxious and agitated. Finally,

---

99 Documented in other accounts as "Lekkert". This would have been between 1914 and 1916.

Rasputin gave her a large sheet of paper on which he had written the following:

"Dear One - Save the one who is languishing in a German prison. Give them two Germans and ask for one Russian. God will help us to save our compatriots - Novych[100] Rasputin."

The next day, Mme Lippert went to see Sazanov. She was convinced her husband would be freed. Sazanov received her, read Rasputin's letter, and said, "In my capacity as Minister of Foreign Affairs, I can easily obtain what you desire, and have no need for this letter. Take it back to Rasputin and tell him that I would have done it without his appeal."

An aide whom Sazanov had summoned reported that six Russian prisoners of war were waiting to be exchanged; Lippert could not be freed before them. Of course, that did not sit well with Mme Lippert. She asked the Minister that her husband be released immediately as he was old and sick. Sazanov said, "I'll have it done by the Red Cross, then."

When Mme Lippert told Rasputin of her visit with the Minister, he appeared irritated, but said nothing since Sazanov's response was promising.

We waited for one week. No news from Sazanov. Mme Lippert went back to Rasputin and asked what to do. He did not like to see his prestige threatened, and if he suffered a refusal he became quite angry. He ran into his office and

---

[100] Novych, or 'novy', meaning 'new' was a name Rasputin gave himself when he started his life in Petersberg.

wrote: "Listen, Minister, I sent you a woman. You told her God-knows-what. Stop this game! Do what was asked and all will be well. Otherwise, I'll knock the wind out of you. I'll tell the One Who Loves Me, and you'll be thrown out!" The words "I'll tell the One Who Loves Me" indicated that Rasputin intended to inform the Emperor of the affair.

Mme Lippert did not dare return to Sazanov with such an insolent letter. The tone in which Rasputin addressed the Minister shocked her, however I finally convinced her to return to Sazanov one more time. She followed my advice and gave him the letter.

"Excellency," she said, "Here is a new letter from Rasputin. Do with it what you will!"

"What did you tell him?" asked the Minister, while opening the envelope. When he read it, he became violently angry.

"What!" he yelled. "Now I must tolerate letters like this from wayfarers such as Rasputin? If you were not a lady of social standing, I would simply throw you out!"

Mme Lippert begged Sazanov to give back the letter. To her surprise, he refused. But even his anger did not stop her.

"If you don't give me back that letter immediately," said Mme Lippert, "then I'll go directly to Rasputin and recount our conversation to him."

She saw that Sazanov appeared embarrassed. "Listen, let's forget that," he said, after a brief hesitation. "I was not myself. Please do not make a scene. Tell Father Grigori that it was only a joke on my part."

Sazanov's sudden reversal had not escaped her. "It would be better," replied Mme Lippert, "if you telephoned him yourself and told him."

"As you know," she said, "they change ministers around here as often as they change gloves."
She picked up the telephone, called Rasputin's number and handed the receiver to the minister.

"You have sent me a very strange letter, Grigori Efimovitch," said Sazanov. "Are you angry with me?"

"How's that?" answered Rasputin. "I did not start this. You have hurt me. Don't try to trip me up. Let us rather be friends."

After several clarifications on the part of each one, the exchange ended with Rasputin saying these words that cemented their reconciliation: "We understand each other well. I have never before written anyone such letters."

Fifteen days later, Lippert was in Petersburg. Our goal was achieved.

~~~~~~~~

Rasputin didn't only help Jews. The case of the Polish magnates[101] was such an example. These businessmen had been exiled to Siberia, by decree of General Brusilov, for allegedly having telephoned the German enemy with information about our positions on the Galician front. A

---

[101] Poland sought independence from Russian rule. Many Poles, priests, businessmen, and academics among them, were accused of lack of loyalty to the Tsar, and exiled to Siberia during World War I.
~~~~~~~~

Galician priest had asked Father Casimir, Dean of the Nevski parish in Petersburg, to appeal to the authorities on behalf of the exiled Poles. Although he knew he should submit the whole affair to the Pope who could request the necessary steps be taken in Petersburg, Father Casimir believed that he would do better to see me. I advised him to see Rasputin whom he had already met at a number of social gatherings.

Casimir, not wanting to meet him alone, made an official, ceremonious visit with his entire entourage. Rasputin felt flattered. Considering that there was no basis for the espionage charges against the Poles, Rasputin asked Casimir to send him the women and children of the exiled men.

"I will tell them what to do to help their people," he explained.

About two weeks later, a delegation of Polish landowners arrived in Petersburg. Four ladies, wives of the exiled magnates, accompanied by their children, were part of this delegation. Rasputin was very warm and welcoming.

"We are all Slavic people," he said, "and I will help you. Tomorrow, I go to Tsarskoye-Selo. Let the wife of the one descended from Bourbon, and one of the delegates accompany me. I'll present you to the Tsarina and you will tell her that you are loyal to the throne and have nowhere to turn."

"And then?" asked one of the Poles.

"I'll do the rest!" answered Rasputin.

The next morning at 8:00 am, I took the Poles to Rasputin's house, in front of which was an Okhrana[102] car with Rasputin inside, waiting to take them to Tsarskoye-Selo. It was during the Great War and the Tsar was still at the front, having taken over as Supreme Commander of all Russian Armies.[103] The Tsarina, who received the Poles in her hospital, welcomed them and asked Rasputin: "What should I do?"

"Write a letter to Papa and send the Poles to deliver it to him at general headquarters. Also, telegraph Voyekov[104] to clear the way for them to see the Emperor."

"All right," said the Tsarina, "Let the Poles give me their petition and I will sign it 'granted.' I will send it to Papa by courier. In this way, it will arrive at headquarters before they do."

My son, Semyon, wrote up the petition and I brought it to the Tsarina who sent it out as agreed. The Poles went to Mogilev. An hour after their arrival, they were received by the Tsar who declared that all of his subjects, whether Russian or not, were equal in his eyes. "I have confidence in you," he said. "In eight or ten days, those exiled will return if the snow storms don't slow the trains down." The Tsar praised the Poles for getting along so well with each other, and inquired into different Polish affairs. Eleven days later, the exiled men returned.

~~~~~~~~

[102] Okhrana – the palace secret police.
[103] This could have been anywhere from late 1915 to late 1916.
[104] The General who was the last chief of the Tsar's personal guard.
~~~~~~~~

Not all of our efforts had such a happy conclusion. One of the more somber episodes of persecution committed by Grand Duke Nikolai Nikolayevich was the cruel treatment he inflicted on the Tzaddiks,[105] highly respected Jewish wise men who were the last to deserve such persecution. After Russia took Lemberg[106] and occupied the Carpathian Mountains, the order was given in Galicia to stop all the windmills that belonged to Jews. The army high command feared that the Jews were giving the enemy information using the windmill blades to signal. But, as Passover was coming, the Jews did everything to obtain authorization to mill flour for the holy flatbread. The military authorities were not so disposed. As chance would have it, just at that moment, the Russians suffered a small defeat. Nikolai Nikolayevich placed full responsibility on the Jews. He decided that the Jews had informed the enemy of the positions of Russian troops by means of the windmill blades. He had the Tzaddiks arrested along with a number of other prominent Jews.

The holy men were sent to Siberia while the others were dispatched to Kiev prisons, as hostages. One can easily imagine the misfortune and suffering of these people taken from Galicia in filthy cattle wagons. The Tzaddiks were not even permitted to say goodbye to their families before being exiled. Nor were they allowed to bring anything. They ate only bread, as they were not given food approved by Jewish law. They had not been allowed warm clothes, and everything had been taken from them. Neither did they have the right to pray. Delegations from the Jewish community were refused authority to see them in the course of their journey to Siberia. In short, nothing was permitted that would ease their suffering.

---

[105] Tzaddiks – pious and wise religious Jews with spiritual power.
[106] In September, 1914, at the start of WW I, Russia captured Lemberg, the capital of Galicia, today known as Lvov, Ukraine.

Halperin, the cantor of the Lemberg synagogue, came to Petersburg to request less harsh treatment of the exiled Tzaddiks. He cited horrible details of what they had endured and I formulated my plan to help these unfortunate pious people. The Petersburg authorities required us to provide precise declarations with supporting evidence, before the matter could be considered. However, before we were able to produce any documents, many of the Tzaddiks died of cold and hunger. Those who remained had to be taken to Werchnerdinsk, Omsk, and Tomsk, but only four made it that far. I presented the Tsar with a plea for mercy for the four survivors, and the order was telegraphed to free these prisoners. But by the time the paperwork arrived in Siberia, every last one was dead.

The Jews decided to protest, in front of the whole civilized world, against these accusations of espionage that were not just limited to individual Jews, but to all Jews. Delegations were sent to other countries to explain the horrible plight of Russian Jews, and to request help. (It was somewhat helpful to Jews that the Tsarina was also suspected of espionage. Agents of the political police intercepted the Tsarina's telephone calls and her activities were monitored. This sometimes eased the difficulty of *our* struggle against Grand Duke Nikolai Nikolayevich and his people.)

Following Bloody Sunday,[107] January 22, 1905, Tsar Nicholas II was called "Nicholas the Bloody." He did not deserve this terrible name. He was a weak man without character. Everything in his life was confused. There was neither order nor any sort of plan. Everything depended simply on who he was with at any particular time. If no

---

107 Palace guards opened fire on unarmed workers during a peaceful demonstration, sparking the 1905 revolution.

other influence opposed yours, you could persuade him to take any side of an issue, important or not. He promised whatever was asked but most of the time did not keep his word. He acted in a contradictory and ridiculous fashion, usually with disastrous results. Most of the time, he appeared indifferent and unconcerned. The cold lack of interest he displayed at decisive moments stunned and even aroused indignation in many people. His behavior was contrary to his duty as a Tsar, a husband, a father, a friend, an officer or a Christian.

However, the *real* "Nicholas the Bloody" was Grand Duke Nikolai Nikolayevich. Few people knew that the Grand Duke was afflicted with an overpowering pathology. He was morbidly cruel and literally bloodthirsty. It seems that this illness first appeared during the Russo-Turkish War, in which he took part as a young officer. In times of peace, he satisfied this thirst by sacrificing animals; he was a passionate hunter and never missed an opportunity to kill one. Rasputin tried to cure him of this morbid penchant and this was the reason for their brief reconciliation. The Great War, unfortunately, gave Nikolai Nikolayevich license to satisfy this frightful inclination. He succumbed to such extremes on the battlefield, in court-martials, and in the cruel persecution of the civilian population. He felt not a hint of responsibility and his power had no limits.

As for his victims, they were generally of a ‘foreign’ race: Jews, Galicians, Poles, or Germans. They were accused of espionage, desertion, or other similar crimes. Then they were hanged, shot, or tortured en masse. The Grand Duke was more interested in cruel repression than proof of guilt. He often struck his subordinates to the point of drawing blood. Not even generals were spared. It is true that sometimes he had to apologize to the latter, but other than that, he unreservedly unleashed his instinct for cruelty. As for the hundreds of thousands of Jews executed and tortured, he alone bears the responsibility in front of God.

Rasputin and I had our own troubles with him. One day, in response to one of my pleas for mercy, I received this telegram from the Grand Duke: "Granted, for the last time. If I receive another request, I'll send you to Siberia." I went to Rasputin, made a big fuss, and complained bitterly of the General's threat. Rasputin smiled. He tried to calm me and stated that there had certainly been some misunderstanding. He immediately tried to arrange, by telegraph, a discussion with the Grand Duke but, three hours later, received the following response: "If you come, I will hang you."

The Grand Duke's threat profoundly wounded Rasputin. From that moment on, he looked for a means of revenge. As for me, I began to fear for my future, and I reproached Rasputin for his attitude which endangered our situation all the more. I finally told him that he had no more succeeded in bringing about peace than he had in obtaining equal rights for Jews. He had only invoked the hatred of all around him — a constantly growing hatred from which no good could come. Rasputin gave this proud response: "A man like me comes only once in a century. My power cannot extend to everything. I achieve what is necessary."

Rasputin had suffered much of the Grand Duke's animosity although their relationship had not always been bad. It was, after all, the Grand Duke's wife who first met Rasputin and invited him to Petersburg. Nikolai Nikolayevich welcomed him at first. Even during the Great War, he granted many requests made by Grigori Efimovitch. Most of these involved returning Germans to their homes after they had been sent to Siberia. These requests came from me through Rasputin. Liberating

Germans from exile was not a popular subject. The Tsarina, a German herself, was behind most of these successful requests to free Germans, however, during the war, it was not appropriate for her to help them.

I had many conferences with representatives of the Jewish cause. We discussed what more we could do in our struggle for equal rights. I did all that was within my power, but the Jewish situation remained as difficult as before. Despite Rasputin's protection and my contacts in political circles, any question of Jewish equality seemed remote.

I arranged for the Tsar to grant an audience to the Jewish delegates who wished to explain to him the terrible conditions in which Jews were forced to live. Here, too, Rasputin came to my rescue. He was the one who persuaded the Tsar to see my fellow Israelites. I was ecstatic and relayed the good news to my compatriots. We resolved to appoint, as members of the delegation, the lawyers Grusenberg[108] and Sliosberg, as well as a deputy to the Duma, Friedmann. However, the Tsar refused to see these representatives, because its members were lawyers and 'revolutionaries.' Rasputin consulted with the Emperor and proposed I send Baron and Moishe A. Gunzburg, and L.I. Brodsky. When we addressed these three men, they were extremely surprised and declined our offer, saying they could not possibly take on the responsibility of speaking to the Tsar inder such grave circumstances. As such, our project was dead in the water.

---

[108] O.O. Grusenberg (b.1866-d.1940) was a prominent Russian-Jewish lawyer who defended Mendel Beilis in the blood libel case, as well as other cases involving minorities and workers. His memoirs detail his struggle to become a lawyer despite anti-Semitic laws.

In the meantime, Nikolai Nikolayevich's politics grew more threatening by the day, and caused great panic. Many Jewish leaders came to ask me to arrange a new meeting with Rasputin. They based their hopes on the fabulous influence of the "Miracle Man" and wanted to know, at the same time, what to expect — what they could hope for from him. I had nothing against meetings of this sort and, as soon as the occasion arose, I relayed to Rasputin that these delegates wished to meet with him again, to seek his counsel and energetic support. He listened to me attentively and announced he was ready to receive the Jewish delegates once again. When I told Moishe Gunzburg of my exchange with Rasputin, he proposed a ceremonious dinner at Sliosberg's apartment. Rasputin viewed the latter as one of the leading Jews, the most trustworthy and reliable. Sliosberg had really done a lot for his fellow Jews, asking nothing in return.

The Jewish representatives assembled at Sliosberg's:[109] among them was Baron Gunzburg, Moishe Gunzburg, Blankenstein, Mandel, Rabbi Maso and many others whose names escape me after all these years.[110] The moment Rasputin entered the room, he was the object of a solemn reception and demonstrations of profound respect. Over the course of the evening, the Jewish delegates, some of them elderly men with long beards, told him of the persecution of Jews by Nikolai Nikolayevich and other anti-Semitic leaders. Rasputin was visibly moved. He could barely hold back his own tears as he tried to calm

[109] In 1928, Sliosberg wrote that he had only met Simanovitch a few times, and met Rasputin just once when the latter came to inquire about Jewish affairs, but that neither he nor other philanthropists ever approached either for help regarding Jewish affairs.

[110] Simanovitch wrote his memoirs in 1928, more than a decade after Rasputin's death.

and reassure the delegates. When the emotions died down, Rasputin declared that he would gladly help, but felt it would be impossible to make any radical changes in a short period of time, considering how deeply rooted anti-Semitism was among Russian leaders.

"The government and the nobility," he said, "are as mean as mad dogs. You must prepare for a long and hard struggle. It is disheartening, but what can I do? I will do whatever I can. Just tell me what I must do!"

"Come to our aid, Father Grigori!" responded the delegates to whom Rasputin's words gave hope.

"This is insanity," said Rasputin, "Look, you are rich and intelligent, and yet you don't know how to curry the favor of people who can be useful to you. You must buy those people upon whom this all depends. You must do all that is in your power, one way or another, to link your interests to those of the men in power who can serve you."

The delegates explained that their leaders — Vinaver, Grusenberg, Kalmanovitch, Rabbi Eisenstadt and Friedmann — were opposed to this type of tactic because, in their opinion, the goal was to *legislate,* not buy, equal rights for all Jews. Certainly, such vast reforms would take time.

"I really don't understand you," replied Rasputin. "There was a time when other Jews —Poliakov,[111] for example — had a great influence. Now, Simanovitch has access to the Tsar. Why not take that path?"

---

[111] Samuel (Shmuel) Poliakov (Polyakov), 1837-1888, was a Jewish civil rights activist and philanthropist, as well as financing and constructing many of Russia's railroads in the mid- to late 19th century.

The delegates continued their accusations against Grand Duke Nikolai Nikolayevich and begged Rasputin to protect the Jews against his persecution. Rasputin had not expected to learn so many things. We submitted to him one report after another of the persecutions suffered by Jews, and example after example of the hatred with which the powerful Nikolai Nikolayevich pursued our unfortunate brothers. We could not contain our tears when recalling the innumerable executions of Jews condemned by military authorities.[112] Rasputin arose and crossed himself. This signified his vow to help us. Profoundly moved, he resolved that, in ten days, Nikolai Nikolayevich would be relieved of his command of all the Russian armies. One of them, either he or the Grand Duke would be removed. "Then the Tsar will himself take supreme command, and then maybe we can do something for the Jews," Rasputin said.

Everyone present was stunned by Rasputin's promise. I proposed that the sum of 100,000 rubles[113] be given to his family. This was unanimously accepted. Rasputin said he would relay all of this to the Tsar. The next day, Moishe Gunzburg deposited one hundred thousand rubles into the bank, under the names of Rasputin's daughters: fifty thousand for each. We soon were astonished at how promptly Rasputin kept his word. Ten days had not yet gone by and Nikolai Nikolayevich was relieved of his post as Supreme Commander of all Russian Armies, and was sent to command troops in the Caucasus Mountains.

This is how it came about: Several days after the conference, I was at Rasputin's home and was struck by his

---

[112] Eyewitness accounts of such events are found in *The Enemy at His Pleasure* by S. Ansky, a journalist who toured the Pale of Settlement during WW I.

[113] Approx. $50,000 dollars at that time.

attitude and mood: He was eating nothing, and drinking Madeira constantly. He was somber and taciturn. At times, he would leap up, making violent gestures with his hands, as if he wanted to punch someone. And he'd yell, "I'll give them a good punch in the ribs!" It was clear to me that he sought vengeance on someone. On other occasions, I had noticed Rasputin bearing a similar demeanor.

He was in a singular state and seemed completely absorbed in his thoughts. That lasted the entire day. In the evening, he went to the baths, as was his habit, accompanied by a palace police officer. He returned home at about 10:00 p.m. He appeared very tired and did not say a word. I knew, at such times, not to bother him with questions. Moreover, I gave orders for no visitors that evening. Quietly, Rasputin went into his office, wrote something on a slip of paper which he folded, put under his pillow, and went to sleep. He fell asleep immediately.

One day, I asked Rasputin, "What are these slips of paper that you sometimes put under your pillow?"

He told me that he was in the habit of writing down his wishes which were realized as he slept. He said this with the utmost solemnity. He firmly believed in the miraculous effect of these scraps of paper, and this belief was almost contagious. Rasputin told me that before he learned to write, he would cut marks into a wooden slate which he would put under his mattress. In this way, he escaped danger more than once. Once he could write, he no longer needed the slate, as the bits of paper served the same purpose.

The next day, when I arrived at Rasputin's apartment, he was still sleeping. A moment later, he entered the room I was sitting in, and I saw that he had a completely different demeanor than the day before. He was in a good mood, welcoming and friendly. In his hand, he held the note that had been under his pillow. He balled it up, rubbing it between his hands, until it was in tiny pieces.

Sporting a wide smile, he said, "You can rejoice, Simanovitch, my force has won."

"I don't understand," I said.

"Wait. You will see what will happen in five or six days. I am going to find Papa and tell him the entire truth."

"And your truth will win over the Tsar?" I asked.

"In three days, the Tsar will know my power and my truth," responded Rasputin proudly. "I need only predict the future."

He asked me to call the palace on the telephone. I got through immediately, as the Tsar had given a standing order to put Rasputin through promptly. A similar order had been given regarding telegrams, so that Rasputin's always arrived ahead of any others.

"What is Papa doing?" Rasputin asked.

"He is busy with the ministers," an aide replied.

"Tell him that a divine message has arrived for the Tsar."

The Tsar was handed the telephone.

"Who is on the line?" Rasputin asked.

"This is Papa. What is it, Father Grigori?"

"I cannot speak of it on the telephone," said Rasputin. "May I come?"

"Certainly. I also need to speak with you," answered the Tsar.

When Rasputin arrived at Tsarskoye-Selo, he was received immediately. Rasputin hugged Nicholas II and pressed his cheek against the Tsar's three times, which was his habit with people he liked. He told the Tsar that the spirit of God had appeared to him in a dream and announced to him that, in three days, the Tsar would receive a telegram from Grand Duke Nikolai Nikolayevich, stating that there was only enough bread to last the troops for three days.

Sitting across the table from the Tsar, Rasputin filled two glasses with Madeira and insisted that they drink from each other's glass. He mixed what was left in the glasses, pouring from one to the other. He gave half to the Tsar and ordered him to drink it.

When these mysterious practices had prepared Nicholas II, Rasputin told him not to put much faith in the telegram's message. The army had plenty of bread. Nikolai Nikolayevich simply wanted to instill fear and panic into the army and the country. Then, under the pretext of lacking bread, he could give the order to retreat to Petersburg and dethrone the Tsar. Nicholas II was profoundly upset, as he believed in all of Rasputin's prophecies.

"What should I do?" he asked anxiously.

"He wants to send me to Siberia," Rasputin responded, "but I will send him to the Caucasus."

The Tsar understood the allusion. You can imagine how stunned he was when, three days later, a telegram arrived from the Grand Duke, announcing that the army only had enough bread for three days. This event was sufficient to determine the fate of Nikolai Nikolayevich. No one could rid the Tsar of the conviction that the Grand Duke planned to attack the capital and dethrone him. Nikolai Nikolayevich was subsequently named Commander of the Caucasus Army, while the Tsar himself took charge as Commander-in-Chief of all the Russian armies. In that capacity, too, he followed Rasputin's counsel.

The Grand Duke spent three more days at general headquarters before being relieved of his post. The Dowager Empress intervened on his behalf, begging the Tsar to retract his decree relieving the Grand Duke of his supreme command, but it was useless. The Tsar was immovable, and gave the order to prepare a special train to take Grand Duke Nikolai Nikolayevich to the Caucasus.

~~~~~~~~

In the matter of Nikolai Nikolayevich's bloody acts, the sad role of his cohort, General Yanushkevitch,[114] must also be told. He was a normal man, but that did not prevent him from trying to rival the Grand Duke in cruelty. He persecuted Jews with a somber stubbornness and passion, with the Grand Duke's blessing. The situation was aggravated by one particular incident. Yanushkevitch had sent an agent to explain to me that the General owned a property that was burdened with a 400,000-ruble mortgage from Fundamental Credit of Tula. He wanted me to ask some Jewish bankers to refinance this loan. I approached the banks, but received a negative response. The result of

---

[114] The military Chief of Staff
~~~~~~~~

this unfortunate incident was that, from then on, the Jews had one more enemy, and a terrible one. He has, on his conscience, hundreds of thousands of Jewish lives.

In his battle against Jews, Yanushkevitch had the support of his friend General Ruzsky,[115] Commander-in-Chief of the Southwest front. In the course of his retreat from a battlefront in the Carpathian Mountains, Ruzsky undertook the most frightening extermination of Jews in Galicia.[116] The atrocities committed by soldiers and Cossacks were too vile to describe. An acquaintance of mine who commanded a regiment during the war told me this characteristic incident: Some Cossacks were sent on a reconnaissance mission, led by a petty officer. The small detachment did not return for three days. Everyone was convinced the men had been killed in an ambush or taken prisoner. The petty officer explained, to everyone's surprise, that his detachment had spent those three days exterminating Jews. He truly believed he was combating Jewish espionage for his country.

General Bonch-Bruevich[117], whom I knew personally, was stationed at the Pskov front and told me that when General Ruzsky was named Commander-in-Chief of the armies on that front, he assured Bonch-Bruevich that all Jews were spies, without exception. According to him, all military defeats were due to Jewish espionage and, as punishment for those crimes, all Jews should be massacred, down to the last one.

Ruzsky's persecution of Jews only increased in magnitude. Nearly every day, I begged Rasputin to find

---

[115] Ruzsky had command of the Third Army, of the Northwest Front, then of the Sixth Army and the Northern Front during WW I.
[116] The region of Austria/Hungary
[117] Expert on Russian sectarianism, defender of Rasputin.

some way to limit the activities of this cruel general. Rasputin decided to reason with him, but Ruzsky got wind of it and began plotting against Rasputin, gaining Grand Duke Nikolai Nikolayevich's support. Soon, it was an open war between Ruzsky and Rasputin.

This was the incident that lit the gunpowder: Princess Tarkhanova requested that Ruzsky release some Jews who were arrested for profiteering from the war. She produced a letter from Rasputin, interceding on behalf of the Jews in question. Ruzsky's subordinate told her that the general could not grant the petition and was indignant that Rasputin had the audacity to impose such demands. However, Rasputin prevailed. The general requested to be relieved of his position, citing health reasons. Conceding that Rasputin was stronger than he was, he attempted reconciliation and arrived at Rasputin's, one day, dressed in parade uniform decorated with medals. His reception, however, was an extremely cold one.

"Listen, General!" Rasputin said, "A thief, that's what you are! You stole your medals from the Tsar. They should never give you back your former post. They should hang you instead! However, I don't want your death! But how can you have the gall to come here? You're an enemy to the Tsar!"

Ruzsky grew pale and fled. Rasputin then turned to the military judge who had accompanied Ruzsky to his apartment and said: "I will no longer receive you if you bring me such bandits."

It was only after Rasputin's death that Ruzsky regained his position as commander-in-chief on the Pskov front. He sided with the revolutionaries and supported them when they forced the Tsar to abdicate.[118]

~~~~~~~~

The son of Zeyev, chairman of Petersburg's synagogue, came to see me regarding the case of the sugar manufacturers. He asked if I could use my influence to help his brother-in-law, Hepner, who had been arrested along with Babushkin and Dobry. All three were Jewish sugar manufacturers from Kiev. They had been accused of selling a large quantity of sugar to the Germans, via Persia, during wartime, although it had been contracted for by the Germans long before the war began.

The military authorities wanted to present these sugar manufacturers, who were all Jews, as guilty of treason. If the accused went before a military tribunal, only the worst consequences would result for all Russian Jews. That is why we needed to aggressively contest the serious accusation against them. I sought out Rasputin. He told me he would willingly help, under the circumstances. Zeyev offered to assume all costs to bring the affair to a happy end, beginning with fifteen thousand rubles he had to spend on a party at the Villa Rode.

I succeeded in interesting Dobrovolsky,[119] with whom I was on very good terms, in the case. He took the affair to the Justice Minister's Chief Adjunct. Several days later, Dobrovolsky advised me to seek legal counsel to oppose the arrest. He was of the opinion that the case could be tried in a civil court. But the military would not yield, taking the stance that the sugar manufacturers had endangered the army's provisions by illegally exporting sugar. The case was so complex that Rasputin, himself,

---

[118] After the revolution, however, Ruzsky was relieved of his command again and executed by the Bolsheviks.
[119] The Senate's State Attorney.
~~~~~~~~

saw no way out and frankly told me that he had no hope. The generals would not listen to him. He told me that I must not count on him, and that I was to go this road alone. It was only after a big argument that he agreed to try to help.

We met with Dobrovolsky and offered him the position of Minister of Justice on the condition that he support our cause. For his part, he promised to dissolve Batyushin's[120] inquiry commission for impeding the pursuit of justice. Rasputin liked this plan, and offered to present it to the Tsarina. In fact, he was able to present Dobrovolsky directly to her. They sought to convince the Tsarina that the activities of General Batyushin and his commission were toxic. Rasputin railed against these useless commissions that wasted effort and time.

I was soon convinced that our case for the sugar manufacturers had had some effect. At the same time, I took steps in another direction. I begged my friend, Rosen, to visit each member of Batyushin's commission. As a former Imperial Prosecutor, he remained on good terms with the members. The goal of these visits was to learn, in the course of casual conversation, the true state of the investigation and inquiry. Rosen succeeded, so that it was soon possible for us to target the weak points in their accusations. This done, we presented a petition to the Tsarina, in the name of Hepner's daughter, in which we shed light on the weaknesses of the allegations. We explained that the Kiev manufacturers had sold the sugar to the Germans long before the war, for distribution in Persia, but that the Russian industrialists had no idea how the merchandise had passed from Persia to Germany. The

[120] Nikolai Batyushin was a general in the Tsar's army and gained a reputation as a 'spy-catcher.'

Tsarina sent the petition to the Tsar at general headquarters, and begged him to set things right.

Nicholas II called General Batyushin to headquarters and told him he would soon be relieved of his duties as president of the commission, and would be reassigned to another position. Batyushin, in an overly excited state, went to General Alexeev and complained. The latter told him to continue with his work as if nothing had happened, and not to be intimidated. Batyushin followed his advice but became more circumspect and sought Rasputin's favor.

As soon as I saw this, I asked for an audience with the fearsome general. Batyushin was now more yielding. We could pluck the entire affair from the military court and put it in the hands of truly competent judges. The sugar manufacturers denied all accusations of treason.

By that time, however, Rasputin had already been assassinated. The Tsar relieved Minister of Justice Maklakov of his duties, replacing him with Dobrovolsky, at my suggestion.[121] Now, I could place myself in his hands and hope he would succeed in putting an end to this affair. Dobrovolsky summoned Kiev's Attorney General to Petersburg, and asked him to submit a report on the case. After a meeting with the Attorney General, Dobrovolsky gave the order to drop the case against the sugar manufacturers. Despite that, it was not possible to liberate the prisoners who had been arrested by order of General Brusilov, Commander of the Southwest Front. He would not hear of their liberation and exiled them to the Narym district in the north of Siberia.

[121] Simanovitch likely would have told the Tsar that this was what Rasputin would have wanted.

We tried to pressure Brusilov, but without success. In despair, Sliosberg sent a new plea to the Tsar, saying that the sugar manufacturers recognized how their actions had aided the Germans, and begged for the Tsar's mercy. It was Protopopov, Minister of the Interior, who gave the Tsar the letter in which he had written, in the margin, a note that did not vindicate the industrialists, but would save them from judiciary proceedings: "The sugar manufacturers are guilty, it is true. But it should suffice that they atone for their error before the people, in their country." They were finally given their freedom shortly before the 1917 revolution.

~~~~~~~~

With regard to the anti-Semitism that ruled Petersburg in and around the royal circles, the young women of the Court were either not anti-Semitic or did not show it. Vyrubova simply shrugged her shoulders when I spoke to her of it; she did not seem to understand.[122] If Nicholas II was hostile to Jews, it was primarily due to his education. Rasputin often told me that the Tsar's relatives, ministers, and dignitaries of the Court, constantly spoke against the Jews. The Emperor himself said that the ministers, in their reports, did not miss an opportunity to rail against the Jews in order to incite him to act against them, and he was deluged with stories about fictional Jewish plots against him. As for the Tsarina, in the beginning, she had not the least idea that the "Jewish question" existed. It was only later that she learned what anti-Semitism meant. A number of Jews were employed by the Imperial Court with no apparent problem or controversy. Everyone knew that the Tsar, upon taking supreme command of the troops, ceased the inhumane hunt of the Jews that was ordered by Nikolai

---

[122] He doesn't consider that she may have found the topic an uncomfortable or awkward one.
~~~~~~~~

Nikolayevich. Rasputin told me that the Emperor did this on his own initiative, and assured that, whenever asked, Nicholas II accorded Jews certain measures, lightening their plight, or reducing punishment.[123]

[123] Yet it is a matter of record that pogroms (raids) on Jews persisted throughout WW I, as documented by S. Ansky.

Grand Duke Nikolai Nikolayevich (left) and his nephew Tsar Nicholas II (right)

Small gathering at Rasputin's apartment. Rasputin is second from left. Maria is at the end of the table, seated in front of the man standing.

Chapter VI

Rasputin and the Ministers

From the moment that Rasputin had a decisive influence on the nomination of Council ministers, he endlessly looked for candidates who could fill these high offices in a manner to his liking. As he was not personally familiar with the hopeful candidates, it was difficult for him to make a choice. This is why he often came to me, asking for suggestions for various vacant and soon-to-be-vacant positions. Our task was further complicated when many of our nominees declined the offer, knowing too well the Tsar's unstable nature. The situation was even more complex during the last years of Nicholas II's reign. The Tsar would telephone Rasputin and ask him, on the spot, to name a replacement for a minister he had just dismissed. When such a situation arose, Rasputin would ask the Tsar to hold on for a few minutes, and then he would ask me to think of someone who would be capable as well as useful to us.

"We need a minister!" Rasputin would shout, very agitated.

I cannot help but smile sadly, thinking of such commonly recurring scenes. Generally, we would have a short consultation. Sometimes, Rasputin's nieces would take part in our discussions, too, and all the while the Tsar would be waiting on the telephone.

One day, one such call came from the Tsar, and Rasputin said, "We need a general." My son, Semyon, who was there by chance, suggested Prince Volkonsky, although he was not a military man. He was Vice President of the Duma. Rasputin gave his name to the Tsar. On the spot, Volkonsky was appointed Deputy to the Minister of the Interior.

I must add that the Tsar told anyone he appointed to a post that Rasputin was the only man who had his total trust. "Rasputin is an emissary from God," the Tsar would say. "Never in my life have I felt such trust and affection for anyone."

Sometimes, when it was particularly difficult to name a choice, Manasevitch-Manuilov[124] would come to our aid. Of course, he tried to choose people he could trust. This was how, for example, Sturmer became Council President. Manasevitch-Manuilov presented him to us as "an old thief and charlatan" and guaranteed that Sturmer would satisfy our requirements.

We were looking, above all, for men who could bring peace with Germany. We had many long talks with Sturmer, and he was only nominated when we felt he was sufficiently prepared. My hope was that Sturmer, once he became Council President, would not oppose equal rights for Jews.

On another occasion, the Tsar was urgently looking for someone to fill the position of Public Prosecutor for the Holy Synod. We recommended Professor Raev who taught at the Superior School for Girls. He was an old, completely insignificant man who wore a wig and had a

---

[124] Ivan Manasevich-Manuilov, son of a poor Jew but adopted by a wealthy Russian merchant, was a journalist, former police agent and was briefly appointed to various special commissions for the Prime Minister. He converted to Lutheranism.

comical appearance. He was President of the Association of Science and Commerce, which I had founded and which, despite its pompous name, was nothing more than a common gambling club where huge parties would go on, day and night.

Rasputin communicated his desires to the ministers by means of little notes in which he habitually inserted the formula, “I will tell The One Who Loves Me.” The ministers considered Rasputin’s demands as they would orders from the Tsar, and generally followed his instructions.

I always went to see Rasputin in the morning. First, we would discuss our plans for the day; then, I would catch up on what had occurred the night before. One day, upon arriving at the apartment, I found Rasputin distraught and agitated. I knew that something must have happened and that, once again, his ‘force’ was operating. In fact, what he told me, point-blank, was frightening.

“Listen, Aron,” he said, “a pogrom will come to Kiev soon. You must take steps accordingly.”

You can imagine how this news upset me! I had many relatives in Kiev and any actions against Jews caused me great worry. When I begged Rasputin to give me more details, he made a very strange statement: “That’s the end for the Old Man,” he said.

We always used the term “the Old Man” when speaking of Council President Stolypin.[125] I concluded that Rasputin foresaw Stolypin’s death. I could make no other sense of his enigmatic pronouncement. He was certain this would

---

[125] P.A. Stolypin was Prime Minister from 1906 to 1911.

occur in the near future. I tried to question Rasputin. Why did they choose Kiev? What can we do to avert this horror? If this was true, I wanted to send a telegram to Kiev, immediately, to alert everyone. To my surprise, Rasputin explained that a pogrom or any such threat could only be avoided if the Tsar did not bring Stolypin to Kiev where he would be assassinated, never to return to Petersburg.

I must admit that, despite all the faith I had in Rasputin's gift of prophecy, I remained skeptical in this case. In spite of the little religious training I had, I did not want to doubt, in my heart of hearts, the possibility of such a miracle in our time. But I did wonder if, at the bottom of it all, there was some trickery to it. Assuredly, Rasputin often surprised me. He told me he had spoken to the Tsar about the upcoming trip to Kiev but had returned very dissatisfied with the meeting. He had warned the Tsar about the misfortune that was about to occur, and advised Nicholas II not to bring Stolypin to Kiev.

"To be perfectly honest," Rasputin said, "I shouldn't alert Stolypin to the danger facing him because he is not my friend. However, the Tsar needs him, and because of that, we must save him. Stolypin doesn't attack me and, for my part, I don't want to set any traps for him either."

This time, the Tsar did not put any faith in Rasputin's words. He did not want, at any price, to leave Stolypin behind. This upset Rasputin who felt that this sealed Stolypin's fate. Stolypin subsequently went to Kiev where a secret police agent, named Bogrov, killed him.[126]

---

[126] Bogrov was a revolutionary terrorist who had once worked for the royal security service, and was permitted by a security guard to enter a theater with a gun, where he killed Stolypin.

Afterward, when I told the entire story to my acquaintances at the Court, some thought that the Tsar had taken Stolypin to Kiev precisely because he believed in the prophecy. I consider this theory groundless. It is true that Nicholas II generally had great faith in Rasputin's prophecies, but it is also possible that, this particular time, he found the prediction too outrageous to merit attention.[127]

Immediately following Stolypin's assassination, the Tsar sent a message to Rasputin: "What must I do?"

Rasputin sent a telegram in reply: "Joy. Peace. Calm. No one will bar your way, Lamb of Peace. The blood of minorities is as precious, in all of the Russian Tsar's lands, as that of our own brothers."

The Tsar gave orders preventing any anti-Semitic agitation in Kiev. The reactionaries were disappointed. There was no pogrom.

~~~~~~~~~

Maklakov[128] did not earn his post as Minister of the Interior by merit of his statesmanship, but solely by his ingratiating behavior toward the Sovereigns. He knew how to amuse the Tsar and the Tsarevitch with his little parlor tricks, but was removed from office for going head-to-head with Rasputin. The circumstances surrounding Maklakov's fall shed some light on the power of the Tsar's 'favorite.'

---

127 Ironically, several weeks before his murder, Stolypin demanded that the Tsar send Rasputin away.
128 Nicholas Maklakov was Minister of the Interior from 1913 to 1915.
~~~~~~~~~

I began a society called Fontanka Prospect. The foundation of this club had some gravitas to it. Count Tolstoy[129] acted as founder, and Baron Roop was elected president. The administrative council united Prince Bermand-Avalov (Cossack officer and, later, General of the White Army of the Northwest) and Count Musvitz Shadorsky (then Cavalry Colonel) with the former statesman, Rosen who was Secretary General of our group. In this club, which served as a meeting place for our members, the only game played was lotto. From time to time, we organized soirées and concerts. I made sure Rasputin frequented our club as much as possible to assure our protection, in the event of any trouble. Rasputin never gambled, but willingly came to the dinners when we invited interesting people. Of course, the fare was fine and abundant. Rasputin always found his favorite dishes there. We knew he did not eat meat, sweets or cakes.

One day, Maklakov gave an order to Nikolayev, a subordinate who ran errands for him, to make a full inspection of our club. Nikolayev confided in us that the ulterior motive of his mission was to find some pretext under which to close us down. At first, we did not want Rasputin mixed up in this affair. Secretary General Rosen was also legal counsel to the reactionary association, The League of the Archangel Saint Mikhail. We scoffed at Maklakov's attack on us, partly because of Rosen's position. Rosen was infuriated and said that he knew a way to prevent the Minister from closing our club.

Two days later, we received a notice from the Prefect of Police advising us that our club was to be abolished for

[129] This could not have been the writer Leo Tolstoy who died in 1910 (Maklakov only became Minister of Justice in 1913), but could have been one of his sons, siblings, etc, as there were many Count Tolstoys among them.

"violations of statutes." This was a declaration of war and we decided to unseat the unpleasant Minister of the Interior. To this end, I telephoned Rasputin: "Listen," I said to him, "they are going to restrict us. Our good life is finished."

"How do you mean?" he asked, surprised.

"They are closing our club because you were attending. They're taking revenge on us."

"Come see me, imbecile," Rasputin said.

When I arrived, I described the affair in such a way that our club appeared to be the victim in a plot against Rasputin. He decided to address himself to Police Prefect Drachuvsky, who had jurisdiction over such clubs. He wrote the following: "My Very Dear Prefect, There was but one place where I could go to relax. Rescind the order to shut down this club. Don't be silly. Don't put a knife to our throats."

Then we sent the Prefect a delegation consisting of Count Tolstoy, Rosen, and Prince Bermand-Avalov. The Prefect courteously received our delegates, but told them that the order had not come from him. He, personally, had nothing against our club and could find no fault with it. It was Maklakov who had given the order. "I was even reprimanded by the Minister for having delayed enforcing the order for two days," added the Police Prefect.

I immediately sought out Rasputin and recounted the entire exchange with the prefect. In order to light a fire under him, I added that Maklakov depicted our group as a den of debauchery for friends of Rasputin, the horse thief.[130]

---

[130] Among the many rumors that circulated about his wild youth,

Rasputin was furious. He paced up and back with great strides, cursing the Minister with all sorts of violent injuries, each more picturesque than the former. Rasputin had, for such moments, an unbelievably rich vocabulary. Even men were embarrassed.

"He is greatly mistaken," shouted Rasputin, "if he thinks to have the upper hand because he has a big mustache that he's always fussing with like a dog, and playing his stupid games around the Tsarevitch. He'll remember me!"

He went to his desk and wrote the following: "Listen well, Minister. Maybe you think you can do whatever comes into your head because the Tsar brought you from Chernikov, you and your big mustache, and because you act the jester. When you arrived from Chernikov, the ends of your mustache were turned up but, today, they are less so and I am the one who is going to take you down a peg. You have shut down my group. For that, I will give you a good punch in the ribs. Thank God, in your prayers, and thank Father Grigori, that I will not inflict anything worse than a punch in the ribs. You were an imbecile. You still are an imbecile. You can go complain. I don't care." — Grigori

Rasputin gave me the letter and telephoned Globachev, head of police security, to send a car. Before leaving for Tsarskoye-Selo, he telephoned Nicholas II, asking to be received immediately, as he had something important to discuss with him.

The Minister of the Interior was relieved of his duties. Rasputin telephoned to tell me the result of his meeting

---

the popular one alleging horse theft was particularly infuriating to Rasputin.

with the Tsar, and I prevailed upon members of our circle to find Maklakov and give him Rasputin's letter.

"Why didn't you give me this letter before I was sent away?" Maklakov asked despairingly of the group members. "I ordered the club closed because Rasputin was indulging in all sorts of excessive behavior there!"

One of the club members responded, "Rasputin knows well that you partake of such excesses in a certain place, yet he's taken no action against you."

Rasputin's way of dealing with the ministers made him popular in society circles. All sorts of people tried to please him in order to realize their own dreams. The groveling that surrounded him was sometimes repulsive. I often saw well-known people — millionaires, dignitaries, and church officials — lower themselves to the point of humiliation. One word from Rasputin was sufficient to determine a man's fate. The desire to obtain riches and advantages, through the all-powerful Rasputin, unleashed all sorts of passions.

~~~~~~~~

Count Sergei Witte telephoned me one morning, and asked me to meet with him to discuss a confidential matter. I had known the Count for years, but had not seen him in a long time. I immediately went to see him, and he received me in the friendliest manner. The Count asked me, carefully turning his phrases, whether he could speak frankly of a matter that had to remain strictly between us. He told me that he had conceived of a plan of great interest to the Jewish people. Completely seduced by this opening, I gave him my word that I would keep our talk secret.
~~~~~~~~

"I need," he said, in an eloquent manner, "for you to arrange a meeting for me — with Rasputin."

He let the silence settle between us for a moment and studied my reaction. I was already used to seeing high-placed people who sought to profit personally from Rasputin's influence. Count Witte's request did not surprise me. I told him I would arrange such a meeting and that, together, we would seek the means to set his project in motion. I suggested that he first curry Rasputin's favor.

It fell to Countess Witte[131] to act as intermediary. Rasputin would send petitioners to her and she would take care to do as he asked. We agreed that she be called by the name 'Madame Mathilda,' without indicating her title or real name, so as not to be recognized by others in Rasputin's salon, especially when they returned to thank him for her help. This made a good impression on Rasputin, and he looked favorably upon Count Witte. I also counseled Witte to rent a discreet lodging where he could meet with Rasputin without calling attention to himself. The Count readily accepted, having already had the same idea. He proposed, to my surprise, an apartment in Rasputin's building.

I must admit to being seduced by the idea of uniting Rasputin and Witte and, in so doing, helping the Count regain his position directing the country's affairs. Witte could be of great service regarding the Jewish question by proposing measures that could lead to a solution. I made him give his word that, if he returned to his government

---

[131] Count Witte's second wife, Mathilda, was a married Jew whom he had urged to divorce her husband so he could marry her. While she converted to Russian Orthodoxy, she was never accepted by society and Witte lost a bit of his social standing in the scandal.

seat, he would work to remove the restrictions imposed on Jews. He promised to make the Jewish question top priority. The agreement between us was thus concluded. For my part, I assured him that I would not tell his wife of his secret encounters with Rasputin. For these meetings, Witte adopted the name of Ivan Fyodorovitch. It was only with the utmost prudence that I laid the groundwork for this meeting. However, Rasputin was too sharp for me. As I was preparing him for the idea of meeting with the Count, without yet mentioning names, Rasputin looked at me with a clever air and said: "I know of whom you speak. It is Witte."

He was happy and flattered that Witte needed his protection and he looked forward to meeting with him. As for finding a comfortable and discreet apartment in Rasputin's building, I went to see Mr. Chaiv who had just such a small, furnished place. I proposed he let me have the apartment for the summer, in exchange for the use of my villa in Sestroretsk, outside of Petersburg. He accepted. I notified Witte and sent him the key by courier, a former soldier who had never before met the Count.

Rasputin and Witte met for the first time in the spring — a Saturday, at four o'clock. They were both quite satisfied with the interview. Rasputin later told me that he first asked Witte how he wanted to be addressed, and they agreed that Rasputin would address the former prime minister as 'Little Count.' The conversation did not take long to get underway. As was his habit, Rasputin came right out with what he wanted in exchange for helping Witte, and they easily came to an agreement. Rasputin said, "The situation is very difficult. You are intelligent and informed. Make a proposition."

Witte explained that he was held in disgrace because he was against the war. Nevertheless, he could not change the way he felt.

"Let me kiss you!" Rasputin cried, delighted. "I, too, am against war. I am absolutely in agreement with you. But what can we do? Papa is against you. He is afraid of you. In any case, I will speak to him about you, and counsel him to put you in charge of ending the war. I have confidence in you."

Later, in the course of that same evening, Witte said that the newspaper, *Novoye Vremia*[132]was causing great harm, as it promoted continuing the war. It had to be rendered harmless.

"Yes, you are right," Rasputin said. "It must be done. We could buy the newspaper and then publish what we want."

"True," said Witte, "but make sure you attain your goal. You know what bad luck resulted when Imperial Palace Commander Voyekov did such business with Prince Andronikov. He gave the Prince money to buy a newspaper and, after that, the new directors had nothing better to do than mount a campaign against me!"

Twelve days later, Rasputin let Witte know that he'd had a conversation with the Tsar on the subject of Witte's nomination.

"I told him," said Rasputin, "that 'Mme Mathilda' does everything asked of her by the people I've sent to her, and that I've spoken to you and that he can trust you."

---

[132] Translation: *New Times*

However, the Tsar could not bring himself to recall Witte to power, and explained his viewpoint thus: "You must know that I'd be exposing myself to grave danger if I entrusted Witte. My relatives would reserve for me that same fate suffered by King Alexander of Serbia. They would assassinate us — my wife and me. Recalling Witte to preside over the Council would signify that I want to make peace with Germany."

"Help me, Father Grigori," said Witte. "Don't abandon me. You are a real Russian and an honest man. The Tsar's relatives do not want him to act on his own and they are already furious with me for having promoted the Constitution nine years ago. The Tsar has not kept the promises he made to the people. That's where he should look for the cause of his difficulties."

Some time afterward, Witte asked me to meet with him. I went to his house and he said to me: "Today, I spoke to the editor of *Novoye Vremia.* He needs money, and asked my advice in the matter. He would be interested in selling a percentage of the paper. Among other things, he asked me to have Finance Minister Bark underwrite *Novoye Vremia.*

"I find," concluded Witte, "that the moment is favorable to assert our influence on *Novoye Vremia* and put an end to the propaganda. If Rasputin can gather a sufficient sum, I will arrange all that. We will take over the newspaper and it will do no more harm. Speak to your Jewish friends about it. They shouldn't miss this chance to disarm such a dangerous enemy."

I recounted this meeting to Rasputin. After a short deliberation, we went to our 'banker'.[133] We also wanted to present the affair to M.M. Kaminka, Moishe Gunzburg

---

[133] Jewish financier Dmitri Rubenstein

and Baron Gunzburg. Rasputin gathered these men of high finance and proposed to them the purchase of this influential, anti-Semitic newspaper. He tried to persuade these businessmen that such a transaction would be most advantageous and, in truth, his speech made a strong impression on all present. They clearly saw that the purchase of this newspaper could be very useful. All of them put great stock in Rasputin's interest in the Jews. Given the influence he enjoyed in the Imperial Court, his approval was of enormous importance.

Witte bought the shares and gave them to Rubenstein who, with some of the others, acquired *Novoye Vremia,* and the affair was concluded. Rubenstein rejoiced that the anti-Semitic agitation, against which the Count had vehemently campaigned, was finished, at least in that arena. For his part, Count Witte was happy not to be slandered and attacked in this important newspaper.[134]

The rapport between Rasputin and the former prime minister lasted until Witte's death. They saw each other often, and it was obvious that Witte never lost hope of returning to power one day, thanks to Rasputin's support. However, the Old Court got wind of the cordial relations between the two men, through its elaborate espionage network developed long ago. The news that Witte sought a reunion with the Young Court, with Rasputin's help, threw Nicholas II's adversaries into great agitation. A huge concern spread through the entire entourage of the Old Court which presumed that Witte would undertake some project to turn the public against them.

---

[134] Other accounts report that Rubenstein was blocked from owning controlling shares by the son of the deceased newspaper owner, who declared the effort an attempt of international Jewry to control the Russian media.

~~~~~~~~~

When Rasputin came to speak to me of his future, I advised him to leave Petersburg and the Tsar, without waiting for his enemies to lose patience. I owned a small piece of property in Palestine, the country of my ancestors, where I hoped to finish out my days. Rasputin also felt attracted to the Holy Land. He approved of my plan to retire there. Before then, we would have renounced the somber, unhealthy and dangerous life in Petersburg, but we felt obliged to remain to continue our good works. Rasputin was determined to put an end to war, and I pursued the goal of equal rights for Jews.

"We must force the Tsar to keep his word," Rasputin said. "He promised to grant the empire a constitution. If he had done as he promised, all of the empire's subjects would have had the same rights long ago. But, at present, we must first think of peace with Germany."

"Attaining peace is a tricky affair," I told him. "You would do better to concentrate on equal rights for Jews. That will even facilitate peace. When the Jewish question has an answer, surely we'll receive money from American Jews who will shelter us."

"Why don't Russian Jews want to give money?" asked Rasputin.

"Because they don't want it said that they *bought* their freedom from the Tsar," I answered.[135] "We will have enough money for our families to leave. Your departure will facilitate general reconciliation and, if I'm not wrong,

[135] The Jewish community wanted their freedom legislated rather than bought.
~~~~~~~~~

the nobility would be glad to allow Jews their rights, in exchange for being rid of you."

"Yes, but Papa doesn't want peace," Rasputin replied. "And, as for Jewish rights, he won't even hear of it. His relatives will not allow him to give the country a constitution. I have told him many times: 'If you accord a constitution, they will call you Nicholas the Great.' But, to that, he replied that a constitution would prevent him from signing a separate peace with Germany. When the Tsar was with me, he searched only for plausible reasons for a separate peace, but he was so fearful of everyone. When he is with me in his office, he looks all around to reassure himself that no one is listening. Myself, I think a constitution would be good for my compatriots. It would only be disagreeable to the nobility. The rest of us peasants need it. Now, when young people finish their military service, they stay in the city instead of returning to the village. If you gave land to the peasants, that would change quickly. It is unfortunate that Papa lets himself be so easily influenced. The last person he speaks to sways his opinion. As soon as we are not there, he forgets what he promised. That is our misfortune."

Rasputin continued: "I think Witte is right. I agree with him. Perhaps I will succeed in getting him nominated. He, in turn, will support me. When I speak to the Tsar now, regarding the issue of the Jews, he does not contradict me. He says, 'listen, Father Grigori, when I have found a minister I can confide in, and when I have brought about peace, I will grant all the reforms I have promised'. I told him that he might give the people what they want, but that he would take it away again, later. And I said that if this is how it is, then it is better to give nothing so that there is nothing you can take away from them."

"Just the same," I yelled at Rasputin, "something must be given to the Jews!"

"And how can you expect me to get for the Jews what I have not yet gotten for the peasants? The Tsar does not dare accord the Jews any rights. He thinks he will be assassinated if he does. And it is true that they assassinated his grandfather.[136] The Tsar has often told me that his ministers were liars, and that their singular mission was to persuade him that everything that happens is the sole fault of the Jews."

This conversation took place in 1915 when Witte was befriending Rasputin and made a great impression on him. For his part, Rasputin knew how to win over the Tsarina and Metropolitan[137] Pitirim. Old Sturmer joined them, and they had the support of the entire Young Court. In that context, Rasputin tried to convince the Tsar of the necessity for a constitutional mode of government that could unify all Russians.

One day, Rasputin arrived at my house, satisfied and joyous. He said he had finally accomplished his mission. The Tsar consented to go to the Duma and declare that he was going to form a cabinet, the president of which would be named by the Tsar himself. The other members were to be designated by the Duma. I cannot say exactly how all that was to come about. Perhaps I had not understood Rasputin, or perhaps he had not explained it well. In any case, he added that once the new constitution was in effect, Jews would have their full rights, with the exception of

---

[136] Nicholas' grandfather, Alexander II, was known for according peasants greater rights and Jews more privileges, although not equality.

[137] Archbishop

holding any leading positions in the army or the state. This was, according to Rasputin, the German system.[138]

I notified Baron and Moishe Gunzburg of what I had learned from Rasputin. No one doubted his word; we all knew he was not a liar. But, alas, we did not count on one of the most important factors — the sad character trait of Russia's last tsar. He would have done better not to have made the promise in light of his lack of will, inability to keep his word, and weakness of character. Returning from general headquarters, Nicholas II told Rasputin that he no longer had the same intentions. He would not go to the Duma. He would not change the form of government. Rasputin always spoke freely with the Tsar, often without first gathering his thoughts. This time, he did not hide his rage, and frightened the Tsarina and Lady Vyrubova with the prophecy that a revolution would occur if the Tsar did not take it upon himself to form a union with his people.

In the end, Nicholas II stated he would follow Rasputin's advice. He even fixed the date to proclaim the constitution. The Tsar arrived at the Duma on the given date but, apparently, was warned, at the last moment, that he would be assassinated if he renounced his prerogative of absolute sovereignty. Unfortunately, I have no further details regarding this last-minute intervention. It is also possible that the Tsar imagined the threat of assassination in order to have an excuse to break his promise.

~~~~~~~~

[138] "In reality, it was a matter of instituting a parliamentary regime in Russia, and creating a cabinet of ministers responsible to the Duma." — A. Simanovitch (This is the only footnote Simanovitch wrote in his book)
~~~~~~~~

When Rasputin arrived in Petersburg, in 1905, he was under the influence of the famous Countess Kleinmichael who had an excellent rapport with Petersburg's high society, as well as the respect of the Court. Many diplomats, state dignitaries, financiers and sophisticated ladies passed through her salon. The old Countess lacked neither intelligence nor presence and knew how to be on the best of terms with all of them. She was a great friend of Countess Ignatiev who presided over the reactionary association, The Starry Room. These two ladies had aligned themselves with Rasputin in order to profit from his influence on the Imperial Couple, but they soon learned that he would not be blindly manipulated. Consequently, they turned Iliodor,[139] the monk, against him. Until then, Iliodor and Rasputin had been on friendly terms. However, from that moment on, Iliodor staged one plot after another against him.

Bishop Barnabas,[140] who owed his position to Rasputin, went to Pokrovskoie to beg Rasputin to reconcile with Iliodor. He told Rasputin that Khvostov, former governor of Nizhniy Novgorod, and friend of Iliodor, was ready to assume the role of mediator between the two. Khvostov hoped to be named Minister of the Interior as a reward for being helpful in the matter. When Rasputin was about to return to Petersburg from Pokrovskoie, Barnabas asked if he would like to meet Khvostov, and he agreed. When Rasputin and Barnabas arrived at the station, Khvostov was

---

[139] Iliodor (born Sergei Trufanov in 1880; died in 1952) was a corrupt monk and priest who began as a friend to Rasputin but ended up plotting assassination attempts against him, even after being exiled.

[140] Also spelled Varnavas. Thanks to Rasputin, Barnabas was made Bishop of Tobolsk despite his lack of educational requirements.

there to meet them, accompanied by his friend, Prince Andronikov.

Barnabas presented Khvostov to Rasputin with these words: "Here's the big man I wired about our arrival." Khvostov and Rasputin began conversing with regard to Khvostov's pending nomination as Minister of the Interior.

"But you would have to withdraw from the reactionary group, The Union of the Russian People," said Rasputin.

"I do not belong to this association," said Khvostov, "but as its members are monarchists, I must support them."

"And on what terms are you with Iliodor?" asked Rasputin.

"He does everything I tell him to do," said Khvostov.

"And if I demand that Iliodor be sent into exile, would you do it?" Rasputin inquired.

"If Iliodor learned that I was against him, there would be no need to exile him. He would leave on his own and you would have nothing to fear."

Rasputin was quite satisfied with Khvostov's explanations and promises. When he returned to Petersburg, he proposed to the Tsar that Khvostov be appointed Minister of the Interior. Nicholas II followed his advice and Khvostov's dream was realized.[141] Rasputin soon saw that Khvostov made an impression on Iliodor. The monk fled to Norway but, from there, he continued his campaign against Rasputin. In truth, Iliodor's 'flight' had been planned in advance, and the monk even received sixty thousand rubles from the Interior Minister's secret fund.

[141] Alexei Khvostov was Minister of the Interior from 1915 to 1916.

The sum was given to him to prevent the publication of documents compromising to the Tsarina.

From Christiania, Norway, Iliodor corresponded with Khvostov for the purpose of organizing an attack on Rasputin. Iliodor had a fanatical follower who would carry out the assassination. It was then that a third party entered the picture: Beletsky,[142] the Adjunct to the Minister of the Interior, who coveted the Minister's post for himself. To gain Rasputin's support for a promotion, Beletsky secretly read the correspondence between his boss, Khvostov, and Iliodor. He reported his findings back to Rasputin.

Khvostov had hired, as his secretary, a little journalist by the name of Rzhevsky.[143] However, Beletsky won over Rzhevsky, such that the latter rendered services to Beletsky that the Minister would have found disagreeable. One day, I received a message from Rzhevsky, stating that he was leaving for Christiania, under Khvostov's orders, to give Iliodor some letters and the money needed to mount another attack on Rasputin. I rushed to see Rzhevsky who showed me the letter from Khvostov to Iliodor. He asked to meet with Rasputin to unveil the huge plot, directed not only at Rasputin but at the Tsarina as well. I think Rzhevsky exaggerated a bit, to feel important. When Rasputin saw the letter from Khvostov, he became very agitated. We talked about what needed to be done. I proposed asking Colonel Komissarov, of the Police Department, to follow the affair. Rasputin agreed. I went to Komissarov and related the entire scenario.

"What would be my reward for cleaning up this affair?" he asked.

---

[142] Stephan Beletsky was Director of the Department of Police in Petersburg, under the Minister of the Interior.
[143] Boris Rzhevsky, also spelled Rashevsky.

“What do you want?” I replied.

“I would like to be promoted to general and named Prefect of Police in a big city.”

Rasputin was ready to fulfill his desire. However, I thought it better if Beletsky uncovered the conspiracy since he was pulling all the strings.

The next day, I took Rzhevsky to see Rasputin who greeted him with a hug.

“Beware of everyone, Father Grigori,” Rzhevsky said. “Neither Komissarov nor Beletsky are worthy of your trust. They will sell you out and behave, perhaps, as Manuilov did with Gapon. As you know, Gapon was betrayed and hanged in Oserki.”[144]

“Counsel me, then,” said Rasputin.

“Negotiate with them, keeping a cool head. Promise you will reward them, but do not trust them. The Tsar must appoint someone totally alien to all of this to investigate this plot.”

The following day, we went to Tsarskoye-Selo, accompanied by Rasputin. There, we saw Vyrubova. The Tsarina arrived moments later and we showed her the letter from Khvostov to Iliodor stating that the murderers were only waiting for Iliodor’s written consent to kill Rasputin. I proposed Army General Belyayev as investigator of the

---

[144] This is a reference to Father Gapon who led a peaceful workers’ demonstration during ‘Bloody Sunday’ of the1905 revolution, wherein soldiers opened fire on the unarmed civilians. A year later, in1906, he was found hanged. The implication is that Manuilov, journalist, former police agent and spy, was responsible for the hanging.

matter. He said he would accept the mission, but wanted a written order from the Tsar. His desire was granted.

Rzhevsky was detained and searched at the Finnish border. This had been planned ahead of time. After having photographed all of Khvostov's letters, they let Rzhevsky go and he continued his trip. From that moment, military censors intercepted all telegrams sent from Iliodor to Khvostov. Upon returning from Norway, Rzhevsky was detained at the border again. He was carrying letters from Iliodor to Khvostov, which contained the names of the three peasants from Zaritzyn who were to kill Rasputin. The peasants were arrested but General Belyayev, at Rasputin's request, simply had them banished to their hometown. When Khvostov got wind of our doings, he swore revenge on me, and it did not take long to come about.

The Tsar had not kept his promise to proclaim to the Duma the introduction of a constitutional regime and equal rights for minorities. Rasputin met with him, hoping that such reforms could be realized. That was on January 6.[145] However, the Tsar did not want to keep his promise. Rasputin, greatly saddened, went to find Metropolitan Pitirim. They telephoned Council President Sturmer, asking him to come to Pitirim's apartment at the Alexander Nevski Abbey where they consulted with each other. Pitirim wrote the most eloquent letter, advising the Tsar to yield to the needs of the times and grant the long-awaited reforms. Pitirim, Sturmer and Rasputin signed the letter. I accepted the mission of remitting this historical document to the Tsar, at Tsarskoye-Selo. Unfortunately, I cannot produce the text of that letter to my readers. I had saved a

---

[145] The year was 1916.

copy but had to leave it behind in Petersburg. However, this letter made a great impression on all who knew of it.

I handed it to the Tsar, himself, at the entrance to the Alexander Palace, and noted that he appeared very worried. He said to tell Rasputin that he would grant the wish expressed by the signatories of the letter. I communicated the imperial response to Rasputin, Sturmer, and Pitirim, who were all satisfied. We expected a proclamation at the January 9 meeting of the Duma. The day arrived and nothing happened. The Tsar went to the Duma that day but made not the slightest mention of the reforms in question.

That night, between the ninth and tenth of January, I was arrested by order of the Minister of the Interior. Khvostov had somehow established that it was I who had given the Tsar the letter signed by Pitirim, Rasputin and Sturmer. When I learned this, I could not help but wonder if the Tsar himself had told him. At the station, they put me in a cell for political prisoners. For sixteen days, no one knew where I was. My family had no news of me and no one would tell them where I'd been taken. At the police station, they presented me with a proposition from Khvostov: take his side in the struggle against Rasputin. I did not want any part of it. My oldest son requested and obtained an audience with the Tsarina, whom he told of my arrest. She was indignant. "This is revolution! Khvostov has acted against the Tsar's will!"

Council President Sturmer and his secretary, Manasevitch-Manuilov, became worried upon learning my fate. Manuilov jumped up from his bed in the middle of the night, yelling, "They could just as well arrest me, too!" Khvostov's orders were completely unexpected. Rasputin was furious and could not forgive himself for having procured for him the position of Minister of the Interior.

My situation was serious. Khvostov wanted to legally send me into the next world. He had falsified documents making me out to be a spy. These were submitted to a military tribunal and were enough to have me executed. By a stroke of luck, I was able to furnish proof that the fraudulent correspondence with enemy agents could not possibly be mine. The accusation was dropped. After sixteen days, I was set free. But within twenty-four hours, I received an order to leave for the Narym district in Siberia. A day later, my family received an order to follow me there. Fortunately, the Tsarina intervened in time and rescinded the orders.

The Tsar, at that time, was at military headquarters. When he returned, Khvostov hastily sought him out to report the story of Iliodor and my arrest, omitting the facts. He blamed Rzhevsky and Beletsky. In the meantime, the Tsar had already been informed of the details. However, he appeared excessively friendly toward Khvostov, who had not the slightest notion that the Tsar was unhappy with him. Their meeting lasted two hours. He pretended to believe Khvostov who left feeling triumphant. Nevertheless, when the Minister returned home, he found a letter, sealed with the Tsar's stamp, announcing his dismissal. He could not believe the decree was authentic. Nicholas II had shown him such hospitality! Khvostov left hastily for Tsarskoye-Selo but was not received.

A new and quite unpleasant surprise was awaiting the now-former Minister upon his return home. Council President Sturmer had sent word for him to come. Khvostov complied immediately. He learned that the Tsar had ordered all of his medals revoked and sentenced him to six months in exile. That night, Khvostov left Petersburg. Before his departure, a search of his offices took place. At Sturmer's request, I assisted. We found numerous documents, important papers, and correspondences, among which were letters from the Tsar, the Tsarina and Rasputin. All of these were burned.

When Khvostov was in his meeting with the Tsar, Nicholas II had already given the order to rescind my exile. It reached me when I got to Tver. However, my brother, who had also been exiled to Siberia with his son, had to continue the journey. Fearing that Khvostov might have me assassinated en route, I had an escort of ten men to accompany me on the return trip.

Due to my relationship with Rasputin, the Tsar did not want anyone to exercise control over my deeds and actions without his knowledge. Khvostov knew this. That is why the Tsar was indignant when he learned I had been arrested and exiled. Rzhevsky had been exiled to the Narym District at the same time I was. Before his departure, however, Khvostov brought his prisoner into his office and beat him badly.

On Rasputin's recommendation, the Tsar appointed Sturmer as Minister of the Interior, although he was already Council President.[146] Rasputin asked Sturmer to assign Colonel Komissarov to a new position. The Colonel became the new Police Prefect of the City of Rostov. Beletsky had hoped to govern the city of Irkutsk, however Rasputin convinced him to stay in Petersburg, promising to create a special post for him as Minister of Police. While waiting for that position, he was made a senator. As for General Belyayev, he was named Minister of War.[147] And so, the promise Rasputin made to him was fulfilled.

---

[146] Sturmer was Council President from January to November, 1916.

[147] General M.A. Belyayev became Minister of War for the new Provisional Government in March, 1917, after the Tsar's

I must add that Khvostov had a particular reason to be angry with me. In 1915, I had turned over to Prince Gelovani, Deputy of the Duma, documents revealing that Khvostov tried to organize uprisings against the Jews. I had received these documents from Beletsky with the promise that I would procure for him the position of Minister of the Interior. Prince Gelovani then brought the documents to Deputy Kerensky who published them. It created quite a sensation. Kerensky brought to the Duma a passionate struggle against reactionary parties, not missing an occasion to fight them.

~~~~~~~~

The hopes we had pinned on the Tsar had fallen like a house of cards, and we felt beaten. We decided we could no longer depend on him, and turned to the ministers. They were easier to influence and one could, at least, seduce them to our side with compensation, such as awards or monetary gifts. As for me, my primary goal was always to improve the lot of Jews, and it seemed easier to attain our freedom of residence, first, than to change an entire regime.

But then new hope took seed. Rasputin told us that the Tsar would now favor making some concessions to Jews. Protopopov had given us his word that he would help us, when we recommended him for Minister of the Interior. For our part, we assured him of paving the way, although his success would depend on his savoir-faire and individual talents. When the Jews heard that Protopopov promised to alleviate their struggle, they sent a delegation which he received, but the Minister did not want to show his hand too early. He received the delegation coldly and showed

---

abdication.
~~~~~~~~

no inclination to assist in their efforts. This greatly displeased the group and drew its animosity.

I had first met Protopopov when he decided to campaign for Minister of the Interior. We soon became good friends. I introduced him to Rasputin whose confidence he earned immediately. The first encounters between Protopopov and Rasputin were at the residence of Princess Tarkhanova. After that, they met at the home of Prince Michovsky. Protopopov's greatest desire was to be a minister. We gave him our conditions: peace with Germany and a better life for Jews. He accepted. I introduced him to important Jewish politicians whose causes he promised to champion and Rasputin often spoke of him to the Tsar, in order to curry interest in this new man. It was not long before his efforts succeeded.

One day, Rasputin, Protopopov and I went to Vyrubova's home at Tsarskoye-Selo. She submitted the candidate to a sort of test, as was her habit. All went well. At the military hospital, Vyrubova presented Protopopov to the Tsarina, upon whom he made an excellent impression. Soon after, he was named Minister of the Interior[148] — the last one of the regime to hold that position.

Before taking his post, I paid him 150,000 rubles without which he would have been insolvent and, therefore, ineligible for the nomination. Protopopov had promised to reimburse me this amount from the Ministry's secret funds, but since he donated 100,000 rubles to Vyrubova's hospital, he could not pay me back immediately. Vyrubova asked Rasputin if he knew of Protopopov's gift to the hospital, and whether he saw any objection. She had

---

148 Protopopov served as the Tsar's last Minister of the Interior, from 1916 to 1917.

only accepted the gift because Protopopov had said it was done under Rasputin's auspices.

It was not unusual for political candidates who received distinctions, due to Vyrubova's influence, to make donations to the hospital she founded. As the Tsarina's Lady of Honor, she sometimes received personal gifts of great value. Mme Rubenstein gave her 50,000 rubles; Mme Reinensohn gave 25,000; Manus, the banker, gave 200,000; Nakimov donated 30,000; and Popov gave 10,000. I offered her various gems, emeralds, and expensive silver vases. Vyrubova explained to the Imperial Couple that her friends' goal, in giving these gifts, was to assure her of a comfortable future since the train accident that had crushed her legs.

Protopopov's nomination raised an uproar in all of Russia. The deputies of the Duma were indignant to see him aligned with the Tsar against representation of the people. In light of this, a worried Protopopov sought Rasputin's advice. Rasputin told him not to trouble himself with all that. He said, "The deputies themselves do not know what they want." In reality, Rasputin feared that much of the Duma's discourse was against him. He advised the Tsar and Protopopov to postpone, as much as possible, the opening date of the Duma, and to keep the Chamber of Deputies on a leash, like a dog that has an insatiable need to bite. That was one of his favorite expressions.

The Tsar, Tsarina and Rasputin all viewed Protopopov in a kindly fashion. The Young Court had previously felt abandoned by its friends and completely surrounded by its enemies. It had been immersed in worry, sensing the danger that was already so close, but unable to deter it. That may seem strange, since the Tsar had not yet been overthrown and had unlimited power. Yet, the atmosphere of the Court had been one of depression beyond all expression, with their circle of friends and supporters receding every day. The Tsar had been increasingly apathetic and indifferent, giving the impression that he was no longer interested in anything. He had exerted no effort to appease his adversaries or to improve the general situation. It was, at this critical moment, that Protopopov arrived on the scene and inspired hope in the Young Court.

Shortly before his death, Rasputin confided to me that the Tsar, once again, had decided to take measures to ease the plight of Russian Jews. According to him, the ministers received instructions to revise all rulings restricting where Jews could live. Interior Minister Protopopov confirmed this information from Rasputin, adding that, above all, the Tsar did not care to draw attention to it. To us, this attitude meant that there would be neither new laws nor ordinances, but simply a renewal of the old ones.

Protopopov then expressed a desire to meet with a Jewish delegation. Warshavski[149] and Sliosberg, were part of this delegation. Protopopov confirmed to them that measures would soon be taken to expand Jewish rights. However, he begged the delegates to consider these talks confidential, in order to avoid attracting attention to the subject. General Kurlov, who held a high position with the Minister of the Interior,[150] was present at that meeting. The assassination of Rasputin put a quick end to all of those preparations. The Tsar then ordered Protopopov to concentrate all the state's efforts on combating the revolutionary movement. The Jewish question was swept aside.

---

[149] A. Warshavski was a prominent Petersburg Jew, active in the *Society for the Promotion of Culture Among the Jews of Russia* and the *Jewish Colonization Association.*

[150] Kurlov was Assistant Minister of Internal Affairs.

Later, when the Revolution broke out, my house was searched and various papers were found that had been drafted by Protopopov. The commission directing the operation[151], upon discovering bills of exchange from grand dukes, ministers, and dignitaries, were inclined to charge me with corruption. But it didn't get to that point. I explained that I could not be held responsible for anything, given that I had no function other than being a Jew with no position of authority.

~~~~~~~~~

Arriving at Rasputin's home at about eleven o'clock, one morning, I saw that something tormented him. He had just come back from Tsarskoye-Selo. I asked what worried him so, and learned that it was top secret. I promised not to betray a single word. It was about a great misfortune that deeply distressed the Tsarina. He said that she held her head in her hands and could not stop crying.

"It's very worrisome, what Papa has done," Rasputin said. "I think he'll do us all in."

I asked him to tell me what happened, but he did not answer. It was nerve-wracking. Finally, he broke his silence and unraveled the details: "A terrible thing has happened. An English general named Kitchener was on his way here.[152] He wanted to help us undertake some action that would put a victorious end to the war, but the Germans sank the boat he was on. They are saying it is our fault.

---

[151] The Provisional Government's Extraordinary Commission.
[152] H.H. Kitchener was appointed England's Secretary of War at the start of WW I. He died in June, 1916 when, en route to Russia to encourage resistance to Germany, his ship struck a German mine.
~~~~~~~~~

German spies must have learned that the English general was en route, and gave this information to our adversaries."

Furthermore, according to Rasputin, the Tsarina believed that she was suspected of this treason, since she was German. She begged Rasputin to use his supernatural powers to discover who murdered Kitchener.

"This was how *I* first learned of the General's pending arrival here," Rasputin said. "My 'force' does not extend to foreigners, but I will clarify the affair and find out who knew of Kitchener's travel plans. They say he was a very intelligent man."

Three days later, I learned from Rasputin that he had met with the Tsar. Nicholas II had appeared somewhat aloof but confided to Rasputin that Kitchener's departure for Russia had been announced to him in an encoded telegram. That morning, he had seen no one but Voyekov, the Palace Commander, and Admiral Nilov. He had lunched with them, and all three had heartily imbibed the wines that were served with the meal.

"Ah! I understand now," Rasputin told the Tsar. "This is what happened: You got drunk and talked to your friends about the telegram. Voyekov would have told the German spy Andronikov who, in turn, had nothing more urgent to do than tell the Germans. It's all clear now!"

The Tsar subsequently questioned Voyekov who confirmed that, in fact, he had spoken to Prince Andronikov regarding the news of Kitchener's arrival. He had hoped, in so doing, that Andronikov might publish an article of welcome in his newspaper. Andronikov was a strange man with an obscure past. No one respected him, yet he had some business dealings with nearly everyone. This man of excessive corpulence was, nonetheless, very fidgety and lively. It was widely rumored that he was a German spy. Despite that, he could give the Germans information on military operations, without a worry.

Prince Andronikov's father was a Georgian, and his mother was from Germany, where he had been raised. He was Protestant, but the difference of the confessional prevented him neither from being on a friendly footing with persons who were highly placed in the Russian Orthodox Church, nor from giving pictures of saints to all he knew. The Tsar and Tsarina had even received icons from Andronikov. He passed himself off as a pious man. It was his cousin, Princess Orbeliani, who had presented him to the Court. Rasputin once remarked, "Andronikov is a big blister which will someday pop. Won't that be a lovely stench!"

Before the war, Andronikov was quite a skirt-chaser but, after 1914, he became homosexual. This is why no one was surprised when his house was full of young men. He filled their purses and offered great hospitality. It is noteworthy that most of those invited were officers. The table was always laden and, at any hour, visitors could eat and drink their fill. The young officers came there willingly and, as they chatted, it was easy to obtain the news of any military orders they had. Andronikov was very close to Colonel Myasoyedov, of the police, and Minister of the Navy Sukhomlinov, both of whom would later be accused of espionage. Myasoyedov would eventually hang and, I believe, the first person to point a finger at him was Andronikov.

I remember another affair wherein Prince Andronikov played a villainous role. He had a relative named Dumbadze who, based on the Prince's recommendation, was ordered by Sukhomlinov to purchase munitions from the United States. This mission accomplished, Dumbadze returned to Russia, but was imprudent enough to have a falling out with Andronikov who subsequently denounced Dumbadze and his friend, an engineer named Weller, as spies and accomplices of Myasoyedov. Both were arrested and sent before a military tribunal.

Weller's grandfather, an old man of ninety, begged me to come to his grandson's aid. Despite my efforts, I could do nothing to prevent the trial. Dumbadze and Weller were condemned to death by the Berdichev War Council. The orders were to be signed by the Tsar and carried out within forty-eight hours. Weller's family came to see me. When they arrived, Princess Tarkhanova, who was related to Dumbadze, was visiting me. She joined up with the Wellers, and we went to see Rasputin.

"And so you see the beautiful work of your Andronikov," I said to Rasputin, once I'd brought him up to date. I knew how much he hated the Prince and hoped to rile him up.

"What should I do?" he asked.

"You must go immediately to the Tsar and ask for mercy for the condemned," I said.

"I'll go then," said Rasputin, "but I will also settle up with Andronikov."

Rasputin called the palace police to send a car, and he left with the Wellers to Tsarskoye-Selo. The family had to wait at the gate but, as Rasputin left them, he told them, "If I find the Tsar, I will get a reprieve in five minutes." As luck would have it, the Tsar was in the palace. The death sentence was commuted to six years of hard labor. Rasputin returned to the Wellers with the good news and, kissing the two Jews, said, "God has graced us. The lives of the condemned have been spared. And now, let's continue to work for them."

However, I feared that Minister of War Shuvayev was neither in a hurry nor had the good will to follow the Tsar's order. So, I asked Rasputin to find the Minister and to have him announce, immediately, to those at general headquarters that the sentence had been commuted. But Rasputin refused to address Shuvayev directly. So, we went to the Minister, bringing along Princess Tarkhanova. Shuvayev received us, had no problem complying, and immediately telegraphed Berdichev. The six years of hard labor were replaced with two years and eight months of detention. After stepping in on behalf of Dumbadze, Rasputin was also moved to clear the Georgians, as a group, of any suspicion of treason. He had a soft spot for these people and was even arranging for his daughter, Marya, to marry one.[153]

The Dumbadze affair had, as its epilogue, a lively little event. Prince Andronikov was a great friend of General Voyekov and Admiral Nilov, both of whom were the Tsar's frequent dining companions. They often drank together and were so comfortable that they often asked the Tsar to intervene on behalf of the Prince. The Old Court favored the Prince because of his ancestry through Prince Shervashidze.[154] This explains how Andronikov could continue his dangerous career with total impunity.

That year, however, during Rasputin's typically solemn birthday celebration, Prince Andronikov was among the

---

[153] This is a reference to Pankhadze who eventually attempted to assassinate Rasputin.

[154] Shervashidze: a Georgian family of nobles, traceable to the 12th century. They ruled the Georgia/Abkahazia region until it became part of Imperial Russia, in the mid-nineteenth century.

crowd of well-wishers pressing around the Tsar's 'favorite.' Rasputin refused to shake his hand and said, "Your hands are covered with blood! I know who you are. You feed human flesh to the fish — you are guilty of the death of the English general.[155] Get out of here!" This caused Andronikov to lose face. He left without responding. The scene had an enormous impression on those present. We could not shake the malaise that hung heavily around us. People of all sorts were, at that time, accused of espionage and many innocents were pursued. But Prince Andronikov could perform his horrible deeds without worrying.

~~~~~~~~

From 1916 on, Rasputin made no mystery of his hatred of war. In his opinion, it was imperative to make peace, and as quickly as possible. When he was told that the Tsar would not hear of it, he would say it was the fault of 'that woman.' He meant the Dowager Empress who energetically lobbied for closer Anglo-Russian relations. This Anglo-Russian alliance hardly seemed a happy one to Rasputin. For him, there was only one way to mobilize proponents of peace with Germany: a rupture of relations between Russia and her current allies. He saw the political situation as very dark: "The ministers are simple charlatans, and the nobles are backbiters," he said. "The Tsar is not counseled and finds no solutions. He sits on the fence, deciding neither for peace nor for war. Perhaps we can find ministers who will support peace efforts, and lead the Tsar in that direction. Mama wants peace, but all she does is cry. Her sister, Elizabeth, is enthusiastic about war despite being German. She even turns people against Germany. She went so far as to ask the Tsar to banish me,

[155] Kitchener
~~~~~~~~

and to put the Tsarina in a convent! Elizabeth, acting as a messenger from Moscow's nobility, came to see the Tsar. The Tsarina chased her away and the Tsar counseled her to return to the convent she founded. I am glad she can no longer continue her schemes. Otherwise, I would feel rather insecure. Now, we have the upper hand."

While the Tsarina's sister was visiting, Rasputin was in a state of great anxiety, especially when he learned of her intentions. He was very agitated and covered many scraps of paper with notes that he put under his pillow. The next day, he felt sure of having conquered his adversary. The Tsar had briskly rejected the Grand Duchess' request but, until then, the situation was so grave that I had thought it necessary to destroy Rasputin's papers that could be compromising if he were investigated. It was a matter of requests addressed to Rasputin, from all corners of Russia and in far greater number than those sent to the Tsarina. Bishop Isidor helped us examine the documents.

During the last years before the revolution, the people's confidence in Nicholas II was seriously shaken. One of the consequences was that the number of requests addressed to the Tsar and Tsarina decreased rapidly. The Tsarina was especially affected by this and sought out such petitioners. Knowing this state of affairs, we asked all who came to us for help and support, to address the Tsarina, thanking her for increasing their probability of success.

Rasputin's pro-peace propaganda awakened discontent among the diplomats of Russia's allies. French Ambassador Paléologue even met with Rasputin but could get no concessions out of the clever peasant. One day, a woman who was an English artist[156] was presented to

[156] This is likely a reference to Danish artist Theodora Krarup (1862-1941) who was commissioned to paint many imperial

Rasputin as one of his ardent followers. She asked permission to paint his portrait. He accepted, and the portrait sittings began, but the work progressed very slowly. Finally, after some six months, Rasputin showed her the door, saying: "I know what you want from me but, malicious as you are, you will not get it." We discovered that this woman had approached Rasputin, under instructions from British Ambassador Buchanan,[157] to learn what she could about the behavior and deeds of the Tsar's 'favorite.'

~~~~~~~~~

When Protopopov was named Minister of the Interior, Rasputin had hoped that he would put an end to the war. "Now that the Tsar has an advisor on whom he can depend," he would say, "we will, perhaps, be able to prevent the useless spilling of blood."

Rasputin went to an arranged meeting with Protopopov, Khabalov,[158] General Globachev,[159] and Nikitin.[160] To Rasputin's surprise, at the last moment, Protopopov brought his ally, General Kurlov. Rasputin opened the meeting by declaring that the Tsar wanted him to undertake an urgent and confidential matter, based on the advice of experienced and stable people. He asked, first, whether he could rely on their assistance.

Protopopov, to whom the Tsar had confided the matter, said, "I have absolute confidence in all those present."

---

portraits. It is the only portrait to show Rasputin in a relaxed pose, smiling.

157 In 1910, George Buchanan was appointed British Ambassador in Russia.

158 General in command of Petersburg troops.

159 Chief of Petrograd secret police.

160 Artillery Commander.
~~~~~~~~~

"However," said Rasputin, "there is someone here who does not inspire confidence. If I had known you were in his camp, I would never have supported your nomination. The person I speak of is Kurlov. I will not speak in his presence."

At these words, Kurlov got up and left. When he had gone, Rasputin spoke again:

"This is a sick man who does everything backwards. The Tsar does not like him. He is suspected of having a hand in the attempt on Stolypin's life. I have complete confidence in all the other generals here. And now, Alexander Dmitrivich, tell everyone what this matter is. What are the Tsar's orders?"

"The Tsar wants me to stage a revolt," replied Protopopov.

"Why does he give *you* this task? This is an affair for generals. How are you going to do this?" Rasputin asked.

"I requested Dr. Dubrovin, president of the League of Russian People and a trustworthy man, to recruit people from the Caucuses whom we could count on. These men are fearless as well as devoted to us, body and soul. They will suppress the riot at the right moment. We'll increase the number of agents from seven hundred men, teach them to handle machine guns, and they'll have orders to shoot the protesters."

"Have you told General Khabalov to pull all of the old soldiers from Petersburg, and replace them with younger recruits?"

"This is not necessary," replied Protopopov.

"I think it is," maintained Rasputin, who turned toward General Khabalov and said, "You must gather, in Petersburg, young soldiers who are commanded by experienced officers. The Tsar will be among them as often as possible, and will seek to bond with them. This done, we will organize a revolt. The soldiers will protect us. After that, the Tsar will be able to bring peace."

"How will you arrange for the people to rise up?" Protopopov asked.

"I'll have my people go into the streets crying '*Bread! Give us some bread!*' That will soon degenerate into a riot. The soldiers will have no trouble dispersing the crowd, but we will tell our foreign allies that we are at the dawn of a revolution. However, I do not think it necessary to reinforce our Petersburg troops. We can be absolutely sure of the garrison."

Rasputin assured everyone that the Tsar had already received an offer of peace from Wilhelm, and that he was considering it with his close advisors. Nicholas II wanted to renew the former peace treaty with Germany, and recognize Poland as an independent state. Russia would receive the part of Galicia inhabited by the Russian Orthodox. The provinces of the Baltic Sea would go to Germany and, in exchange, Russia would have free passage through the Dardanelles Straits. However, the Tsar declared that he could not bring peace before a revolt broke out.[161]

A woman by the name of Laptinskaya,[162] who was an agent of Deputy Guchkov's, wrote a draft of the plan. News of

---

[161] The implication is that the Tsar could use the revolt as an excuse that his foreign allies might accept to make peace with Germany, rather than simply turning his back on his allies.

the project of a staged revolt soon spread through Petersburg. Protopopov continued with the preparations and assigned the tasks, although General Kurlov found it strange. Just at that time, Rasputin was assassinated and the entire project was abandoned.

~~~~~~~~

Our choice of ministers sometimes went horribly awry, as in the Rubenstein affair. In 1914, when war against Germany was declared, Goremykin was President of the Council of Ministers in Russia. This old man, completely impotent, owed his eminent position to his wife's influence with Rasputin. She rarely left the apartment of the Tsar's 'favorite,' and did her best to show herself in a good light. Afterward, when Goremykin was relieved of his functions, she succeeded, once again, in regaining for him the post of Council President. Mme Goremykin took care of furnishing Rasputin with boiled potatoes, which she considered her sacred duty. She knew ten different ways to prepare them, and the potatoes were brought so quickly, that they arrived still steaming. She also sent him soups, fish, apples and rolls. These attentions cemented her rapport with Rasputin.

One day, Rubenstein,[163] the well-known but ambitious and vain Jewish Petersburg banker, expressed a desire to meet Goremykin. I counseled him that, to do so, he must give the Minister a hefty donation to build a military hospital. Rubenstein followed my advice, asking Rasputin to present his donation to Goremykin. He offered the sum of two hundred thousand rubles and Mme Rubenstein was named president of the directing committee for this hospital.

[162] Akilina Laptinskaya was a devotee of Rasputin's.
[163] Dmitri Rubenstein was a Jewish banker, financier, supporter of Rasputin and philanthropist.
~~~~~~~~

Rubenstein, thus, often had occasion to meet with Goremykin. Naturally, that made other local bankers jealous but this served Rubenstein well, giving him greater prestige among the well-to-do of Petersburg. He made a big deal of knowing Goremykin and never missed an opportunity to mention it. When one of his biggest clients was in his office, he telephoned the Council President, asking news of his wife, simply to impress his visitor who then bragged to everyone about Rubenstein's wonderful relations with the Council President. This gave his clients greater confidence in him.

Rubenstein, having acquired a majority interest in the Bank of Junker & Company, celebrated this event by giving a grand ball. One of his guests was Leo Brodsky. Rubenstein had invited him, hoping to sell some of his shares in the Bank of Junker. When Brodsky saw, among the guests, Goremykin, Protopopov, Rasputin and other highly placed people, and when he heard his host speak to them so familiarly, he declared that he was ready to purchase stock in Junker & Company.

Rubenstein was a marvel at making himself useful to know, and never missed the chance to position himself advantageously. At gala fundraising events, he was never the last to arrive and always gave generously. We had a mutually beneficial relationship: I introduced him to Rasputin, with whom he felt it important to remain on good terms, and Rubenstein always assisted Jews in financial need whenever I requested it.

One day, the Tsarina begged Rasputin to recommend a banker to take charge of her confidential, financial affairs. Naturally, Rasputin asked me, and I proposed Rubenstein. Rasputin sent for him and asked if he would be capable of taking charge of very important and confidential matters for the Tsarina. Rubenstein excitedly swore that he would honor any such issues with the utmost confidentiality, and would rigorously keep secret any affairs entrusted to him. To my great satisfaction, he succeeded in convincing Rasputin that he was the man for any confidential missions concerning the Tsarina. Rasputin told the Tsarina that he had found an excellent banker, Rubenstein, who belonged to an old Jewish family, was related to the famous composer,[164] and was an exceptionally gifted financier. The Tsarina left the choice to Father Grigori, and Rubenstein was congratulated on his new assignment.

This was his task: The Tsarina had poor relatives in Germany whom she usually helped. However, during the war when she could not send money to them, she worried herself sick about them. She needed a discreet means of sending money. This was a delicate and dangerous task, but Rubenstein accomplished it with the greatest discretion, much to the Tsarina's satisfaction.

Thanks to his ties with Rasputin, Rubenstein also acquired a certain importance in the Court. Each of these two men sought to serve each other mutually. Rasputin had no need of Rubenstein for himself, but often requested him to help people in need until they established themselves. Rubenstein never turned his back on any of Rasputin's requests but, as it was not physically possible to accommodate all of the people Rasputin sent, he opened a large office at March Square. The necessity for this was clear to no one — not even to Rubenstein. In this office, the employees had nothing to do but draw regular salaries. But Rubenstein's reward was that Rasputin praised him to the skies as an intelligent banker, and bragged about it to

---

[164] Brothers Anton Grigorievich (1829-1894) and Nikolai Grigorievich (1835-1923) Rubenstein were composers, pianists and conductors.

everyone. No one knew the confidence the Tsarina had placed in him, but Rubenstein was loose-lipped enough to spread the word, declaring that he was the banker of the Imperial House. For his part, Manuilov, Council President Sturmer's secretary, watched this situation and carefully defused this 'rumor' that was so useful to Rubenstein.

Soon, the banker received a terrible blow. He had bought all the stock in an insurance company called The Anchor, and then had sold it all to a Swedish insurance company, at great profit. He sent the Swedes the architectural plans of the factories that were insured by The Anchor Company, some of which were owned by Ukrainian sugar manufacturers. Following the example of Nicholas II, the hunt for spies had been spreading all over Russia, creating numerous innocent victims, and provoking a general upset. Naturally, at the border, any postal transmissions and travelers to Sweden were subjected to rigorous scrutiny. As soon as the border guards saw Rubenstein's building plans, they were sure they had hit upon a vast spy ring, organized on a grand scale.

Sturmer had just become Council President,[165] so old Goremykin was no longer there to help Rubenstein. The banker was no longer on good terms with Rasputin, as some of his financial activities had set Rasputin against him. Rubenstein was arrested by military order. The news of his arrest sent ripples through Russia. This action against such a well-known banker was especially upsetting to Jews as it fueled the rumor that we were all spies. Rubenstein's friend, Wolfsohn, was also arrested.

The imprisonment of Rubenstein had a terrible effect on the Tsarina. She feared the cause of his arrest to be one of

---

165 Early 1916.

the missions she had entrusted to him, and was only relieved of those fears when she was convinced the charges had nothing to do with her. But she still could not help worrying that her relationship with Rubenstein, if known, would create a scandal. This caused her great anxiety. The Tsarina dispatched State's Attorney Valuyev to general headquarters to end the affair. She advised him to address himself to General Gurko with a request to shed light on the matter.

Gurko declared that, in his opinion, Rubenstein's arrest was arbitrary. He supposed that the army high command had arrested the banker to cast a poor light on Jews. Rubenstein faced being hanged. Gurko knew the file. He made out a long and detailed report that stated that Rubenstein had done nothing to violate the wartime ordinances. But General Ruzsky, an avid anti-Semite, was not of the same opinion. Fearing that Rubenstein would be freed if kept in Petersburg, Ruzsky sent him to Pskov Prison, along with Wolfsohn. Batyushin's interrogation committee was in charge of the preliminary hearing, which aggravated the whole affair.

This turn of events greatly worried the Jews. Representatives of Jewish society organized a series of meetings. I was invited to one where I was told I could be of great service to the Jewish people. I was the only Jew who could approach the Imperial Couple and, thanks to my rapport with Mme Vyrubova, the ministers, and Rasputin, was the only one who could improve the situation. This scandalous affair had to be ended immediately, as it appeared to be as dangerous as the 'ritual murder' trial. I was fully aware of the gravity of the situation and understood that nothing must be spared to protect Jews from the danger that threatened them.

Before all else, I sought to pave the way for a reconciliation between Rubenstein and Rasputin. To my great satisfaction, Rasputin was favorably disposed toward Rubenstein. I brought Mme Rubenstein to talk to Rasputin. She swore that her husband was innocent, spoke of the constant surveillance she was under, and cried bitterly. Rasputin was warm and attentive toward her and immediately took her to Tsarskoye-Selo to see the Tsarina who received them at the military hospital.[166] Rasputin asked the Empress to come to Rubenstein's defense, as he was innocent and unjustly imprisoned. The Tsarina asked Mme Rubenstein for details of the matter and then said:

"Go home in peace. I will go to general headquarters where I will tell my husband everything. I will wire you the result."

Mme Rubenstein was very touched by these kind words. We presented a legal request for Rubenstein's release and, to our great surprise, the most well-known lawyers refused to draw it up. Even those who, until then, maintained good relations with Rubenstein, did not want anything to do with him. All were afraid of the high command. However, the Tsarina could do nothing without a formal request. In desperation, I asked my eldest son to draw up the papers and gave them to the Tsarina. In the Jewish New Year, I received the following telegram from her: "Simanovitch, my congratulations. Our banker is free. — Alexandra"

The next day, Mme Rubenstein went to Pskov. She thought her husband would be released, but there was no news. She had rejoiced too soon. We researched and found the reason why he was not freed. Rubenstein had started a bank with the Voyekov brothers but the enterprise

[166] The Tsarina often performed nursing duties at the hospital, along with her elder daughters.

was not a success and the two brothers, who lost more than eight hundred thousand rubles in the affair, blamed Rubenstein, and viewed him as their enemy. One of the Voyekov brothers was commandant at the Imperial Palace. When the Tsar's order to release Rubenstein arrived, he did not obey it but hid the imperial order in his pocket.

When Nicholas II returned from general headquarters, I informed him of this. He was outraged at Voyekov's conduct and told me to present a new request. Written in the margin, in the Tsar's own hand, was a note to competent authorities to execute the order immediately, without consulting Voyekov. Rubenstein was finally released. When the Tsarina learned that Voyekov was permitted to get away with ignoring the Tsar's orders, she was furious and made a lively scene. The Tsar remained silent, without trying to defend his friend, Voyekov. I had the impression it was not the first time such a scene had taken place.

~~~~~~~~

With regard to the nomination of candidates, my friend, Rosen, once explained to me why reactionary governors from the provinces were so successful with the Tsar: Whenever a governor was appointed who enjoyed the support of the League of Russian People, the Tsar would be deluged with telegrams from all over Russia. Agents of the League would send them. To counteract this maneuver, I consulted President Orlov of the Moscow branch of the League. For a modest sum, he agreed to send the Tsar telegrams of thanks when one of Rasputin's choices was appointed to a position. Of course, the costs associated with this endeavor were my responsibility.
~~~~~~~~

Oil Portrait of Rasputin (1916)
By Dutch artist Theodora Krarup

The Romanov family (1913)
The Tsar and Tsarina are center, with daughters Olga, Tatiana, Maria, Anastasia, and son Tsarevitch Alexei.

Chapter VII

Assassination Attempts

I knew the extent to which Rasputin was hated by his enemies. His safety, therefore, was a constant source of worry. I could clearly see that this peasant's life would end tragically. Globachev[167] was in charge of a special service that had been organized to protect Rasputin and guard his home around the clock. When Rasputin went out, it was never without the discreet accompaniment of the secret police who noted all they observed and made a detailed report to their boss.

Rasputin's protection was the same as that for each member of the Imperial House. This service consumed large sums of money. Only trained personnel, worthy of absolute confidence, comprised this group. As for my role, I tried not to let him out of my sight, even for an instant. We met several times a day and I went to his house in the evenings, when he was not at the Imperial Palace or at Vyrubova's home. Moreover, we spoke frequently on the telephone. There were numerous assassination attempts, most of which were concocted by Iliodor, Rasputin's former friend. The attempt initiated by Khvostov was just one of many.

In the course of Rasputin's nocturnal activities, various incidents and conflicts were not uncommon. One early morning, we were returning after spending the night at the Villa Rode. I was accompanying Rasputin to his home when, at Komeno-Ostrovski Street, some people threw large blocks of wood under our car, hoping for a

[167] Chief of Petersburg Political Police.

catastrophe. Fortunately, the chauffeur had the presence of mind to steer around the obstacles, saving us but knocking down one of the troublemakers. The conspirators took flight, but we called an officer who pursued them and arrested one. As for the groaning female conspirator who was hit by the car, we took her to the hospital where it was confirmed that she only had contusions. Rasputin consoled her and gave her money. The police arrested one of the men who named all of his accomplices. They were all simple peasants from Zaritzyn, home of Iliodor. It was Iliodor who convinced them to attack Rasputin, but their intention was, allegedly, only to play a dirty trick on the Staretz, not to take his life. Rasputin declined to lodge a complaint against these aggressors, and no further legal action was taken, except that they were sent back to their native province.

~~~~~~~~

Approaching Rasputin to make a request was not easy for strangers. Obviously, one could come to his home during his receiving hours, but few were admitted as guests. Therefore, those interested in speaking to him often tried to befriend his daughter, Marya. The young girl, who was sweet and kind, but not exactly pretty, still lived in a childish and naïve dream world. One man who sought to get close to Rasputin through Marya was Davidson, the reporter. Basically, he was looking for sensationalist stories for his newspaper. Rasputin felt he had ulterior motives and did not permit him to visit Marya.

In the summer of 1914, just before the war started, Rasputin returned to his native village to see his family, as he did every year. That year, however, Davidson also left for Pokrovskoie, and on the same boat as Rasputin and his daughters. Aboard the boat, he could approach Marya and
~~~~~~~~

speak familiarly with her. By the time they arrived at Pokrovskoie, the friendship was sealed.[168]

All the while, Davidson knew of Iliodor's latest plot against Rasputin, and wanted to be the first to report the next attempt on Rasputin's life. The battle between Rasputin and Iliodor was then at its peak. Iliodor wanted to try, one more time, to do away with his triumphant adversary. One of his followers was a woman named Guseva[169] with whom Rasputin was acquainted. She was a peasant with a long, hooked nose.[170] Iliodor gave her the mission of assassinating Rasputin. She accepted, arriving in Pokrovskoie some time before Rasputin. Initially, she visited him without raising any suspicion.

One day, Rasputin received a telegram from Petersburg. He was always in the habit of tipping the messenger but, this time, a family member received the telegram, so the courier asked if his tip had been forgotten. Learning that one hadn't been offered, Rasputin came out to speak to the messenger. Guseva waited for the right moment. She approached him and said, "Grigori Efimovitch, give me charity. I beg you, in the name of heaven."

Rasputin dug into his wallet. Guseva stabbed him. He was only wearing a lightweight shirt, and the knife easily penetrated his stomach. Seriously wounded, Rasputin tried to retreat back into the house. His innards seemed to be

---

[168] Marya Rasputin recounts the same story, adding that Davidson flirted with her on the trip to Pokrovskoie, in order to gain access to Rasputin.

[169] Khioniya Guseva, a former prostitute, became a follower of Rasputin until his split with Iliodor with whom she sided. She denied that Iliodor was involved in the attack, and was eventually sent to an asylum for the insane.

[170] Other accounts, as well as a photograph, depict her as having no nose at all, but simply nostrils in her face.

oozing from the wound. He tried holding it all in with his hands. Guseva pursued him. She wanted to stab him a second time. He mustered the strength to pick up a large piece of wood in his path and, hitting her on the arm, knocked the knife from her hand. At the sound of his cries, people came running and, circling her, inflicted their own punishment. They wanted to lynch her but Rasputin asked that she be spared.

Davidson's published reports of the incident put an end to his romance with Marya. Her father prohibited her from speaking to him. Grigori Efimovitch was severely wounded, but the doctors found his recovery miraculous. He treated himself with certain remedies that he mixed and to which he attributed his recovery.

Many people in Petersburg thought that if Rasputin had been there when the Great War was declared, he would have known how to prevent it. I share this opinion. The Tsar often followed Rasputin's advice, and Rasputin was openly anti-war. With his wound preventing his return to Petersburg, he telegraphed the Tsar of his desire to avoid war, at all costs. However, a telegram did not have the power of Rasputin's presence. The news of the declaration of war threw Rasputin into such a violent frenzy, that his wound re-opened. He rushed a second plea to the Tsar, begging him to avoid war, but it was already too late. After the Archduke's assassination at Sarajevo[171] Rasputin told me that he had frequently tried to convince Nicholas II of the futility of warring with Austria over the Serbs.

---

[171] The assassination of Serbian Archduke Ferdinand sparked World War I, as Russia supported the Serbs against Austria, and Germany supported the Austrians against Russia, following which each nation's allies joined the fray.

"You were born in an unhappy era," Rasputin told the Tsar, agitated. "The people have not yet forgotten what happened at Khodynka[172] and in the unfortunate war with Japan.[173] We cannot undertake a new war. Pay your enemies! Give them as much money as you like. Give the Austrians four hundred million rubles, but do not go to war! War will surely be the end of us all."

Rasputin had little sympathy for the Balkan states. When Ferdinand of Bulgaria came to Petersburg in 1913, he visited Rasputin because Nicholas II refused to see him. Rasputin got him in to see the Tsar, but not with good results. Ferdinand left, looking dismayed and uneasy, having sought to influence the Tsar by signaling the possibility of a new war in the Balkans. Rasputin, however, wouldn't hear of it. "As long as I live," he used to say, "there will be no war."

~~~~~~~~

Rasputin, who lived life with a passion, had excellent rapport with all the ladies in the capital who were known for their taste for pleasure. The mistresses of grand dukes, ministers, and bankers were all his friends. He knew, therefore, all the scandals and illegitimate liaisons of influential men, the night secrets of anyone important, and he used this knowledge to spread his influence in these important social circles. All the women of Petersburg who deserved to be called "lively"— loose women, actresses, music hall singers, aristocrats smitten with the joyous life — were proud of their relationship with the darling of the Imperial Couple.

---

172 At Nicholas II's coronation celebration at Khodynka Field, in 1896, hundreds were trampled, as a mob of souvenir-seekers rioted.

173 The Russo-Japanese War was fought from 1904 to 1905.
~~~~~~~~

They were astonished by his incredible success and his ability to open doors for their more-or-less shady deals to promote their own careers or those of their protégés. When Rasputin, in the dead of night, would telephone these friends to meet him at some elegant restaurant, they would seize such opportune moments to make requests of him for their friends, lovers or family. They could obtain almost anything from him on such occasions. Then the party would quickly degenerate into an evening of excess.

The owner of a grand and elegant restaurant called the Villa Rode, which was situated far from the city's center, on the right bank of the Neva River, built a house especially for Rasputin's nocturnal orgies.[174] There, one could find gentlemen and ladies of high degree, as well as women of the world trying to compete with actors and singers. It was rare not to have a cabinet minister or candidate at these parties. Usually, bohemian musicians would be there because Rasputin loved bohemian songs. He was also a passionate dancer and performed Russian dances admirably and tirelessly. No one could surpass his endurance.

When Rasputin would go to these joyous festivities, he would stuff his pockets with gifts for the women — iridescent scarves, candies, silk ribbons, perfumes, powder boxes, cologne, etc. At the restaurant, he would hang up his coat and, without further invitation, the women would empty his pockets and share the gifts. Delighted, he would exclaim, "The bohemians have robbed me!" Rasputin enjoyed seeing his scarves on the shoulders of singers and knowing that the women around him wore no perfumes other than the ones he gave them.

---

[174] The term 'orgy' is used loosely by Simanovitch and can mean anything from celebratory excess to sexual activity.

Once, in the course of one of these festivities, an assassination attempt was made on Rasputin's life. Some officers and young people entered the room. At first, all was calm, but when Rasputin strode to the center of the room to ask someone to dance, a few officers suddenly arose and showed their sabers. The civilians with them pulled revolvers from their pockets. Rasputin jumped aside, shot them a terrible look and bellowed, "You want to kill me!"

The conspirators became immobile, as if paralyzed. They could not unlock their eyes from Rasputin's. Everyone was quiet, so enormous was the impact of the moment. Rasputin declared, "You were my enemies. Now, you are no longer. You have seen my strength triumph. Do not rejoice at being able to leave now. There is no power that can make you act against me again. Go home. I want to stay here with my friends and relax."

The young people kneeled and begged his forgiveness.

"I will not forgive you," said Rasputin. "It is not I who made you come here tonight. I did not rejoice when you arrived, and I will not be sad when you go. Go now. You are cured. Your bad intentions are no longer."

The conspirators simply left and that ended the affair.

~~~~~~~~

I had long feared Rasputin's assassination and, in a way, expected it. I had often been alerted to the intentions of his enemies, and had taken measures with such regard to detail that I believed I'd foreseen every possibility. However, all of that was useless given the first echoes of another plot against Rasputin.
~~~~~~~~

There were many circles in Petersburg where games of chance were honored. Such games were presided over by known personalities in high places. These men saw serious profits, but had nothing to do with the general operation of the games. I was the owner of one such gaming club, called The Fireman's Club (having nothing to do with firefighters), which met at the home of Baroness Ignatiev, on March Avenue. I had two young men serving as waiters at my club — Ivan and Alexei.

The President of our club's board of directors was Mr. Tomilen, Elder Mayor of Pskov,[175] who had just become President of the Russian National Club which was in our neighborhood. He, therefore, had to leave us but wanted to take my two waiters, Ivan and Alexei, for his new club. I was happy to let them go, knowing they would inform me of whatever they heard in that club. I considered it very important to keep current on everything, so I had ears all over town. This seemed necessary in order for me to best serve my clientele.

One day, Ivan, my former employee, arrived with news of some secret meetings there, which had made him suspicious. He could not provide details, as it was Alexei who had served during these clandestine gatherings, but one thing he knew for certain was that the topic of these talks was always Rasputin.

"Listen, Ivan," I told him, "here's five hundred rubles. Give some to Alexei, and tell him I would like all the details of these meetings. I'll pay you both handsomely if you can inform me of exactly what they're plotting." Ivan and Alexei knew that I could be very generous in these situations.

---

175 Pskov had one or two mayors at any given time.

Two days later, Alexei came to see me and told me what he had learned. Apparently, Deputy Purishkevich,[176] well known for his anti-Semitism, presided over these meetings. Also in attendance were Grand Duke Dmitri Pavlovich,[177] Count Tatischev,[178] young Prince Felix Yussupov,[179] former Minister of the Interior Khvostov, the reactionary Deputy Shulgin, and many young officers whose names Alexei did not know, but he had heard them called 'Grand Duke.' They spoke of Rasputin and mentioned the names of English Ambassador Buchanan,[180] the Tsar and the Tsarina. They were saying that someone had to be thrown out. The general impression we got from this information was that a plot was being hatched against both the Tsar and Rasputin. Purishkevich seemed to be at the bottom of it.

The reactionary Deputy Purishkevich had two reasons to hate Rasputin, and me as well. First, it was at my urging that Rasputin influenced the Tsar to stop the deputy's government subsidy. When Purishkevich learned that I was the one responsible for depriving him of his subsidy, I became his sworn enemy. The other reason for his enmity was the situation involving Rosen, a former Imperial Prosecutor who was also a friend of mine and played an

---

[176] Purishkevich was a monarchist who was a member of the Duma from 1902 to 1917 and one of Rasputin's murderers.

[177] Grand Duke Dmitri Pavlovich Romanov was cousin to Tsar Nicholas II and grandson of Tsar Alexander II. He participated in the murder of Rasputin.

[178] Count I. L. Tatishchev was aide-de-camp and friend of Nicholas II. He was killed by Bolsheviks in 1918.

[179] Prince Felix Yussupov was a Russian nobleman who married Irina, the Tsar's niece. He was one of Rasputin's murderers.

[180] There is a theory that Buchanan and the British Secret Intelligence Service were behind Rasputin's assassination because of Yussupov's friendship with a BSIS agent, and because Buchanan knew of Rasputin's death only hours after the fact, telephoning Grand Duke Nicholas Mikhailovich the news. There is, however, no hard evidence to substantiate the theory.

important role in the League of the Archangel St. Michael, which was under Purishkevich's leadership. Rosen had the task of judging the importance of all complaints and claims against Jews that were sent to the League. I would obtain these documents from Rosen before anyone else could see them and burn all the ones with potentially horrible outcomes. Only the minor ones got through to the League. In the end, Purishkevich found Rosen suspect and had him followed. They surprised Rosen at my house and found his big briefcase filled with these anti-Semitic complaints that we were going to burn. He was relieved of his position as secretary of the League, which was not a great loss for him since he received two thousand rubles a month from me, in addition to his other income.

Alexei's report was very worrisome. I promised him a handsome sum if he could bring me ample details regarding the conspirators. I told him there was even the possibility of employment at the Imperial Court. He was thrilled at this and said he would communicate as soon as he had learned more. I took him to see Rasputin who listened to Alexei's report with rapt attention, as he had always known Purishkevich to be his enemy. We thought that, with Alexei's help, we could avoid any difficulties from Purishkevich and his friends. Each day, Alexei gave me updates on the progress of the plot, noting which members of the Duma took part in these meetings.

I had always had good luck with my informants. This time, I had the help of another of my employees, Gevski Bukstab. Gevski had a doctor friend who treated diseases of the flesh[181] at his clinic on Nevski. One of his patients was Purishkevich, to whom he gave injections of Salvarsan.[182] I begged Bukstab to ask his doctor friend

[181] 'Diseases of the flesh' is a euphemism for sexually transmitted diseases.

what the deputy was plotting against Rasputin. We were hoping that Purishkevich, being the gossip he was, would not be able to resist the temptation to reveal his secret to the doctor. Bukstab saw the doctor every day and promised him a large sum if the doctor learned details of the plot.

One day, the two of them arrived at my house, greatly agitated. They said that Purishkevich had lain down to relax after one of his injections. The doctor chatted with him, saying that Rasputin was a calamity for the country and that it was high time to do away with him. Purishkevich assured him that Rasputin would not be counted among the living much longer, and even spoke of delivering the Russian people from him. The entire Duma was in complete agreement. Soon the Tsar would no longer bother the Duma with Rasputin's constant requests. "You will see what's going to happen in three days," concluded Purishkevich.

I warmly thanked the doctor for this precious information and went straight to Tsarskoye-Selo. I met with the Voskoboinokov sisters who were favored by the Tsarina. I told the sisters of Purishkevich's plot, and to let the Tsar know that the doctor must be summoned for questioning. A coup was in the works, without a doubt. The situation was dire.

A few days later, I arrived at Rasputin's apartment and found three officers at his home: the Eristov princes, who were brothers, and Simeon Pankhadze, fiancé of Rasputin's elder daughter, Matryona. Rasputin loved the Georgian people and was please to give his daughter's hand to a Georgian officer. Pankhadze and the Eristov brothers had

[182] Salvarsan was an arsenic-based antibiotic for syphilis.

come to Rasputin's home to invite him to a celebration that evening at Count Tolstoy's[183] home on Troitskaya Street. The officers assured him it would be very festive. He consented to join them. He found a huge crowd at Count Tolstoy's home. Everyone was drinking a lot. Some guests were completely drunk. Suddenly, Rasputin noticed that Pankhadze was pulling a gun from his pocket. Rasputin looked straight into his eyes and said, "You want to kill me, but your hand won't obey you."

Hearing this, the Georgian, crazed, turned the gun and shot himself in the chest, though not fatally. There was general panic among the witnesses. Some surrounded Pankhadze, trying to help him. Others tried to calm Rasputin who would not listen to their words. He simply put on his coat and went home. Later, we discovered that Pankhadze was an agent for the National Club, and only became engaged to Marya to facilitate an attempt on Rasputin's life. His motives were only discovered after the bungled assassination attempt. With Vyrubova's help, Pankhadze obtained an audience with the Tsarina, to enter a plea in his own defense. The Tsarina occupied herself with preventing judicial action against him.[184]

Upon returning home from that attempt on his life, Rasputin summoned me and told me all that had happened. He was not troubled in the least. On the contrary, he seemed in a very good mood. He said, "There. The danger has passed. The assassination attempt is done. Of course, Pankhadze is no longer my daughter's fiancé. Now, he'll return to his homeland."

---

[183] This could not be the author, Leo Tolstoy, as he died in 1910, and Marya Rasputin only became engaged to Pankhadze during WW I, which started in 1914. However, there were other Count Tolstoys among Leo's siblings and children.

[184] The Tsarina likely did this at Rasputin's request.

He was completely convinced he had nothing more to fear. I, on the other hand, was of the opposite opinion. I understood very well that the conspirators would not stop after yet another failed attempt. In fact, the danger now appeared to be even greater. I guessed, with good reason, that Pankhadze had been given special permission to leave the front for Petersburg for the sole purpose of assassinating Rasputin.[185]

When I returned home, I learned that Rasputin had been invited to tea with one of the Grand Dukes. This news shook me and I needed to warn Rasputin to be on guard. If Grand Duke Dmitri Pavlovich or Prince Yussupov were taking part in this 'tea,' there was no doubt that Rasputin could expect some problem. I went straight back to his house to tell him to exercise the greatest prudence.

"Be careful for your life, there," I exhorted him.

"Rest easy," Rasputin replied. "I've already beaten one assassin. I can stand up to dilettantes like the princes. I will go to them and show them the power that assists me so that the Tsar will see that I am stronger than all of them."

"No," I said. "We cannot permit you to go. They'll kill you."

"No one can keep me from going," he said, obstinately. "I will wait here for the Little One. He will come to get me, and we will go there together."

"Who is the Little One?" I asked. I had heard this name many times, but Rasputin refused to tell me who it was.

---

[185] Actually, Rasputin himself had intervened to have Pankhadze stationed with the reserves in Petersburg instead of serving at the front.

He seemed very agitated and paced the room with long strides.

"Grigori, they'll assassinate you," I said. "It may be today, or tomorrow. Follow my advice and disappear. Otherwise, you are lost."

As I said these words, the telephone rang. Rasputin answered, and an unknown voice asked him, "Can you tell me when Grigori Rasputin's funeral will be?"

"You'll be buried first," Rasputin answered, and he hung up the telephone.

"You see?" I continued. "They're already burying you. Listen to my advice, I beg you. Set aside your plans. You cannot accomplish what you wish. Two hundred years ago, you could have done something, but today, it is impossible. I do not want to argue with you, but I will tell the truth to the Tsar, the Tsarina and Vyrubova. Perhaps they'll succeed in convincing you."

"Listen," said Rasputin, "today I will drink twenty bottles of Madeira. Then I'll go to the baths, and then I will go to bed. During my sleep, God will show me the path to follow. God will tell me what I must do and, after that, no one can further endanger me. And now, you can go to the devil!"

Rasputin had a case of wine brought to him, and began to drink. Every ten minutes, he emptied a bottle. When he had consumed most of the case, he went to the bathhouse across the street from his apartment. When he returned, he went directly to his bedroom without speaking. When I returned the next day, I found him in the strange state that always seemed to befall him at critical moments in life. He had, before him, a large bowl, filled with Madeira, which he emptied in one gulp. I asked if he felt 'the force' increasing within him.

"It is my force that will conquer, and not yours," he answered.

At that moment, Lady Vyrubova appeared. She was very anxious, and asked, "Are the Red Cross nurses here?"

Rasputin, visibly embarrassed, whispered to me, "Tell her that they've already been here."

They were speaking of the Tsarina and one of her daughters, who had come to visit Rasputin disguised as Red Cross nurses to beg him not to accept any invitations without first talking to me. I had alerted her regarding Rasputin's strange state.

I had also relayed my concern to Protopopov who assured me that my fears were groundless and that no danger threatened Rasputin, for the moment. He added: "I will personally oversee this affair. The Tsarina gave me the order to prevent Rasputin from leaving his house. All security measures have been taken, and Rasputin gave me his word of honor that he would stay home all night. There is really no reason to worry."

Protopopov spoke with such conviction that I was somewhat reassured. However, I took my own precautionary measures. After all the visitors were gone, I asked Rasputin to undress and I put away his coat, boots and hat. I asked Osipenko, Pitirim's secretary, to stand guard over him. His house was surrounded by government agents who were ordered not to allow him to leave. Protopopov arrived to see that orders were being followed. Rasputin was in bed. He asked Protopopov to dismiss

Osipenko, since his presence was not needed. Protopopov acquiesced. Bishop Isidor, who had been visiting, also left.

Just before Protopopov left, Rasputin said to him, "Listen, dear friend, I am lord and master of my word. I have given it and I can take it back."

Hearing this strange declaration, Protopopov was more than a little surprised but, convinced that it was a joke, he left. Nevertheless, Rasputin knew how to render our precautions useless. He went outside, gave the agents large sums of money, and convinced them to leave, saying he was going to bed. They believed him and went to a nearby restaurant.

At midnight, Rasputin telephoned me. He said, "The Little One has just arrived. I am going to his place."

"In the name of heaven," I cried, horrified, "stay at home. They want to kill you!" This name, 'The Little One,' filled me with fear.

"Do not be afraid," answered Rasputin. "Come soon. We will have tea. I'll call you at two o'clock."

There was nothing more to do; the die was cast. I had no hope of stopping him. Too anxious to sleep, I sat near the telephone with my sons. Two o'clock, then three o'clock passed. Nothing. Unable to contain my anxiety, I told my sons, "You'll see — they've murdered Rasputin!"

Finally, accompanied by my eldest son, Semyon, I went to Rasputin's apartment. Having awakened his daughters and nieces, I declared bluntly:

"Your father has been assassinated. We must find his body."

The girls broke out in sobs.

I asked them, "Who is The Little One? Surely you must know."

"Father has sworn us not to tell," they said.

"He has killed your father!" I cried.

"It's Yussupov," admitted Marya, the elder daughter.

When I heard this name, I held my head in my hands in despair. Now, I understood everything. I had absolutely no doubt that Rasputin was the victim of a horrible plot.

"But how did he ever get near your father who so hated him?" I asked Marya.

"It was Marie Golovina who reconciled them," she answered, to my great surprise.

This seemed, to me, incomprehensible. Mme Golovina was not only a sincere admirer of Rasputin, but also a fanatical follower. I could not bring myself to believe that she could be involved in the plot. I immediately sought her out to convey my fears to her.

"Grigori has been assassinated," I told her.

She did not want to believe me. "No. Grigori lives. You are wrong," she kept repeating.

I asked her what the purpose was in bringing Rasputin and Yussupov together. It was clear she knew nothing of the conspiracy. She told me that Yussupov's parents, unhappy with their son, Felix, and his penchant for homosexuality, had sent him to study in England. They did not permit him to return to Petersburg until after the death of his older brother who was killed in a duel over a woman. Felix's parents asked Rasputin to cure him of his homosexuality. The treatment had some measure of success. However, Felix subsequently spurned Rasputin who opposed his marriage to Irina, the Tsar's niece. Rasputin did not approve of the match.[186]

A union between Felix and Irina would give the House of Romanov access to the Yussupov fortune. The Yussupovs were wealthy Tartars. Rasputin had often said that this family was not of Russian blood, and counseled the Tsar against permitting the union, adding that Felix Yussupov could not be a proper husband. Felix knew Rasputin's position, and was extremely irritated by it. There was a loud argument between the two, after which they no longer saw each other until Marie Golovina reunited them. Yussupov had even wanted to buy a pearl necklace from me for Irina but the purchase never came to fruition. Rasputin was against any transactions between Yussupov and me, even stating that I should have nothing to do with his enemy.

The Tsarina was resolutely averse to the marriage. According to Rasputin, when the event took place anyway, she attended the ceremony, but did not exchange one word with Nicholas for a long time afterward.[187]

---

[186] Felix sometimes dressed and went out in women's dresses when he was a teen, and was known to pursue young men, even after his marriage and the birth of his daughter, despite which Irina and Felix seemed to have had a happy marriage. Felix's brother, Nicholas, was killed in a duel with the husband of a married woman with whom Nicholas was having an affair, with Felix's encouragement.

[187] Other accounts mention the Tsarina's extravagant gift to Irina of expensive diamonds.

When Felix ended his studies at the Military School of Petersburg and was promoted to officer, the Tsar did not want him in the Imperial Guard because of Yussupov's homosexual tendencies. The latter needed Rasputin to intercede on his behalf, knowing that the Tsar would not refuse him. Consequently, he enlisted the aid of Mme Golovina to plead his case to Rasputin.

"And so, I reconciled the two," Golovina declared proudly. "Today, Felix invited Rasputin to his home. Grigori promised to cure Princess Irina of her illness. At this moment, they are undoubtedly dining together and celebrating their reunion. Murder is out of the question."

I knew that Princess Irina was not even in Petersburg. Rasputin was surely drawn into a trap. But Marie Golovina did not want to believe me. She was certain that, after their dinner, Rasputin would happily return home. It was useless to continue talking to her. I hurried to Protopopov, woke him and told him everything.

"But Rasputin gave me his word of honor that he wouldn't leave his apartment," the shocked Minister said.

I told him how Rasputin had lured the guards away from their posts and slipped away. Protopopov knew he had serious reason to worry about Rasputin's situation. He alerted the criminal police, as well as the political police, and a foot search commenced all over the city. I went to Bishop Isidor, in the section of the city near the Yussupov Palace. He, too, had no doubt that Rasputin had been assassinated. He had already heard stories that shots had been fired at Yussupov Palace during the night. The conspirator's palace was put under special surveillance, with guards posted at the perimeter of the property. The police officer on duty the prior night had reported that an unknown person, claiming to be Purishkevich, had given the officer fifty rubles, admitting that he had killed Rasputin. "I delivered Russia from a monster," Purishkevich said, adding, "He was a German sympathizer and wanted peace. Now, we can proceed with the war. You must be patriotic and keep quiet."

The officer did not attempt to arrest Purishkevich but returned to headquarters and made his report. The Chief of Police summoned one of Yussupov's servants to explain what had transpired in the palace the prior night. The valet was pale and agitated. He could give no details, but stated that he had seen a car, driven by Grand Duke Dmitri Pavlovich, arrive. Yussupov and Rasputin were in the car with him. Sitting next to the driver was Purishkevich, with his face poorly disguised. All got out of the car. The valet opened the door and was ordered by the Prince to leave them.

Yussupov's cousin later gave further details. The conspirators, other than Yussupov, were Grand Duke Dmitri Pavlovich, two sons of Grand Duke Alexander Mikhailovich,[188] and Purishkevich. Yussupov's father and former Minister of Interior Khvostov awaited news of Rasputin's death in another part of the palace,. Also assisting in the attempt were Yussupov's cousin, and the dancer, Vera Karalli. One of Yussupov's brothers-in-law hid behind a curtain in the adjoining room. He aimed a gun at Rasputin's head and shot him in the eye. After that, the others fired shots at the crumpled victim. Only Vera Karalli refused. She screamed, "I don't want to shoot!" Her cry was heard in other rooms.

---

[188] Princess Irina Yussupov's brothers.

When the accomplices saw Rasputin on the ground, motionless, they assumed he was dead. They put his fur coat on him, rolled him in a traveling blanket, and hid him in the basement, planning to dispose of him later. But despite eleven gunshot wounds Rasputin was not dead. When he came to, he crawled out of the basement and into the garden surrounded by high rock walls. He looked for an exit and even tried to scale the wall but could not. The dogs in the palace garden began barking furiously. This drew the assassins out to the garden where they discovered Rasputin. They found a clothesline for drying laundry, cut it into pieces and tried to tie him up. Despite his wounds, he put up a desperate struggle. Grand Duke Dmitri Pavlovich finally succeeded in binding his hands and feet. The assassins knocked him out and dragged him, unconscious, into the car. He was driven to the icy Neva River and thrown off a bridge, into the not-yet-frozen water.

At about eight o'clock in the morning, before we found the body, I went to Yussupov Palace, accompanied by Bishop Isidor. We asked to speak with young Felix. When he appeared, he seemed very pale and nervous.

"What have you done to Rasputin?" I demanded. "Did you go with him to see the gypsies?"

Prince Yussupov did not dare look me in the face. "I don't know," he stammered. "Yes, we dined together, but he stayed with the gypsies."

"Please tell that to the Tsarina," I replied. "Her Majesty is very worried. She wants to know what happened to Rasputin."

Yussupov followed my suggestion and, minutes later, gave me a letter declaring that he knew nothing with regard to Rasputin.

"I know nothing at all," he kept repeating.

I took the letter. However, in the meantime, I noticed blood stains on the floor.

"What is this blood doing on the floor?" I asked him.

He responded artfully, but without looking at me: "We killed our dog. That's of no importance."

"How is it, then, that your neighbors heard many gunshots and someone screaming, 'don't kill him'?" The police had provided me with a few details they had learned.

"Ah, that was my cousin and Mlle Karalli," answered the Prince. "They were very upset when we shot the dog."

I asked several other questions to which he responded in the same fashion. I could get nothing out of him.

When we began looking for the body, it was difficult to find the exact spot where Rasputin had been thrown into the water. However, my son found one of Rasputin's boots on the bridge. Then we also saw trails of blood, which led to a crevice in the ice. About half a mile down river, we found Rasputin's body on the ice. He was covered with a thin layer of snow. It seems he had pulled himself out of the water and then froze. He still had on his fur coat. The coat had bullet holes in eight different places. His right hand was no longer tied, but raised above his head, his fingers bent, as if making the sign of the cross. Most likely, he had partially freed himself from the ropes while still in the car. When they threw him in the water, he was still alive.[189] The date was December 17, 1916.[190]

Soon after the discovery of Rasputin's corpse, the following people arrived on the scene: Minister of the Interior Protopopov, Chief Globachev of the political police, City Commandant General Khabalov, General Balk, and Chief of Police Halle. In their presence, the body was transported from the scene by car, placed in an iron coffin and transported to a chapel between Petersburg and Tsarskoye-Selo. His daughters and nieces arrived. I also went, accompanied by my sons. In the chapel, we saw Rasputin's devotee, Akilina Laptinskaya, who was really an agent for The National Club. Strangers were not permitted into the chapel by order of the Tsarina. The Tsarina wanted to attend the funeral without being seen by strangers. Rasputin's daughters had brought clothing and linens that were used for washing and dressing the body.

Nicholas II was at general headquarters when it happened. The assassination was communicated to him by telegram. He received notification before the corpse was found, and sent back an order to break up all the ice between Petersburg and Kronstadt, an impossible task. He hastened back to Petersburg. Rasputin's death plunged him into a profound despair. "I am lost!" he said. Everyone

---

[189] A number of the details and the sequence of events in Simanovitch's account of Rasputin's murder are erroneous (though widely accepted at the time), especially in light of recent forensic evidence regarding the actual cause of death (close range gunshot to the forehead) which until recently was thought to be drowning. It is also highly unlikely that Simanovitch was on the scene before the police who were alerted shortly after the gunshots were heard. There is still much speculation about the actual events and cause of death.

[190] By the Julian calendar. By the Gregorian calendar, it was approximately two weeks later.

attempted to console him, but nothing could tear him away from his profound sorrow. He was convinced that Rasputin's death would inevitably lead to his own demise.

After burials, services for the dead were often repeated, attended by the entire Imperial Family. The only ones admitted to these ceremonies were part of the Imperial Couple's intimate circle. In the church at the Tsar's palace, funeral services for Rasputin took place several times. The Tsarina and her daughters sobbed the whole time. The body was buried secretly at the palace chapel. Members of the Imperial Family helped transport the coffin, including Tsarevitch Alexei who held the coffin's black ribbon. Everybody cried.

The body had been embalmed and, before closing the coffin, a saint's picture, bearing the signatures of the entire Imperial Family, was placed on Rasputin's chest. Many people knew these details. Consequently, in the first days of the revolution, Rasputin's body was taken from the coffin and burned. An officer, named Belyayev, learned of the saintly image with the signatures and, knowing it would attract collectors, resolved to obtain it for himself. He first had to find where Rasputin was buried. He approached Rasputin's daughter, Marya, passing himself off as a follower of her father's. In this way, he extracted the secret from the young girl, but could not carry out his plan until the revolution began. When it did, he led a mob of revolutionaries to Rasputin's tomb, and opened the coffin. Belyayev took the picture, but burned the corpse. The crowd thought Belyayev's actions were driven by revolutionary sentiment, and they cheered him.

Not long before his death, Rasputin asked me to summon his friend, the lawyer Aronson. He said he wanted to make out his will. I was surprised by my dear friend's request.

Aronson spent the evening in our company, and Rasputin dictated the following letter, including a chilling prediction: "The spirit of Grigori Efimovitch Rasputin Novych of the village of Pokrovskoie. I leave this letter to Petersburg. I foresee that I will leave this life before the first of January. I want to make known to the people of Russia, to Papa, Mama, their children, and to the Russian land, what actions they must take. If common assassins or my brother peasants kill me, then you, Tsar of Russia, have nothing to fear. Stay on your throne and govern. Moreover, you, Russian Tsar, will have nothing to fear for your children. They will reign in Russia for centuries. However, if the nobility assassinates me, their hands will remain stained with my blood for twenty-five years. They will leave Russia. Brother will rise against brother and they will hate and kill each other. And for twenty-five years, no aristocracy will exist in the country. Tsar of the Russian lands, if you hear the bell toll signifying that I am dead, you should know this: If anyone in your family causes my death, none of your children or your family will remain alive more than two years. You must reflect, study well and act prudently. Think of your health, and tell your relatives that I paid for them with my blood. I will be killed. I am no longer among the living. Pray! Pray! Be strong. Think of your blessed family! — Grigori."[191]

Rasputin had entrusted me with this prophetic document, which I took to the Tsarina. I do not know what impression it made; she did not speak of it. She only begged me not to show it to the Tsar. I gave it to Pitirim for safekeeping. The Tsar only knew of this declaration after Rasputin's death. I imagine, at that point, the Tsarina told him of the letter. After Rasputin's murder, the Tsar felt himself to be in serious danger. His relatives' attitudes

---

[191] There has been much debate as to the authenticity of this prediction as coming from Rasputin.

toward him became even more menacing. He held a series of meetings with representatives from the police department.

From that moment on, the Tsar feared more for his life than he ever had. Terrible premonitions plagued him, and he no longer had the will to live. This is the only way to explain his passive abdication of the throne. He had been convinced of the inevitability of the revolution even before it happened. Rasputin's sinister prediction played a role in this, and doubtless had a depressing effect on Nicholas. This prophecy became a reality as did most of the pronouncements he made.

Chapter VIII

After Rasputin's Death

Soon after Rasputin's burial, Nicholas II summoned me. He questioned me at length about Rasputin's last days and the circumstances surrounding his murder. He was particularly interested in the conspirators' ulterior motives. I told him all I knew, including Rasputin's intention to retire as soon as peace with Germany was reached, and his wish for ministers who would not impede peace. The Tsar listened attentively. He asked if one of the ministers had taken part in the murder or had prior knowledge of it. I responded that Minister of Justice Makarov and Minister of War Shuvayev had a close rapport with the conspirators, and that they were most likely well informed.

"But they said nothing to me," the Tsar remarked sadly.

The next day, Makarov and Shuvayev were dismissed. Later, I was called more often to see the Tsar. He wanted more precise details regarding the murder. He also wanted an idea of the general impact of the assassination on Petersburg society. However, foremost on the Tsar's mind were Rasputin's pronouncements during the last days of his life. He wanted to fulfill the desires of the deceased. Rasputin had not liked Makarov and had wanted to replace him with Dobrovolsky. The Tsar carefully followed all of my suggestions regarding important posts, including the appointments of Dobrovolsky as Minister of Justice and Belyayev as Minister of War.

The choice of Dobrovolsky proved a grave tactical error on my part that resulted in the second arrest of Rubenstein who had been released just prior to Rasputin's assassination. While Rasputin was still alive, I had the idea of nominating Dobrovolsky, the Senate's Attorney General, for the position of Minister of Justice. He was an obese man who gave the impression of being narrow-minded and heavy-hearted, but we obtained many things from the Senate thanks to his support. He loved money more than anything and rendered services in exchange for 'gifts.' Petersburg was full of people like this. I wanted Dobrovolsky to be Minister of Justice because I thought that he would do as I requested once he was indebted to me. Having been mixed up with I-don't-know-what villainous affairs, his reputation had suffered and he was not well received by leading society figures. This is why it was so difficult for me to get him nominated as it was met with an angry response from the press and high society.

This nomination occurred only after Rasputin's death, and solely by my advice to the Tsar that this was Rasputin's wish. I had not the least suspicion that Dobrovolsky had ties to the Old Court, but I subsequently learned that he typically frequented the home of Baroness Rosen, where he often encountered Mme Rubenstein. In the course of a spiritual séance (which were common at Mme Rosen's home), there was a dispute between the banker's wife and Dobrovolsky. The argument alienated them from each other and he said he would not free Rubenstein this time. Dobrovolsky had deeply disappointed us. He was barely in office when he began to act counter to our interests. From the first meeting the Tsar accorded him, he insisted on pursuing the Rubenstein matter, saying that, in his opinion, the banker was guilty of military espionage. The result was that the Tsar, weak and indecisive as he was, did not stick by his decision to dismiss legal action against

Rubenstein. Instead, he agreed with his new minister to jail the accused.

This action by Dobrovolsky was a huge and disagreeable surprise. We did not know what to do. I went to see him and vehemently reproached him. I lost my head. I told him that he would not remain Minister of Justice for long. I was carried away by my rage. I even went so far as to pound my fist on the table. Nothing worked. The old fox recounted our exchange to the Tsar in a provocative manner. However, he did not dare break ties with Vyrubova and the Tsarina. I gave the Tsarina a faithful account of what had transpired between Dobrovolsky and me. Upset and in despair, she put her head in her hands and cried:

"Ah, Simanovitch! What have you done?"

The nomination of a partisan of the Old Court could have had disastrous consequences for her. She was in danger of being caught funneling funds to her relatives in Germany. It was only after a great while that she recovered from the blow of my regretful actions, enough to cry repeatedly, "You've done us in, Simanovitch. We're lost!"

I dropped to my knees and said, "I beg Your Majesty to forgive me! But things can still be set right. We must get rid of Dobrovolsky!"

The Tsarina asked me to find Minister of the Interior Protopopov, our confidante, and ask his advice. Dobrovolsky's treason upset him also, since getting rid of him would not be an easy task as long as the Tsar thought he was Rasputin's choice. Moreover, Dobrovolsky knew how greatly the memory of Rasputin played in the Tsar's mind. This only fueled his hostile attitude toward us. Protopopov called Dobrovolsky and reproached him, but

Dobrovolsky stood firm and was content to lay the blame for everything squarely on the Tsar. Given the difficulty of the situation, I decided to resort to the most classic means of corruption. Protopopov agreed, and we resolved to execute our plan immediately.

The following day, I went to the bank with Mme Rubenstein. She took one hundred thousand rubles from her account. I had brought some jewelry, knowing that Dobrovolsky's favorite daughter had just gotten engaged. The Minister could not resist the temptation for long. He accepted the one hundred thousand rubles, a pearl necklace, and a pair of diamond earrings for his daughter. He promised he would halt the case against Rubenstein. However, he did not keep his promise; he only had Rubenstein transferred from the prison to a hospital, which was just a little better. In addition, the revolution had begun. When Kerensky placed himself at the head of the Provisional Government, Mme Rubenstein finally obtained her husband's freedom, thanks to Zarudny, a lawyer who was devoted to her.

~~~~~~~~

On one occasion, I told the Tsar, "Rasputin did not trust General Alexeev."[192]

"Impossible!" Nicholas responded. "Who did he trust more?"

"General Gurko," I answered.[193]

---

[192] General Mikhail Alexeev (also Alekseyev) (b.1857-d.1918) was the Tsar's Chief of Staff in the Imperial Russian Army.
[193] General Vasily Gurko (b. 1864-d.1937) was Alexeev's Chief-ofStaff in the Russian Imperial Army.
~~~~~~~~

"I can't remove Alexeev from his position," the Tsar said. "He knows all of our military secrets. I'll have to tolerate him."

Rasputin's death threw the Tsar's court into a panic. Now, Protopopov seemed to be the only man who could avert the danger of revolution. The royals, concerned about the Duma's threatening attitude, needed to calm the people's representatives. Vyrubova proposed reconciliation between Protopopov and Duma President Rodzianko.[194] This idea was very agreeable and easy to effect, or so Vyrubova convinced the Tsar.

One day, when Rodzianko came to Tsarskoye-Selo to give his report, the Tsar also called in Protopopov. The Minister and the Duma President met in the Tsar's office. Nicholas reproached Rodzianko for being adversarial toward Protopopov, especially as they had to work together. If Rodzianko did not want to do battle with the Tsar, he would have to reconcile with Protopopov. But, despite the Tsar's demands, Rodzianko refused to shake hands with Protopopov. Nicholas was beside himself. He rose abruptly, turned his back to Rodzianko, and said to Protopopov, "Come, Alexander Dmitrivich. Let us go!" The two of them left the office without saying anything further to Rodzianko.

Several hours later, Protopopov sent his second to challenge Rodzianko to a duel. The latter accepted. When Protopopov informed me of his demand for a duel with Rodzianko, I tried to dissuade him of this insane idea but he would not hear of it. The Tsar had left for military headquarters soon after his meeting with Protopopov, most

---

194 Protopopov and Rodzianko not only held differences of political opinion, but the latter hated Rasputin while the former was Rasputin's ally.

likely to avoid the opening session of the Duma. In his absence, I proposed that, at the very least, Protopopov inform the Tsarina of his intentions. He telephoned her and brought her up to date. She was furious, and spoke to him in English for nearly an hour. She said that Protopopov had conducted himself worse than Rodzianko had but she could not bring herself to tell him that he would surely lose to Rodzianko. We all felt that the eventual death of Protopopov could only have the worst consequences for us.

In response to an anguished letter from the Tsarina, Nicholas II summoned Rodzianko by telegram. In Petersburg, this gave rise to rumors that the Tsar intended to ask Rodzianko to create a cabinet accountable to the Duma. Nothing could have been further from the truth. In fact, the Tsar ordered Rodzianko to renounce the duel with Protopopov. Rodzianko wrote his adversary, declaring that he would only cancel the duel if Protopopov submitted to the Tsar's wish that it not take place, which he did. I was very happy to have the whole affair ended. For Protopopov's dueling seconds, I ordered some impressive jewels as souvenirs of the canceled duel.

Following this incident, there was an era of stormy reorganization of the ministers, but I can no longer remember the details of all the changes.[195] There was a moment when Rodzianko's party seemed to have the upper hand. Sturmer, President of the Council of Ministers, was replaced with Trepov, who accepted on the condition that future nominations be made by the Council President rather than by the Tsar. Even before taking office, Trepov met with Protopopov, Dobrovolsky, General Belyayev, and Raev, asking them to submit their resignations. However,

---

[195] In the last two years of the Tsar's reign, some forty cabinet ministers were cycled through the thirteen positions.

Protopopov said he was placed in office by the Tsar and would only step down by order of the Tsar.

Protopopov sought me out and brought me up to date. The situation was worrisome. I thought that the principal danger was that Rasputin's posthumous influence would be negated. I wanted to maintain his influence at all costs, and told Protopopov that we could only save ourselves by reviving Rasputin's legacy. Stunned, he could not imagine how I could do that, but I submitted my plan to him and he enthusiastically accepted. Among other things, Rasputin had been in the habit of telephoning the palace every day at 10:00 a.m. After Rasputin's death, Protopopov continued these daily telephone conversations in an effort to conduct himself in the spirit of Rasputin. However, since he was not as well-versed in Rasputin's views as I was, he asked me to be present and assist him during these conversations.

More importantly, Rasputin had a habit of marking down, on slips of paper, the names of different candidates and the positions for which he felt they were suited. Shortly before his death, he discussed with me his plan to form a cabinet that would satisfy our need for equal rights and an end to the Great War. The situation was difficult and the number of potential candidates was limited. At the critical moment, when it seemed our suggestions were losing ground, I remembered Rasputin's letters and notes that I had kept. The Tsar was very familiar with Rasputin's handwriting, so I knew he could validate the authenticity of the notes.

"Where are these notes?" Protopopov asked.

I told him that, after Rasputin's demise, all documents, including important and confidential correspondence from the Imperial Couple, were secured at a location far from the apartment. Upon the Tsar's return to Petersburg, I informed him of this, too. He praised me for having taken such precautions. I had given some of Rasputin's papers to Princess Sofia Tarkhanova, who was on intimate terms with Protopopov. The rest were hidden with Metropolitan Pitirim, which is where we found the notes we needed. The names of Dobrovolsky, General Belyayev, and Raev were written down, but all of those candidates had already been placed.

Finally, we saw the names of several people who seemed perfect for the vacant positions. Our candidate for the office of Council President was Prince Golitsyn, an old and decaying yet loyal friend of Protopopov's and a charming gentleman as well. Among Rasputin's papers was a photograph of Prince Golitsyn, with an inscription by Rasputin. The words 'the old man' on the photograph were code for President of the Ministers. This more than adequately met our needs. We were sure that the Tsar would take this posthumous suggestion. The respective mistresses of Golitsyn and Protopopov were friends and, when the latter became minister, the two women resolved to procure an equally high position for the Prince, so that neither friend would be left behind socially.

With Rasputin's posthumous validation of Prince Golitsyn, we went to Vyrubova. We persuaded her that Rasputin desired the nominations of Prince Golitsyn as Council President, Pokrovsky for Minister of Foreign Affairs (even though he knew no foreign languages), and Voynovsky for Minister of Communications. Vyrubova, surprised by our communication, immediately submitted our list of candidates to the Tsarina who was very pleased to see a list devised by Rasputin himself. She sent it by special courier, with her own cover letter, to the Tsar at general headquarters. Nicholas summoned Protopopov, showed him Rasputin's list and asked whether he knew the candidates. The Tsar knew nothing of these men. Protopopov pretended he was seeing the list for the first time. He told the Tsar that he knew all the names and felt they were the best candidates one could imagine.

The next day, Trepov, who had been Council President for about a week, was obliged to leave, and Prince Golitsyn, a relative unknown, was instated in his place. Protopopov was very happy with our success in persuading the Tsar to do this. Several days later, however, he surprised me with some bad news. He told me that, at the first cabinet meeting, Minister of Justice Dobrovolsky had proposed that I be exiled to Siberia. Apparently, I was a nuisance and interfered with the activities of the ministers. It did not suit them to depend on me, so they judged the moment opportune to act against me. Protopopov replied that he would not join a discussion of that nature. The Tsar told the police not to interfere with my activities, and the affair ended there.

Unlike the protocol until that time, the new cabinet did not meet with the Tsar. As far as I can remember, the Tsar received Prince Golitsyn only once. However, all the newly named ministers knew that it was in their best interests to pay a visit to Vyrubova since her approval was considered important. The Golitsyn cabinet was the last of the Tsar's reign.

~~~~~~~~

Some consider the conflict between the Old and Young Courts to be evidence that the 1917 revolution leading to the Tsar's abdication came from higher up — in fact, from the Tsar's relatives in the Old Court. They initiated the movement against Rasputin. However, the shots fired by
~~~~~~~~

Yussupov and Grand Duke Dmitri Pavlovich hit not only Rasputin but also, indirectly, the Imperial Couple. It was only a brief time before the conflict moved from the palaces to the streets of Petersburg.

The goal of eradicating Rasputin's influence by murdering him was not realized. The murderers' actions had the opposite effect. Rasputin's influence outlived his body and grew greater. Imbued with the glory of a martyr, more than ever, the deceased was a saint in the eyes of the Tsar and Tsarina who wanted to follow his advice to the letter. The Tsarina assembled all of the letters and notes Rasputin had sent them, as well as conserving the ones found after his death. At the start of the revolution, when she saw that her collection was in danger, she put all of Rasputin's papers into my hands for safekeeping.

Rasputin's death did not, in the least, ease tensions between the Grand Dukes and the Imperial Couple, but fueled them. A veritable conspiracy was formed, at the head of which was Yussupov's father-in-law, Grand Duke Alexander Mikhailovich, cousin to the Tsar. All of the Grand Dukes stuck together, with the exception of the sons of Grand Duke Vladimir. The conspiring Grand Dukes conjured a plot to declare the Tsar insane and to put the Tsarina in a convent, putting Grand Duke Nikolai Nikolayevich on the throne until the Tsarevitch came of age. This plan soon was abandoned, with another emerging in its place. According to the new plan, the Dowager Empress would take the throne after the Tsar's abdication, and proclaim her son, Grand Duke Mikhail, as heir to the throne.

All of these ideas were aired so openly that the political police had no trouble following the Grand Dukes' discussions. The frequent exchange of letters and telegrams between them used clear and strong language. The ladies of the Old Court participated in these conversations as much as the men. In their salons, the subject of overthrowing the Tsar was daily conversation.

The Tsar knew very well that a plot against him was brewing but did nothing about it, largely because, in his farewell letter predicting his death, Rasputin pleaded with the Tsar to abstain from punishing his murderers. The will of Rasputin was sacred to the Tsar who limited himself to sending Dmitri Pavlovich to the front, and exiling Yussupov to his home.[196] This only encouraged the Grand Dukes to plot further. The Tsar received almost daily threats of overthrow from his family. Grand Duke Alexander Mikhailovich appeared once at the Imperial Palace, with his two sons, both of whom had a hand in Rasputin's death. He insisted on speaking to the Tsarina. At first, she refused to see him but finally acquiesced. She was not feeling well that day and received the Grand Duke in her bedroom. As the Imperial Couple expected trouble from the Old Court, the Tsar remained in the adjoining room with his two oldest daughters. When Alexander Mikhailovich began speaking to the Tsarina in a threatening tone, Nicholas appeared with his daughters. He was calm and in control. The Grand Duke sputtered and mumbled that Protopopov should be dismissed and that the entire cabinet should be reappointed.

I arrived later that day, along with Rasputin's daughters who went to retrieve the fur coats that the Tsarina had bought for them. The girls joined the Tsarina's youngest daughters, Maria and Anastasia, in the rooms reserved for Grand Duchess Elizabeth. As for me, I went into the

---

[196] The Tsar was likely less influenced by Rasputin's wishes than by his fear of the Old Court's wrath if he severely punished the murderers who were members of his family.

infirmary which was within the palace walls. There, I saw Mme Vyrubova who was terribly overwrought. She told me about the scene that had unfolded in the Tsarina's bedroom. I took Rasputin's equally upset daughters home, and went to see Protopopov. He called the palace and, for about an hour, spoke to the Tsarina in English. He insisted that it was necessary to act immediately and severely against Alexander Mikhailovich, but he could not get consent from the Tsarina. The rupture between the Imperial Couple and the Old Court progressed until, eventually, the Tsar and Tsarina would no longer receive his family at the palace. It was finally ordered and strictly enforced that no Grand Duke be permitted to approach the Imperial Couple.

Chapter IX

Nicholas II

I always found Nicholas II pitiful. He was, without a doubt, an unhappy man. He could not intimidate anyone and his personality inspired neither veneration nor respect. However, he made a good first impression and was quite likeable. He was simple and welcoming in a way that made you forget he was Emperor. In his private life, he was modest and without pretension. But his character was full of contradictions. He had two great faults which would cause his ruin: he was weak-willed and lazy. He had confidence in no one and was wary of everyone. His misfortune, above all, was not having the stuff of a king — of being nothing more than an average man.

Rasputin had told me that the Tsar declared, "For me, loyalty only exists in children under two years old. As soon as they reach three, parents begin to hear their lies. All humans, men and women, are liars." Rasputin often tried to dissuade him of this, but to no avail. It was this attitude of the Tsar's that caused people to lose confidence in him. In the course of conversation, Nicholas II would seem conciliatory and ready to oblige, but one was never sure that he would keep his word. Those in the Emperor's entourage tried to see to it that his promises were kept, but he did not concern himself about it in the least.

Nicholas II was convinced that he had been wronged and that no one would tell him the truth. He felt hurt and scoffed at by everyone. This was the tragic side of his life. Knowing that his own mother and all of his family hated him, he never stopped living in fear of the Old Court of the Dowager Empress, and even believed his life to be in danger. He was constantly haunted by the fear of some conspiracy in the palace, feeling that he and his wife would be thrown from a window like King Alexander of Serbia and his queen.

Nicholas II was bored by the Court's rigid etiquette imposed on him by his high rank. Sometimes he escaped. It was a true pleasure for him to frequent the cafés of the capital, where the patrons would behave with their typical boldness and lack of inhibition. Goulesko,[197] for example, earned the good graces of the Tsar by composing a happy song about the officers in the Emperor's entourage who had forgotten to pay their bill in a house of pleasure. The refrain, "Give me my three rubles" pleased the Tsar enormously.

The Tsar's younger brother, George, was proclaimed heir to the throne during the first years of Nicholas' reign (before the Emperor had a son). However, George died of an illness in his chest at Abbas Tuman, in the Caucasus. The direct causes of his death were imprudent activities and excessive fatigue. Hellstrom, who had accompanied him to Abbas Tuman, bore some responsibility, as it was he who had engaged the Grand Duke in a boating race that was beyond his strength.[198]

---

[197] Goulesko was famous as the director of a Rumanian gypsy orchestra.

[198] Grand Duke George (b.1871-d.1899) had been diagnosed with tuberculosis at the age of 19 and died at the age of 28 when he went out alone for a motorcycle ride.

Hellstrom entered the Russian Navy as a second captain. He was the illegitimate son of Alexander III and a lady of the Court,[199] and fiercely resembled the former emperor in a striking fashion. The Dowager Empress, Maria, widow of Alexander III, could not look at him without becoming emotional. He received a pension from the cabinet and was subsidized by the Dowager Empress and the Grand Duke Mikhail. Empress Maria, though very irritated with him due to his part in George's death, often received him for visits anyway, after that affair. He constantly complained of his illegitimate birth, damning it for keeping him from attaining the throne. However, he led a carefree life devoted to pleasure.

Few know about the intimate details of the life of Nicholas II. The Imperial Family avoided everyone. They distanced themselves from the extended family and admitted only their closest friends to their circle. Each year, that circle became smaller and, by the end of his reign, Nicholas' family was completely isolated. The Tsar, himself, was extremely taciturn and gave no indication as to his thoughts, which lent him a sphinx-like appearance. Those closest to him did all they could to hide his faults. In high society, he was considered a well-mannered man, sweet and tender, who loved his wife and children, and lived a retiring and peaceful family life. The reality, however, was otherwise.

Nicholas II had many faults as Tsar, but many more as a man. His greatest weakness, alcohol, transformed this sweet, tender, well-bred man into a monster and ferocious

---

[199] While the illegitimate children of other tsars are documented, none are recorded for Alexander III or Nicholas II, and no association of the name Hellstrom with Alexander III was found by this writer.

beast. Nicholas was often dead-drunk, and his face appeared almost inhuman when under the influence. At these times, he was frightening. He would go overboard in his sensual pursuits and his mistress would be the victim of painful tortures and atrocities because, in the sexual domain, he was not a normal man. His passion for alcohol was intricately linked with sexual sport.[200]

Before Nicholas II ascended to the throne, he had two mistresses; the ballerina, Mathilde Kschessinska,[201] who had several palaces and a fortune in the millions, and the beautiful dramatic artist, Labunski[202] who was always covered in diamonds. This was no secret among Russian society. However, almost no one knew that he continued to see Kschessinska even after his marriage and coronation. Neither Kschessinska nor Labunski loved Nicholas II but they secured fabulous favors and gifts from him by giving generously of themselves. Tragic destiny pursued not only the Tsar and his advisors but also placed its heavy hand on all the women who allowed the Tsar into their intimate lives. Only these two of the Tsar's mistresses escaped his influence in time. In so doing, they succeeded in separating themselves from the sad destiny of the unhappy monarch.

The women who were Nicholas Romanov's mistresses after he attained the throne, not only did not obtain great favors, but had to submit to great pain and degradation. I will only mention his two principal mistresses who had to suffer the consequences of the alcoholic perversity of

---

[200] There are no other accounts and no evidence that the Tsar was an alcoholic or sexual deviant.

[201] Kschessinska was Nicholas II's mistress before he married the Tsarina.

[202] This writer found no evidence that Labunski was Nicholas' mistress though they may have known each other.

Nicholas II. They were Mme Vyrubova[203], lady of honor and friend to the Tsarina, and the beautiful Georgian Princess Sofia Orbeliani. Each sincerely loved the Tsar, and both lost use of their legs. Even after the execution of the Tsar, tragedy continued to pursue his mistresses who, although still living today,[204] are in ill health, with no support, and leading horribly painful lives.

Both Vyrubova and Orbeliani had a panic-stricken terror of his love of alcohol and the resulting sadistic behavior. He would break into their houses in a drunken fury and torture them. The servants of these unhappy women kept quiet only because their mistresses told them to and because they feared reprisals from the Tsar. The Tsarina not only closed her eyes to the Tsar's affairs, but even protected these women. She felt great tenderness toward Lady Vyrubova and Princess Orbeliani. When both lost the use of their legs (the former in a train wreck[205] and the latter through rheumatism), the Tsarina herself looked after them and never ceased thinking of them as her best friends. Despite her generally cold manner, the Tsarina's kindness was not surprising, considering that she was no longer the woman she had been before the birth of the Tsarevitch.

While the Tsar's mistresses feared him, it was a different story with the intimate life of Nicholas II's advisor and friend, Grigori Rasputin. If only a rare few knew of the Tsar's amorous adventures, Rasputin's love life was known to the entire universe. Even now that historians and

---

[203]After the revolution, Mme Vyrubova was certified as a virgin by the Extraordinary Commission's physician. Although she was an occasional companion to the Tsar on walks when the Tsarina was unavailable, there was no evidence of any impropriety, nor was there with Princess Orbeliani.

[204] Circa 1928

[205] She was confined to a wheelchair but eventually was able to walk with a cane.

authors are drawing attention to him, clarifying the role he played in the reign of the last Tsar, most people are interested in him as a character from the scandal columns of the newspapers. Affairs between a Siberian mujik and high society ladies lent themselves to gossip. Rasputin had quite a number of flings and, incredible as it may seem, these woman of all social classes left satisfied and happy. This is explained not so much by Rasputin's extraordinary physique, as by the consideration he showed the fairer sex. He not only loved women but sympathized with them, helped them and defended their interests. He always said that, in all family quarrels and misunderstandings, the woman is right.

When women came to him complaining of miserable lives due to tyrannical husbands, he generally recommended a rapid divorce and would see to it that the trial process was simplified in the woman's favor. "If a woman wants a divorce," Rasputin would say, "she must have her freedom immediately, because life as a couple is unbearable to her. If the husband wants a divorce, his is either lying or cheating. He doesn't want to feed his wife and children, or he has a mistress."

Knowing his amiable disposition toward women, many came for help with a divorce, and he never refused. The bureaucratic machinery began to work with amazing speed. This is how hundreds of women gained their freedom, thanks to Rasputin. He not only helped his mistresses, but all women who addressed him. He refused them nothing but since he did not carry money, he would write notes to his banker friends who always satisfied his requests to help his protégées. All the women who came for help left happy. Beneath his crude manners and coarse appearance, hid a true gentleman with a big heart. "It's a great sin to wrong women," Rasputin would say. "A man can be a swindler in politics, business or trade, but he must always be honest and noble with women."

According to him, innocence, youth and beauty were female currency, and a man who profited from those assets should reimburse and defend the woman because one can always return money and well-being, but it is impossible to restore youth, innocence and beauty. In giving these, a woman irrevocably gives all. While Rasputin supported the rights of married women, he was even more protective of women who did not have the security of a legitimate marriage. He held the opinion that one's word was worth more than any written law, and that a man should respect the honor and rights of an unmarried woman, even more than those protected by law and social opinion. He felt that the illegitimate woman believed in one's word of honor and promise — believed in the nobility of emotions. In Rasputin's mind, the woman was almost always right when arguing with a man; maybe, among thousands of women, one might be wrong.

So, women were drawn to him not only for material aid, but also for the sweetness and understanding they found in this nearly illiterate mujik. That was the source of his popularity which the scandal newspapers explained in their own way. Rasputin scorned the way Nicholas treated his mistresses, as well as his atrocious habits. He made long speeches to the Tsar, imploring him to be sweet and tender with his mistresses — not to see them when he was in a drunken state, and not to beat and torture them. The Tsar's mistresses were left feeling morally and physically ill, while Rasputin's mistresses were healthy, happy and content. Nicholas II brought his mistresses nothing but pain and displeasure. Outside of his personal faults, he was a doomed man whose bad luck touched all those around him. Rasputin's 'divine grace,' on the other hand, made those around him happy. Even now, after the downfall of the Imperial throne, the Tsar's ex-mistresses are pursued by ill destiny, leading miserable lives, while Rasputin's women enjoy happy lives.[206]

From the day he was crowned to his abdication and subsequent horrible death, Tsar Nicholas II's entire reign was encumbered with wars, revolutions, plots, assassinations, intrigues of all kinds, and the family's misfortunes. There were two predominant causes of all these calamities: the political situation of the era and the character of the Tsar. The first is, by far, the most important cause. However, without discerning how much of these morbid events was NicholasII's fault, one cannot deny that his character played a considerable role in Russia's history and the world's.

Nicholas inherited an immense empire from his father, Tsar Alexander III, who had ruled with an iron hand. Nevertheless, Nicholas had neither his father's character nor his system of government. Under Alexander III, everything was clear. Barely educated, but gifted with great intelligence, Alexander III had several positive qualities essential to a monarch. He was strong and firm, but neither stubborn nor arrogant. Nor was he presumptuous. Tsar Alexander III did not consider himself capable of governing an entire empire all alone. He knew how to consult his ministers and choose his allies, giving them the means to act, within limits, and to work peacefully. This sort of politic is the measure of a stable and consistent situation, which allowed Russia to roll along without catastrophe. During his long reign, there was

---

[206] This may have been true of Rasputin's mistresses (who are not named) but, in the early 1920s, the communists took his wife's home and, in 1930, exiled her and son Dmitri to northern Siberia where they died in poverty.

neither war nor revolution, and Europe regarded its giant neighbor with fear and respect — as being potentially dangerous, yet peaceful. The title of 'The Peacemaker,' given to Alexander III, was not the vain flattery of courtesans, but characterized the Tsar better than any other title.[207]

Nicholas II was just the opposite of his father. He was wary, weak, with a rare stubbornness, and determined to govern Russia alone. He suspected and saw constant evidence of his diminishing prestige as Tsar. He doubted and disliked strong, intelligent ministers, surrounding himself instead with mediocre and incapable men. If we also add that Nicholas II so believed in mysticism that it ruled his decisions, we see that his reign became an infinitely sad spectacle. From the start of his reign, Russian politics were hesitant, enemies reared their heads, and the prestige of great power diminished visibly. The Russia that had supported and protected the iron hand of Alexander III against so many enemies, now began to slip into a bottomless abyss.

Nicholas II had no confidence in his ministers and they, in turn, never knew what did or did not please the Tsar. In Alexander's time, today's 'yes' was always tomorrow's 'yes'; in Nicholas' time, today's 'yes' often became tomorrow's 'no.' Given these uncertain politics, conscientious dignitaries could not fulfill their duties and, despite the most flattering propositions, they refused any Council positions offered to them. By the end of Nicholas' reign, it was impossible to find anyone willing to accept nomination.

---

[207] The title of 'Peacemaker' was actually given to Tsar Alexander III solely because there were no wars during his reign. He was, however, one of the most austere and tyrannical tsars, instituting new restrictions and encouraging pogroms.

There was another reason to avoid these positions. Advisors to Nicholas II had a high fatality rate. The list began with the assassinations of Council Ministers Bogolepov, Sipiagin, and Plehve, in the first years of the Tsar's rule, and ended with Stolypin's assassination, Witte's poisoning, Goremykin's strangulation, and finally, the death by firing squad of the last Council Ministers — Shcheglovitov, Protopopov, Khvostov and others. The massacre of one hundred and one dignitaries was carried out in Kislovodsk Park.[208] Bolshevik Commissar Bullei specifically chose this number of victims, to evoke the one hundred one cannon blasts that had been symbolic of the Tsar's grandeur. Generals Ruzsky, Radko-Dmitriev and others who were the last to serve and counsel the monarchy, were killed. In addition to these names, there were ladies of the Court who were burned alive with the Tsar's family in Ekaterinburg.[209]

I remember well that Sukovkin categorically refused the position of Minister of Internal Affairs when it was offered, although it would have crowned his administrative career. Rasputin had offered the same proposition to Ordovsky-Tanaevsky, Prefect of Tobolsk. However insignificant his position in Tobolsk, he also declined the great honor. This occurred quite often and, more than once, Rasputin had to appeal to their patriotism as well as to their personal ambition.

"What are you afraid of?" Rasputin would ask them. "Revolutionaries? Bombs? Death? So, you will die for

[208] This may refer to the 1918 mass execution of imperial bureaucrats and officers at Pyatigorsk. In Kislovodsk, the Bolsheviks killed people in the hospital.
[209] The Tsar's family and entourage were first shot and then burned.

your country, for your Tsar, for your people. Sacrifice your life for Russia!"

Rasputin embroidered his discourse with quotations, excerpts from the Bible, and examples from ancient history. Nevertheless, neither quotes nor appeals for patriotism could conquer their fears of reputedly fatal positions. It became very difficult to find candidates. The intelligent, independent and honest people declined, so we had no choice but to address ourselves to unstable people and adventurers whose reputations were not exactly intact.

Everything that Nicholas touched, from near or far, came to an unhappy end. His coronation ceremony at Khodynka Field ended with the bloody trampling of people grabbing for souvenirs. His railroad through Manchuria led to the Russo-Japanese War. The peaceful assembly of workers, led by Father Gapon, brought a petition to the Tsar, only to come face to face with a firing squad and, finally, the hanging of Father Gapon himself.[210] (When Manasevitch-Manuilov, Secretary to the Council President, was given the order to send Father Gapon far from the Finnish border, he may have taken it to mean 'beyond the borders of this world.') During the Great War, when Manasevitch-Manuilov was arrested, he asked Rasputin to beg the Tsar for mercy on his behalf. In his petition, he asked for his freedom and a dismissal of the whole affair, in light of the service he had rendered the government by disposing of Gapon. The government, considering his past services, promptly liberated him. Rasputin had told Manasevitch-Manuilov, more than once, that Father Gapon's blood would cover him and that he would find death in the same place as his victim. That, like many of Rasputin's

[210] This is a reference to the 1905 revolution.

predictions, came true during the Revolution when Manuilov was shot at Oserki.

Every step was in error. Every reform was defeated. Every nomination was fatal. Is it then surprising that terrorist revolutionaries paradoxically decided to protect Nicholas II from assassination attempts? In their opinion, the monarch was the best revolutionary. Each of his actions pushed Russia further into the arms of revolution and anarchy. They were right. The revolutionaries viewed Rasputin in the same light, since he was the source of information on all that happened at Tsarskoye-Selo. The revolutionaries, considering the size of the Romanov dynasty, preferred to deal with the weak and unlucky Nicholas than with a successor who might prove to be of strong will and character.

All the plots and attempts against Nicholas and his friend and counsel, Rasputin, emanated from the Old Court. The Tsar's constant fear of attacks from revolutionaries was misplaced. Everything coincided in such a manner that Nicholas could not extricate himself from the fatal circle of events. The intelligent and honest men who could help him were put off by his paranoia, and the insignificant people in his entourage pushed him to commit unpardonable acts, encouraging his weakness and whims.

Tsarina Alexandra Feodorovna also played a fatal role during her life and reign. Ambitious, authoritarian, wary, hysterical and neurotic, her religious fanaticism approached mania. She was in complete possession of her husband's soul and constantly fueled his beliefs and suspicions. She and her entourage manipulated him and obliged him to sever relations with his family. This woman was Nicholas II's bad luck charm, the source of his troubles, and the inspiration for a number of inopportune decisions.

In these strategic conditions, all of a sudden, by a fairy-tale path, appeared a Siberian peasant — Grigori Rasputin. All of Russia accepted this fact as a sinister foreboding.[211] All of the gossip and anecdotes made this peasant the source of evil and the symbol of the monarchy's downfall. When Grigori Rasputin first appeared at the palace, the knot of tragic events to come had already been tied. Hypnotists, clairvoyants and other charlatans were familiar to the palace. Politics turned like a weathervane, and there is no reason to believe that events would have followed another path if Rasputin had never existed.

The incredible power and strange end of Rasputin, the Siberian peasant who was advisor and conscience to the Tsar, makes one wonder about the grotesque capriciousness of the mysterious forces ruling the lives of men. We seek explanations. We find a series of bizarre circumstances which throw some light on this disconcerting power. But, in the end, any explanation of this unique piece of history is insufficient. Rasputin's fate was strangely linked to that of the Imperial Family.

Whenever the Tsar asked Rasputin about his country life at his home in Pokrovskoie, Rasputin was in the habit of replying that he strongly wished the Tsar could see his village for himself. The Imperial Family had great interest in Rasputin's home but, certainly, no one expected that they would actually go there. Yet, fate had determined that they be banished precisely to the province of Tobolsk, very near Pokrovskoie. In the Russian Empire, there were many

---

[211] Perhaps not all of Russia, as Rasputin had a great following among many peasants who had long known him as a gifted healer before he went to Petersburg.

places to which the Tsar could have been exiled but the Provisional Government chose Tobolsk. When the Tsar was transferred from Tobolsk to Ekaterinburg, his journey stopped briefly in front of Rasputin's home, not by request of the Tsar but strictly by chance. The military guard prevented him from visiting the house but Rasputin's family came out to greet him. What is even more ironic is that two years after Rasputin was killed by relatives of the Tsar, the Imperial Family was betrayed and killed with the help of Rasputin's son-in-law. The Imperial Family perished in the same cruel fashion as Rasputin and, like him, their bodies were burned.

Despite his outrageous life, Rasputin was a good family man. It had been too late to give his son a good education, but he gave his daughters all the culture the city had to offer. They went to one of the best girls' schools in Petersburg, and were raised strictly. The eldest, Marya, who is now[212] in Paris, resembles her father most remarkably. His enthusiastic spirit lives in her. This character trait of his was well known, even among those who attempted to exploit him.

Marya was a close friend of the Tsar's daughters who, despite their high rank and rigorous court etiquette, were very simple and without pretension. In the close circle of the Imperial Couple's intimate friends, these girls lived a monotonous existence and knew nothing of life. Their view of the world was severely limited by the high walls surrounding the palace. Their reading was carefully chosen, so as not to stir any inappropriate interests. To them, Marya must have seemed as a creature from another world. She encountered many interesting people and enjoyed much more freedom than they did. Her stories

---

[212] Circa 1928

awakened a great curiosity in the young princesses. For example, she could recount her amorous longings with captivating charm. The princesses impatiently awaited her visits to the palace. The tales of this young girl were the height of happiness for the Tsar's daughters. The Tsar delighted in the friendship between the girls, and Rasputin's daughters felt at home in the palace.

After Rasputin's death and shortly after the revolution, his daughter, Marya, married Soloviev[213] who was a military officer. The marriage between Marya and Soloviev, who became adjunct to Gorichkov, President of the Duma's Military Commission, was celebrated solemnly in the chapel of the Tauride Palace. Many members of the Provisional Government were in attendance. Soloviev had known Rasputin and passed for one of his devotees. Like Davidson and Pankhadze, Marya's first two loves, Soloviev had only ulterior motives for marrying Marya. At that time, the Imperial Family was in exile in Tobolsk. Soloviev knew that they had jewels and diamonds of enormous value. The Tsar's banishment was unexpected, as the Imperial Family had hoped to be permitted to leave for England. Everything was ready for this journey, including personal effects which were packed. Kerensky had permitted the Tsar to take his valuables, and his baggage did not have to go through customs agents. Suddenly, the order was given to take the Imperial Family, not abroad, but to Siberia. Their baggage followed them to Tobolsk. Soloviev offered his services to the Provisional Government for this mission. Once again, Marya became an unwitting co-conspirator. With her help, Soloviev hoped to become intimately close to the Imperial Family in order to conduct surveillance on their activities and to prevent their flight.

---

[213] White Russian officer, Boris Soloviev, was son of the Treasurer of the Holy Synod. He married Marya in October, 1917.

Soloviev, son of the President of the Holy Synod, had completed his studies in Kiev and was promoted to officer during the Great War. He was one of the first officers to submit to the Duma after the revolution. He made a brilliant career for himself and gained the trust of Minister of War Guchkov, as well as other ministers of the Provisional Government. However, that earned him very little money, so he conceived a plan that could bring him a larger fortune. He took Marya to Tyumen, a village situated between Ekaterinburg and Tobolsk. As a precaution, he passed himself off as a representative of a fishing club. Upon his arrival in Tyumen, Soloviev had Marya and her sister, Varya, convey to the Imperial Family that he had been sent to Siberia by Vyrubova and Count Rostovzev, the Tsarina's former secretary, to help them escape. This news put him in good stead with the Imperial Couple who deemed Rasputin's son-in-law to be a trustworthy man.

Once Soloviev had the Tsar's complete confidence, he let the secret monarchist society know that he was in full control of the Tsar's liberation from captivity. Thanks to this lie, he was able to control all of the Tsar's correspondence, which he reported to the Provisional Government and, after its fall, to the Bolsheviks. He succeeded in corrupting the Imperial Family's chaplain, Alexei Vassiliev, through whom Soloviev transmitted only certain news to the Tsar. When the delegates from the monarchist organization came to Tyumen to organize the Tsar's escape, Soloviev appealed to them to abandon their plans. When they did not agree with him, he turned them in. Their arrests served to intimidate others. All money sent to the Tsar passed through Soloviev's hands. In the beginning, he remitted the full amounts to the Tsar, but then he appropriated other sums in the most shameful manner and even convinced the Tsarina to turn her diamonds over to him, to sell.

The Tsar had been abandoned by many of his dignitaries, but there still remained groups eager to liberate and move him abroad. One of these organizations had been formed by Tugan-Baranovski.[214] The group had solid financial backing and often sent men to map and plan the Tsar's escape from Siberia. The leaders of this group understood the danger facing the Tsar and his family, and knew it could only be avoided by a rapid departure. Not far from the house in Ekaterinburg where the Imperial Family was imprisoned, this group rented a shop in which they installed a bakery. Their intention was to dig a tunnel from the bakery's basement to the Tsar's house. These efforts were actively pursued. Nevertheless, events were such that their plans were not realized in time.

In Kiev, a 'sacred guard' was created to save the Imperial Family. Hetman Skoropadski[215] had reason to be unhappy with the Tsar as he had been the former commander of a guard regiment in which Dmitri Pavlovich had served as an officer. Following a public scene, Skoropadski had punished the Grand Duke and was subsequently relieved of his command. Despite that, the Hetman did not hinder the activities of the monarchist organization. In fact, his intervention opened a dialog with the government, regarding the transportation of the Imperial Family to Germany. The head of the German troops, General Eichham, and Ambassador Mirbach invited the Tsar to come to Germany and even sought permission from the Soviets to this effect. General Keller and Vassily

[214] Mikhail Tugan-Baranovski was a Ukrainian economist, social theorist and politician.
[215] Skoropadski was the last Hetman (Cossack ruler) of Ukraine which merged with the Russian federation at the end of 1918.

Vsevolozhsky worked side by side with Tugan-Baranovski, to liberate the Imperial Family. I knew Tugan-Baranovski very well. During my own escape from Petersburg to Kiev, he made his apartment available to my family members who stayed behind. I saw him, for the last time, in 1920, in Danzig, where he told me the details of his efforts to free the Tsar's family from the hands of the Bolsheviks.[216]

Soloviev knew that he would be betrayed eventually. Consequently, he amassed as much money and as many diamonds as he could, to escape abroad. As he had never been interested in freeing the Tsar, Soloviev revealed all of the monarchists' activities to the Bolsheviks, including copies of letters detailing a plan to move the Tsar to Oriental Siberia, which was under the rule of Semenov.[217]

In Siberia, no one had ever seen a Russian Tsar. The arrival of the Imperial Family awakened great curiosity in Tobolsk, where the lives of the Imperial family were the main topic of conversation. The streets were always full of people around the house where the family was held. Soloviev spread the rumor that the Tsar and his family would soon be executed. This further sharpened the public's interest in them. The Bolsheviks were worried about this. At that moment, Soloviev knew he was finished. He went to Oriental Siberia with his wife, Marya, who knew nothing of his activities and was treated most brutally by him. But Semenov had him arrested and he had to part with most of the diamonds to buy his freedom. After that, he went to Japan, Czechoslovakia, Germany, and finally Paris. He died of tuberculosis in Paris, at

[216] Simanovitch is mistaken as to the year as Tugan-Baranovski died in 1919 en route to France.

[217] Also referred to as the Russian Far East, "Oriental Siberia" extended from Lake Baikal to the Pacific Ocean.

Cochin Hospital where I visited him many times, and where he recounted his schemes while in Siberia.

Commissar Yurovski played a decisive role in the Imperial Family's murder. He, too, was motivated by greed. Yurovski was a jeweler by profession. After the Imperial Family's transfer to Ekaterinburg, he became a Bolshevik commissar, in charge of prisoners. He authorized the Tsar and Tsarina to sell their jewels to his friend, Krumnos. He knew that the Imperials possessed many priceless gems. He worried constantly about the rumors that the Soviets might take the Tsar to Moscow, to bring him before a tribunal, which would prevent him from getting his hands on the jewels. On the other hand, there was talk of the monarchists liberating the Tsar.

Neither possibility was to his benefit, so he decided, along with Commissars Beloboradov and Goloshkin, to kill the Tsar and his family so he could steal their jewels. All three acted contrary to orders from Moscow.[218] The President of the Central Executive Council sent them to the capital to submit a report. There is no doubt that Yurovski's greed had an effect on the sad fate of the Imperial Family. Yurovski appropriated the jewels and shared them with Beloboradov and Goloshkin. The settings were broken up and taken away. I learned all of these details from Simon Golub, a jeweler who knew Krumnos. Golub was in Ekaterinburg when the Imperial Family was exterminated. The night of the murders, he was in the neighborhood and clearly heard gunshots and screams.

---

[218] Yurovski not only acted on orders but, ironically, was subsequently given the job of cataloging the jewels and personal effects of the Imperial Family for the Bolsheviks. In his memoir and statements, he reported feeling conflicted about killing the family although he felt that too many Russians had suffered and died for the Romanovs.

Yurovski said that the Tsar's daughters did not die from their gunshot wounds, and had to be finished off with bayonets. Apparently, the girls had tried to defend themselves. For Yurovski, witnesses such as Simon Golub and his brother Vladimir were dangerous. That is why Vladimir was gunned down. Simon saved himself and went to America where I met him in 1922.[219]

In the same year, I obtained permission for Rasputin's younger daughter, Varya, to enter Germany. She left her native Pokrovskoie and went to Moscow, having been authorized to go abroad by the Soviet government. However, when she arrived at the train station, she was held and searched. In her bags, officials found precious notes on the Imperial Family's life in Ekaterinburg. She had lived near the royals then, visited them frequently, and was privy to intimate details of their lives. I do not know exactly what happened to her after she was held in Moscow. I only know that Varya is dead. This news came to me with no details regarding the circumstances of her death.[220]

---

[219] Simon Golub & Sons remains a worldwide manufacturer of diamond jewelry.

[220] Some reports state that Varya died mysteriously of poisoning while detained by the Soviets.

Chapter X

After the Fall of the Tsarist Government

After the fall of the tsarist government, a group of soldiers arrived at my apartment, looking for ex-Ministers Sturmer and Protopopov. Of course, they found neither, and left. Then, I had a visit from my friend, Mme Tarkhanova, who told me that Kerensky[221] had ordered me to leave Petersburg immediately. Nevertheless, I preferred to stay on. I moved to a modest hotel owned by a friend, and spent two peaceful days before a military attachment found me. This troop was led by a student named Buchman whose acceptance to law school I had facilitated. It seems that Buchman had volunteered for this detail because he knew me personally. At the hotel, I was registered as 'Jifmanovich.' Buchman saw me, aimed his gun at me, and declared me his prisoner.

"What do you want of me?" I asked him.

"You didn't want me admitted to medical school," he answered.[222] "But now I know your schemes and I am arresting you."

---

[221] Kerensky was Prime Minister of the Provisional Government until it was overthrown by the Bolsheviks.

[222] It may have been that Simanovitch could not get Buchman into medical school, but could get him into law school. Either would surely have required special permission, beyond the quota of Jews allowed, since Buchman found Simanovitch's help necessary.

The only thing to do was submit to my fate. They drove me to a cave where I learned that Sturmer and Pitirim had also been arrested by the revolutionaries, and were imprisoned in the Alexander Nevski Monastery. They transferred me there, as well. From the monastery, they took us to the Duma. An enormous crowd pressed toward the building. I could hear them shouting, "It's Pitirim and Rasputin's secretary!" A young clerk received us. No one knew where to take us, so they enclosed us in the room with all the ministers.

"You all know well that I concern myself only with Jewish matters. Why was I arrested?" I asked.

"You have illegally given many people an unfair advantage," they said. "You must answer to this charge."

Several hours later, I was brought before Deputies Krupenski and Markov III who were holding my family and Rasputin's daughters, all of whom had been arrested at their apartments and taken to one of the palaces. On the table, in front of Deputy Markov III, I saw most of the jewels that I had hidden in a strongbox at my apartment. They were pieces of immense value. The two deputies told me that my jewels were being confiscated. My son, Semyon, demanded that they itemize every diamond and pearl confiscated, but they sent him from the room. Finally, they dismissed me, too. I never knew what became of my jewels, but I imagine they disappeared into the pockets of the two deputies.

In the middle of the night, I was interrogated about Rasputin's role and the intimate life of the Imperial Couple. I gave no details, and declared that I had never been anything but a jeweler to the Court, except when I could render assistance to my fellow Jews through my connections. The next day, they freed my entire family. The lawyer, Sliosberg, filed a complaint to Kerensky about my arrest, maintaining that I could only be cited as a witness. On Kerensky's order, I was taken from the room of arrested ministers, and into the loge of the Duma meeting room. There was great chaos there. Everyone was talking and shouting. Sliosberg told me, by way of his son, that I had nothing to fear because the Jews I had helped were coming to my aid. I signed the telegram that the lawyer had prepared, stating that I had committed no illegal acts, and sent it to Kerensky. It just so happened that Kerensky was a good friend of Deputy Prince Gelovani for whom I had done a favor long before the revolution. Gelovani had, at that time, requested an end to the surveillance on his lawyer friend, Boreversev, and I saw to it. In light of that, I thought I could expect some leniency from Kerensky who did, at least, accept the complaint against my arrest.

However, just as I learned this news and was anticipating being released, Grand Duke Cyril brought in a naval detachment as an act of loyalty and submission to the Provisional Government. This sparked a frenzy in the room. Duma President Rodzianko stood before him and was greeted by enthusiastic shouts. Social Democrat Deputy Cheidze jumped on a table and made a heartily applauded speech of which I retained only these few words:

"Citizens, I remind you that right there, in the street, used to be a policeman. You were afraid of him. I was, too. Nicholas II was Tsar by the grace of God, but we have dethroned him. Hurrah!"

The noise and emotions in the room escalated. The police who were stationed in the Duma noisily protested these declarations and threw empty bottles, as well as other objects. Since I was caught in the middle of the fray, I was taken to be an instigator and carted off to Peter and Paul Prison. The complaint I filed against my original arrest was forgotten. Others arrested were taken to Prison of the Cross.

My sons sought help from some prominent Jewish politicians who played an important role in the revolution. They were not eager to help me, not wanting to call attention to their past dealings with me, someone associated with the tsarist regime. Nevertheless, they could not refuse me their support, and I was transferred from Peter and Paul Prison to Prison of the Cross, where communication with the outside world was easier. In this prison, Minister of Justice Peraversev came to see me. He said he knew that, under the Tsar, I was very powerful and that I could have made a colossal fortune. He had not yet filed a formal complaint against me, but would be working on it shortly. After that, I had a visit from the lawyer, Feitelson, who promised to have me transferred to Petersburg Prison.

"We will arrest your wife," he said. "She will serve as a hostage. You will be quite free within Petersburg Prison. You will not even appear on the list of prisoners. The arrest of your wife will be officially motivated by your so-called escape from Prison of the Cross."

It was a good plan. Once my wife consented, I accepted. I asked for the return of my confiscated jewels, but they were nowhere to be found.

In my new prison, I took steps toward my liberation. I argued for my release in exchange for the sum of two hundred thousand rubles. This sum was given to

Peraversev, and I was released. A little later, my wife was also freed. I had to sign a promise to leave Petersburg as soon as possible. It was a promise I did not keep.

Soon afterward, all members of the Imperial House — grand dukes, ladies-in-waiting, and any other members of the Court — were all relieved of their responsibilities. I was no longer being followed, but to lift the order exiling me from Petersburg, I had to pay another forty thousand rubles through my lawyer, Kvolson. This was the sum for the services of attorney Sokolov who, at that time, was a member of the Council of Petersburg Workers.

Under the Bolshevik regime, I no longer felt safe in Petersburg. I transferred my family to Moscow and then to Kiev, as the Ukraine was under the hetman government, the current hetman being Skoropadski.[223] To reduce the risk of this trip, I resorted to a ruse. I pretended I had a broken arm and had a plaster cast put on it. I carried an official document stating that the cast could not be removed before a certain date. Moreover, I had a medical note confirming that I had broken my arm. In the plaster cast, I hid one thousand carats of diamonds and a million rubles. I purchased a seat in a train car reserved for Ukrainian invalids, and rode to Karkov. From there, I went to Kiev where I discovered my worst enemy and Rasputin's murderer, Purishkevich, was staying. The Akazatov brothers had warned me that Purishkevich wanted me dead.

---

[223] The term 'hetman' literally means 'head man' and was the title of the chief Ukrainian Cossack, just as 'tsar' was the emperor's title. Hetman Skoropadski's anti-Socialist Ukrainian government, which lasted less than a year (1918), fought to preserve its autonomy before becoming part of the Russian federation.

I sought out Count Keller, Commander of the Northern Army[224] in Kiev, whom I had known well in Petersburg, for protection against my enemy. He reassured me, gave me a military guard, and advised me to address myself to Hetman Skoropadski's cousin, General Vsevolozhsky, who commanded a division of the Northern Army. The general received me in a friendly fashion and promised to protect me from Purishkevich. He also proposed that I join his division. Vsevolozhsky could not overlook the fact that, although Purishkevich remained a monarchist, he had sided with the revolutionaries against the Tsar. The mere mention of Purishkevich's name would enrage him.

At a restaurant banquet, Vsevolozhsky told me that the northern division had completely separated itself from the rest of the volunteer army. The division tried to maintain military discipline and did not partake of pogroms and pillaging as the southern division often did under the influence of Purishkevich. In the absence of pillaging, the northern division lacked provisions, which General Vsevolozhsky advised me to supply. In return, he would warn me of any upcoming anti-Jewish activity. This proposition pleased me enormously. We had every reason to fear pogroms. At that time, Kiev was the meeting place for all reactionary groups who wanted to wreak vengeance on Jews who were being blamed for causing the revolution.

My personal funds would not be sufficient to purchase provisions for the northern division. Consequently, I proposed that a casino be opened in Kiev, under the protection of the Commander of the Northern Division. The general approved my proposal. We rented Rots Restaurant and installed a casino there. That soon

---

224 This was part of the White Army, comprised of supporters of the monarchy, which fought the Bolshevik Red Army during the five years of civil war that followed the revolution.

generated large revenues. The former assistant to Moscow's Chief of Police was appointed as Kiev's Chief of Police. He was our man, so we had nothing to fear from the police. The casino's take grew to about ten thousand English pounds per day.[225] Officers of the northern division were the administrators, and guarded the peace and order of the game rooms. For our part, we could help many fugitives and give out food as well as necessary sums of money. I even organized games amongst the rich escapees, which brought in six million rubles.[226]

During the uprising in Kiev, Jewish soldiers were placed in the Northern Division. They took no part in military operations but oversaw order in the city, and protected the Jews from pogroms. One day, Belyayev, who had burned Rasputin's body, came to see me. He told me, confidentially, that he had ordered a detachment to Kiev. Two officers from the Southern Division's White Army wanted to organize a pogrom, to be directed by Purishkevich, and asked that nothing stop them. Other officers from the Southern Division, namely Bermondt-Avalov and the division's political strategist, Tugan-Baranovski, were against the whole plan but were unable to prevent it. I met with these two men. Tugan-Baranovski said, "You, too, have armed men. You could stand up to Purishkevich yourselves." With the consent of Count Keller and General Vsevolozhsky, two hundred men were sent to the suburb of Podol which, having a large Jewish population, made it a target. The detachment was comprised solely of Jews from the Northern Division. Only the commanding officer was Christian.

In the meantime, Purishkevich was posting signs in the streets, calling for a pogrom. General Vsevolozhsky, in

---

225 Approx. $50,000, at that time.
226 Approx. three million dollars, at that time.

keeping with his promise of protection in exchange for feeding the division, gave the order to remove Purishkevich and his men. The pogrom was squelched and Purishkevich was ordered to leave Kiev within three days. However, the detachment sent to the suburbs to protect the Jews was still there so, to avoid any pillaging, I quickly had to obtain provisions for them.

After that came the overthrow of Skoropadski. Petlyura's Ukrainian gangs[227] occupied the city, and I had to flee to Odessa with my sons. However, I later learned that when it became obvious that the occupation of Kiev by Petlyuria's men could no longer be prevented, Count Keller went to his superior and proposed a retreat to the Kuban region. All of the officers agreed with him. All of the division's valuables were packed in sacks that the officers had to carry on their weapons. They readied for their retreat while they waited to be joined by another detachment.

A Petlyurian advance group entered Kiev, but all General Keller knew was that some gang of bandits wanted to attack Jews, so he ordered his men to aim at the intruders. He soon realized that this was part of Petlyura's gang, and that he had missed his chance to retreat and would pay dearly for it. Count Keller ordered his officers and soldiers to disperse around the city. He and his aides, as well as the division's valuables, went to St. Michael's Monastery. There, he was advised to put on a German uniform and leave Kiev with the German troops, but Count Keller did not want to remove his Russian uniform. The Petlyurians discovered him shortly thereafter. He and his aide-de-camp were arrested, taken to Sofia Square, and shot. The

---

[227] Simon Petlyuria (also Symon Petliura) was President of the Ukrainian National Republic during the Ukrainian war for independence from 1917 to 1921.

Petlyurians then confiscated the Northern Division's valuables.

Before Petlyura's army came to Kiev, I had escaped to Odessa where I found myself in the company of Vsevolozhsky, Commander of the Northern Division, and his bureau chief, Dobrinski. A detachment of the volunteer army, under the command of General Grishin-Almazov, arrived in Odessa. I was staying at the Victoria Hotel while the Northern Division officers were housed at the Hotel of Commerce. I had large sums of money on me because you could not get anything without money. Rumors had circulated already that I was spending a lot of money. One day, there was a knock on my door. Two men, armed with hand grenades, quickly entered my room. One of them handed me a letter from the famous pillager, Mishka Japonchik[228] who had a huge army of thieves. The head of the group wanted fifteen thousand rubles from me.

"Listen to me," I said. "You came to me in vain. I am one of you. It would be preferable if Mishka came himself and sat down to tea with me, to discuss the affair calmly. Rzhevsky and Belyayev, who you know well, are my friends, so we can make a deal."

Surprised that I knew of the rapport between Japonchik and Belyayev, the bandits believed me and left after I gave each one three hundred Ukrainian rubles. There had already been some suspicion that Belyayev and Rzhevsky were collaborating with Minister of the Interior Khvostov. Several days later, I was in a Jewish cabaret, managed by my friend, the impresario Fischsohn. There I saw

---

[228] Mishka Japonchik (also Yaponchik) was an Odessa gangster who was freed from prison at the start of the revolution and, in 1919, was permitted to form his own unit in the Soviet Army. He was killed in an ambush two months later.

Rzhevsky and Belyayev. They were very absorbed in conversation. I had to put myself in good stead with them, or I would not have a peaceful moment in Odessa. We sat together and drank a lot. In the course of conversation, Belyayev said to me, in a low voice: "Do not fear, Simanovitch! When we leave here, some shots will be fired, but there is no danger."

I wanted to know what was happening, but he said nothing more. After the meal, we left. Rzhevsky did not want to leave on foot, so he hailed a car and we said our amicable farewells. But at the moment he got into the car, Belyayev pulled out his revolver and killed him on the spot.

I asked Belyayev, "Why did you kill him?"

"I killed him," he replied, "because he had plotted against Rasputin."

It is true that Belyayev owed Rasputin a debt of gratitude. During the Great War, Belyayev had been condemned to prison following an incident with his brother. His mother came to Rasputin, asking the Tsar's mercy in the matter, which was granted. Upon his return to Petersburg, Belyayev often came to Rasputin's home where he was warmly welcomed. At that time, he was a contributor to the *Vecherniy Vremya*[229] newspaper. Then, when the revolution came, he was arrested again and put in Prison of the Cross. That is where I saw him. His head was bandaged and he had wounds and more bandages all over his arms. I asked him what happened. He told me he had been arrested in Moscow but had tried to flee, whereupon he was severely beaten.

---

[229] The Evening Times.

It was odd how he had come to be arrested in Moscow. During the first days of the revolution, Belyayev received an order to search the home of former Council President Sturmer. In the process, he stole many jewels from Sturmer's home. Sturmer's son filed a complaint, and the order was given to arrest Belyayev. It was just prior to that that Belyayev sold, for forty thousand rubles, the icon with the Imperial Family's signatures that he had stolen from Rasputin's tomb. As he knew nothing of Sturmer's complaint, he believed he was being arrested for the theft of the icon. He volunteered the entire story, thinking the judge already knew about it, but he only added one more theft charge. The picture with the signatures was found in Katherin Reshetnitova's shop. It was taken to Kerensky but I do not know what he did with it.

When Belyayev killed Rzhevsky, however, he was only using Rasputin as an excuse. He certainly had other scores to settle with Rzhevsky, especially when the latter sided with Japonchik in a quarrel with Belyayev. The murder of Rzhevsky, who was protector and aide to the bandits, enraged Japonchik who then ordered that Belyayev be found. Having learned that I had dined with Belyayev in Fischsohn's cabaret, Japonchik sent two men to ask me where he could be found. Belyayev was actually in the room and, as I had no idea what these men wanted of him, I pointed him out. They thanked me and asked Belyayev, under some pretext, to go out into the street with them. He followed them and was shot and killed.

~~~~~~~~

The famous affair of the sugar manufacturers heard its final echo in January of 1919 in Odessa. Hepner, Rosen and I arrived there with many other refugees. Rosen was in financial need, so I asked the rich Hepner to give him the
~~~~~~~~

twenty thousand rubles which Zeyev and Hepner's son-in-law had promised Rosen in Petersburg. Hepner refused. Rosen then complained to Orlov, a judge on Batyushin's commission, who was employed in counterespionage for General Denikin. After that, during a search of Hepner's house, the letter I had addressed to him was found, requesting that he remit the sum of twenty thousand rubles to Rosen, as agreed. Hepner was arrested. At the time, Odessa was occupied by the French,[230] and when they learned that Hepner had helped the Germans during wartime, they put him in prison until they evacuated the city.

One night before I left Odessa, I was dining at the London Hotel with Prince Nizheradze, General Vsevolozhsky, and the former adjunct to the governor of Moscow, General Markov. Suddenly my archenemy, Purishkevich, arrived. I jumped up and grabbed my revolver. Prince Nizheradze told Purishkevich that he would kill him if he laid a hand on me. Purishkevich responded that he had no ill intentions toward me, and even felt that we should make peace.

It wouldn't last long. Several days before the evacuation of Odessa, General Markov offered me fifty tickets on the French ship, *Prodigal*. In addition to my sons, I brought twenty uniformed officers. The ship was full of Russian monarchists and police officers. Thanks to the military uniforms of my associates, we were well received. But once the *Prodigal* lifted anchor, some of the officers and former policemen tried to rally a pogrom against the Jews. I had my three sons with me and was filled with anxiety.

[230] The French occupied Odessa from 1918-1919, as one of 14 nations that participated in the allied intervention during the post-revolutionary Russian Civil War. These allied nations supported the pro-tsarist White Russian Army.

However, the Northern Division officers calmed me. They promised to protect us in case of danger. The hostility on board increased. They yelled, "Kill the Jews!" We were the only Jews on the ship. I decided to put an end to it.

To our great surprise, we saw that the agitated army and police officers had encircled the well-known journalists, Elfimov, Lutoshin, and Bonch-Bruevich, threatening to kill them. Believing the first two to be Jews, and the third to be a Bolshevik agent (since he was the brother of an influential Bolshevik), they wanted to throw Elfimov and Lutoshin overboard, and shoot Bonch-Bruevich. I explained their error to these men and the officers apologized to the journalists. However, Bonch-Bruevich's fate was still uncertain. I asked him if he had any money. He said he had several thousand English pounds that he would readily part with for the sake of his life. We dispersed three thousand francs and five hundred English pounds among the military and police officers, which succeeded in calming them all. They took a new vote and decided to forego the execution of Bonch-Bruevich, but to deliver him to Denikin's men,[231] upon arriving at Novorossiysk. General Markov was charged with this task. However, once in port, the General let Bonch-Bruevich leave, and announced to the Novorossiysk government that the officers aboard the ship were transporting merchandise they had stolen from the volunteer army's storehouse. The guilty were soon arrested.

During my stay in Novorossiysk, the famous General Shkuro visited. He was still an army commander, but his army no longer existed. A choir of gypsies and a Rumanian orchestra, directed by Jan Gulesko,

---

[231] General A.I Denikin fought in the Russo-Japanese War, WW I, and commanded the White Army during the Russian Civil War after the 1917 revolution.

accompanied him, but in the whole army, there remained only two trumpet players; all the others had fled.[232]

The bourgeoisie of Novorossiysk organized a banquet in honor of the General. At that occasion, he asked the city to donate two hundred million rubles to form a new anti-Bolshevik army. The rich merchants and bankers of the city supported him and were ready to raise the necessary funds. However, the General had drunk a little too much, and imprudently spoke of missing his Cossacks whom he had permitted to pillage and plunder the general public. He complained that his men had become so rich from thieving that they lost all will to fight the Bolsheviks, and abandoned their posts to return to their respective villages. Only the Rumanian orchestra and gypsy choir remained loyal to him. This sad story had the effect of a cold shower. There would be no funds for General Shkuro.

Soon afterward, General Mamontov arrived at Novorossiysk. He was famous for his impassioned battle against the Bolsheviks. One day, after we had gotten to know each other, Mamontov told me that he had acquired large sums of money in his campaigns against the Bolsheviks, but did not want his comrades to know this, because he should have shared those sums with them. He asked me to buy any diamonds owned by the big sugar manufacturers who had come from Kiev. Since they all needed money, one might suppose that they would willingly sell their jewels. He entrusted me with several million rubles, which I kept in the shop of my friend,

---

232 Shkuro had resigned from the White Army after General Wrangel relieved him of his command. He went into exile in France. During WW II, he formed an anti-Soviet Cossack unit of Russian émigrés, allied with German Nazis, but was captured by the English and turned over to the Soviets who hanged him in 1947.

Feldman. Negotiations with the industrialists were quickly concluded. I bought the jewels and turned them over to the General.

Unfortunately, my large purchase of jewels quickly became common knowledge in the city. Two officers from Mamontov's division presented themselves at my lodgings, demanding that I remit the jewels that they pretended belonged to the Imperial Family's treasure. I refused, and they tried to enter by force. I defended myself, taking the gun of one officer and hitting him on the head with it. The noise alarmed his accomplice, who was also subdued. We notified the city governor who had them arrested. General Mamontov felt obliged to reveal to my attorney the entire truth about the jewels. He made a special trip to apologize to me for the trouble caused by my actions on his behalf.

Later, I learned that Mamontov had brought from his campaign in Kursk an enormous quantity of silver and gold icons, as well as two cases of money. His men had confiscated valuable objects from churches and citizens under the pretext of saving them from the Bolsheviks. Mamontov kept everything for himself and thus provoked discontent among the soldiers.

~~~~~~~~

One day, I had a visit from an old Petersburg acquaintance, Skvorsov, the former editor of the reactionary publication, *Kolokol*.[233] In Petersburg, he had led anti-Jewish demonstrations and wanted to continue his propaganda in Novorossiysk. When I asked his motive, he said he hoped to make money this way. I asked him to name the sum he required. After some haggling, he declared that he would abandon his anti-Semitic projects for the sum of ten

---

[233] The Bell.
~~~~~~~~

thousand rubles. When I remitted the amount to him, he confided that Purishkevich was in Novorossiysk.

Purishkevich had published a brochure titled *The Murder of Rasputin*. It was being sold for fifteen rubles per copy. A thousand of these pamphlets had been left in a cabaret for distribution among the patrons. When Purishkevich demanded that the cabaret owner pay him the money from the sale of his pamphlets, he was surprised to learn that I had prevented his pack of lies from being sold. He was enraged, and, wanting the ultimate revenge, hired some of his followers to kill me. Among these agitators was a good friend of mine, young Prince Dadeshkiliani, who informed me of the plot. I was obliged to surround myself with guards and never went out without an armed escort.

One day, an enraged gang attacked me in the street. My men and I pulled out our revolvers and fired. One of the aggressors was wounded and the others fled. I filed a complaint with the authorities, with whom I was on good terms. Subsequently, Purishkevich was expelled from the city. However, he returned a month later and announced a public meeting. I had to prevent this meeting that was certain to have a clearly anti-Semitic tone by suggesting to a Jewish able seaman, Fedor Batkin, that he hold his own important conference. Batkin had acquired great celebrity for his speeches in the first days of the revolution. He loved appearing in public, and quickly accepted. I rented the same hall as Purishkevich, but for the prior evening. Batkin publicly attacked Purishkevich in front of a receptive crowd.

The next evening, when Purishkevich came to speak at his own conference, my friends and I staged a violent demonstration against him. We yelled and threw things, and he could not say a word. The following day,

Purishkevich came to see me flanked by two officers with the obvious intent of killing me. I escaped through the back door and, at my request, Purishkevich was again arrested and expelled from the city.

Some time later, Purishkevich returned to Novorossiysk but fell ill with typhus and was hospitalized. As chance would have it, my younger son was also afflicted with typhus and in the same hospital, at the same time, but neither Purishkevich nor I was inclined to renew the conflict. The hospital personnel were all Jewish, and Purishkevich's presence made them all a bit nervous. The nurses were monarchists and considered Purishkevich to be a traitor by adhering to the revolutionary movement. The hospital staff said, "It's not worth spending the time to cure Purishkevich." However, he was very robust and began to heal. I was told that two of the nurses who detested him gave him champagne to drink following a relapse, hoping to hasten his death,. I was greatly relieved to learn the news of his demise, [234] as he could have killed me on any given day.

[234] Purishkevich died of typhus, in Novorossiysk, on February 1, 1920.

Chapter XI

God's Emissary

It is incredible that, once inside the Court, having become familiar with the Imperial Family, Rasputin planted deep, solid roots in this unstable soil. The Imperial Court's mystical aspirations for miracles gave Rasputin easy access to the Court, to start. However, his formidable influence did not occur overnight. Five years would go by before he achieved his influential position. It was only in his last five years that his full power was unleashed.[235] As his influence grew, he took on the importance of a non-crowned monarch.

Everyone knows the pain and problems suffered by the Imperial Family because of Grigori Rasputin. Everyone knows that, in the final years of the dynasty, the army, the nobility and the Grand Dukes formed a bloc and launched a furious attack on the Tsar's 'favorite.' But the Imperial Family, with mud on their faces and under threats of a revolution, courageously defended the man of God and, in shielding him, suffered those blows, themselves.

Many explain Rasputin's influence on the Imperial Family solely by his ability to help little Alexei, thereby winning the hearts of the parents who constantly feared for their son's health. Rasputin often alleviated the Tsarevitch's symptoms but the results were far from a cure. He charmed the child as completely as he did the parents.

---

[235] Rasputin spent a total of eleven years (1905-1916) at the Tsar's Court.

Rasputin only encouraged the spoiled boy's pranks. He advised him to be firm and pursue his desires, never to obey anyone, never to submit his will to another, and never to depart from a decision once it was made. Of course, the child was delighted with this educational system which gave him absolute freedom of action. Moreover, Grigori told the parents that he was not a simple little boy, but heir to the throne, the future Tsar and, as such, he should be firm, independent and obstinate. He told them that Alexei would only become a true and powerful Russian tsar by acting according to his own desires and believing in his own ideas. The little prince adored Rasputin, obeyed only him, loved to listen to his lectures, and always eagerly awaited the arrival of his friend to whom he told his secrets and complaints about Mama and Papa. When Rasputin was killed, the child's sorrow knew no limits. He demanded, sobbing, that the assassins be punished immediately for their crime, and that they must atone for their sins on the gallows.

Rasputin had fit the description of God's emissary, predestined for the House of the Romanovs, sent to shield the Imperial Family from enemies and other sorrows by means of his counsel and commandments. His very manner was intimidating to men accustomed to the superficial trappings of veneration and blind obedience. He had an independent and authoritative attitude, gave his advice as orders, and was unshakably obstinate.

Having conquered and nourished the soul of the indecisive Tsar, Rasputin never lost sight of the Tsar's biggest weakness: Nicholas II's tendency to agree with whomever he last consulted. Consequently, Rasputin stayed nearby when the Tsar made decisions, so as to watch that he didn't fall under another's influence. This often meant physically being with the Tsar until the decisive moment of his signature on a decree, ensuring that Rasputin's counsel would be the last one the Tsar heard. To this end, he had two allies: Vyrubova and the Tsarina herself. Mme Vyrubova, the closest and most intimate friend of the Imperial Family, kept Rasputin current on all of the thoughts, feelings, and secrets of the Tsar's home life. She even made a gramophone disc to transmit Rasputin's words to the Tsar and Tsarina. His other ally, the Tsarina, saw a friend and savior in Rasputin. She would transmit his words to the Tsar in writing when the latter was under the influence of the military commanders at Stavka.[236] Nearly every day, she wrote the Tsar twenty-page letters, begging him to give such and such order, or to enact this or that reform, and always underscoring that it was the counsel of "Our Friend." Even when the Tsar was away from his direct influence, Rasputin still had the last word because, despite the influence of others, the Tsar would be mesmerized by the Tsarina's letters or Vyrubova's words on her gramophone discs.

To clearly understand the extent of Rasputin's influence on the Tsarina, one must recall the solitude that engulfed her from the early days of her marriage, which intensified after the birth of the Tsarevitch, and reached threatening proportions during the war. The young Tsarina knew that the Dowager Empress had always hoped that her son, Mikhail, would attain the throne, and she desperately wanted to produce her own heir to the throne, knowing that none of her daughters could assume the crown. So, when Tsarevitch Alexei was born, the Dowager Empress could not abide that little Alexei had ruined her dreams, and relations between the Old Court and the Tsar's family grew into overt hostility.

---

[236] Stavka: headquarters of the Supreme Commander of Russian armed forces.

The Dowager Empress, Maria Feodorovna, frequently traveled to Denmark where she spread all sorts of rumors about the Tsarina who then severed ties with her husband's family, allowing none of them access to government business. She feared for Alexei, perhaps more because he was heir to the throne than because he was her son. It is significant that Alexei was almost never allowed to see his grandmother or the Tsar's other relatives because the Tsarina feared that he might be killed, poisoned or kidnapped.

The Russian Tsar was a very average man who was a good father, enjoyed family life, and who took no pleasure in his tasks as head of state. He was neither authoritative nor ambitious, unlike the Tsarina who was assertive, proud and arrogant. She saw Russia as her own domain, mixing issues of state with her duties as wife and mother. She only wanted ministers appointed whom she found personally sympathetic and agreeable. She considered them not as men called to govern an immense country, but as part of her household entourage. She was, however, a great patriot, wishing only for the glory and grandeur of Russia.

The Grand Dukes, most of whom were unemployed and idle, considered the Treasury funds as a cake to be shared, and believed that the interests of the dynasty were more important than those of the current monarch. They certainly met fierce resistance in the Tsarina. With the exception of a few Grand Dukes who were unconcerned with politics, the others formed a bloc of opposition. Their accusations against the Tsarina began in the Grand Dukes' palaces and spread among society, the army, the peasantry — all of whom accepted the rumors as facts. The Grand Dukes, accustomed to directing politics and occupying important positions, were furious that the Tsarina had reduced their influence to zero.

The Grand Dukes came up with all sorts of plots and plans, and wrote the Tsar letters threatening the Tsarina. Their hatred of the Imperial Couple was not even diminished by the Tsar's abdication, after which the Imperial Family was completely isolated. At first, the abdication seemed to be a favorable thing to the Grand Dukes. They were sure this would stop the gears of revolution, as well as re-establish the Romanov dynasty. They understood, only too late, how wrong they were. Only a rare few, such as the family of the Elder Maria Pavlovna,[237] remained loyal to the Young Court and did not spread rumors. They were devoted to the Tsar's family with all of their hearts.

When revolution broke out and the Imperial Family was exiled to Siberia, having been abandoned in a revolting fashion by friends and family, only Maria Pavlovna and her sons made great sacrifices for them. Risking danger, they left for the Caucasus, sold their jewels, and organized an escape for the Tsar. They sent hundreds of thousands of rubles to Siberia, but their money fell into criminal hands and the imperial prisoners only received a tenth of it. This complex and dangerous plan crumbled, despite enormous expenditures, and ended in treason: The Imperial Family perished.

The sacrifice of Maria Pavlovna's family was a lesson and reproach to other Grand Dukes who cowardly sought refuge for themselves while not lifting a finger to save the Tsar's family. When Cyril went to the head of the Duma to save the Imperial Family, the other Grand Dukes tried to

---

[237] A prominent Petersburg hostess (born 1854; died 1920), she was married to a son of Alexander II and, therefore, was an aunt to Nicholas II.

blacken his name and discredit him. They treated him as if he were crazy and a traitor to the dynasty.

The personality of the Tsar's 'favorite' was not understood. It was unjustly falsified and compromised. If one believes in destiny and some sort of justice, Rasputin was sent *not* to precipitate the loss of the monarchy, but for the health of Russia and the Tsar. He was misunderstood, spurned, and ferociously killed. This cruel fate saved neither Russia nor the Tsar. Providence had sent compensation for Nicholas' character in the form of Rasputin. Uneducated and nearly illiterate, Rasputin possessed a rare and lucid intelligence, an enormous will, a profound knowledge of men, and the gift of foresight that could be called a miracle.

Rasputin proved a thousand times more reasonable and full of foresight than did the educated and respected politicians with their futile strategies. He often gave the Tsar practical and reasonable advice, proposing state reforms that were stronger and more profound than those of liberal parties. Wasn't Rasputin right to try to abolish the death penalty, saying that for every hundred condemned, ninety-nine are innocent? Wasn't he right to tell the Tsar not to try to run the country alone, but to let the ministers govern while the Tsar reigned?

Although he felt his death approaching in the year before his murder, Rasputin could not accept it, being an energetic and healthy man. He went to great pains to avoid such premonitions. He knew that Nicholas would not live forever and that, eventually, Alexei would occupy the throne. In that event, Rasputin, who was only forty-six in 1915, would have many years ahead of him as a sort of non-official regent.

He had met with the Tsar concerning Alexei's future as Tsar of the peasants. Rasputin wanted to separate the nobility and the Grand Dukes from power, to do good things for the peasants, and to establish an idyllic monarchy with Alexei as official sovereign. Rasputin could remain powerful but from behind the scenes. The dreams of the peasantry could only be fulfilled by radical social reforms. This is why Rasputin defended the monarchy and was afraid that Nicholas II would be dethroned. He understood perfectly that the dissolution of the monarchy and overthrow of the Tsar would be his loss as well.

In the end, the Tsar's favorite advisor was harassed and beaten by people defending their own interests. Providence took pity on Nicholas II and sent him a liberator and a prophet. But a prophet's lot is uncertain. They are misunderstood by their contemporaries, as Rasputin was. Fate had paired an unhappy and weak Tsar with a hardy, intelligent and humanitarian man, but contrary to popular opinion, the tragic destiny of Nicholas II's entire entourage was in no way precipitated by the man who was predestined to play the role of 'Savior of the Monarchy.'

Rasputin awoke, in all who approached him, the most diverse sentiments. In some, he evoked a strange fear; in others, a profound repulsion. Still others filled with bitter hate at the sight of him. Over the years, I met with Rasputin both day and night. I knew him better than anyone did. I can confirm that he did not see his time with the Tsar as lasting long. He often felt uncertain and worried. Assuming that his role in Russia's affairs would cease one day, he often pondered his future. He was less fearful of being assassinated than of falling into disgrace. He tried to reassure himself, through his faith, that his ‘force’ would triumph over all the conspirators. However, this belief had no basis.

Rasputin had confidence in my experience and common sense. He was fond of me and, for my part, I also felt close to him. I never saw him do anything evil or wrong. In fact, his mission was to be good to everyone. If Nicholas II was a bad tsar, Rasputin was not to blame. With my assistance, Rasputin helped thousands of people, with a real and sincere goodness, and with no personal profit motive. Numerous were those he saved from misery, death, humiliation and suffering. This I will never forget. I have neither the right to judge nor to condemn him. No human being is without faults, and Rasputin was more honest than most of those around him.

Translator's Afterword

Aron Samuilovitch Simanovitch (aka Aaron Simanovich) finally settled in Paris where, in 1944, at the age of seventy-two, he was taken from his home by the Nazis, during World War II. He died at Auschwitz-Birkenau concentration camp, as recorded in Yad Vashem's Central Database of Shoah Victims' Names. His eldest son, Semyon (aka Salomon), according to some records, was shot and killed by the Nazis at Mont-Valéries in 1942. Other records state that Semyon died at Sobibor concentration camp. Aron's younger son, Ioann (aka John), escaped to Monrovia, Liberia where, until sometime in the late 1960s or early 1970s, he operated a Russian restaurant called "Rasputin."

When Simanovitch's family settled in Paris, they maintained a close relationship with Marya Rasputin and her children who also lived there. To this day, some of the grandchildren and great grandchildren of both families are closely bonded.

CPSIA information can be obtained
at www.ICGtesting.com
Printed in the USA
LVHW052305100122
708213LV00017B/2501

9 781484 925850